by Miwa Ueda

1

Pocket Edition

TOKYOPOP Presents
Peach Girl 1 by Miwa Ueda
Chix Comix Pocket Edition is an imprint of Mixx Entertainment, Inc.
ISBN: 1-892213-62-1
First Printing April 2001

10   9   8   7   6   5   4   3   2   1

This volume contains the Peach Girl 1 installments from
Smile Magazine No. 2.3 through No. 3.2 in their entirety.

Translator - Dan Papia. Retouch Artist - Jinky De Leon.
Graphic Designer - Akemi Imafuku. Graphics Assistant - Steve Kindernay.
Senior Editor - Michael Schuster. Editor - Jake Forbes. Associate Editor - Katherine Kim.
Production Manager - Fred Lui. Vice President of Publishing - Henry Kornman.

Email: editor@press.TOKYOPOP.com
Come visit us at www.TOKYOPOP.com

TOKYOPOP
Los Angeles - Tokyo

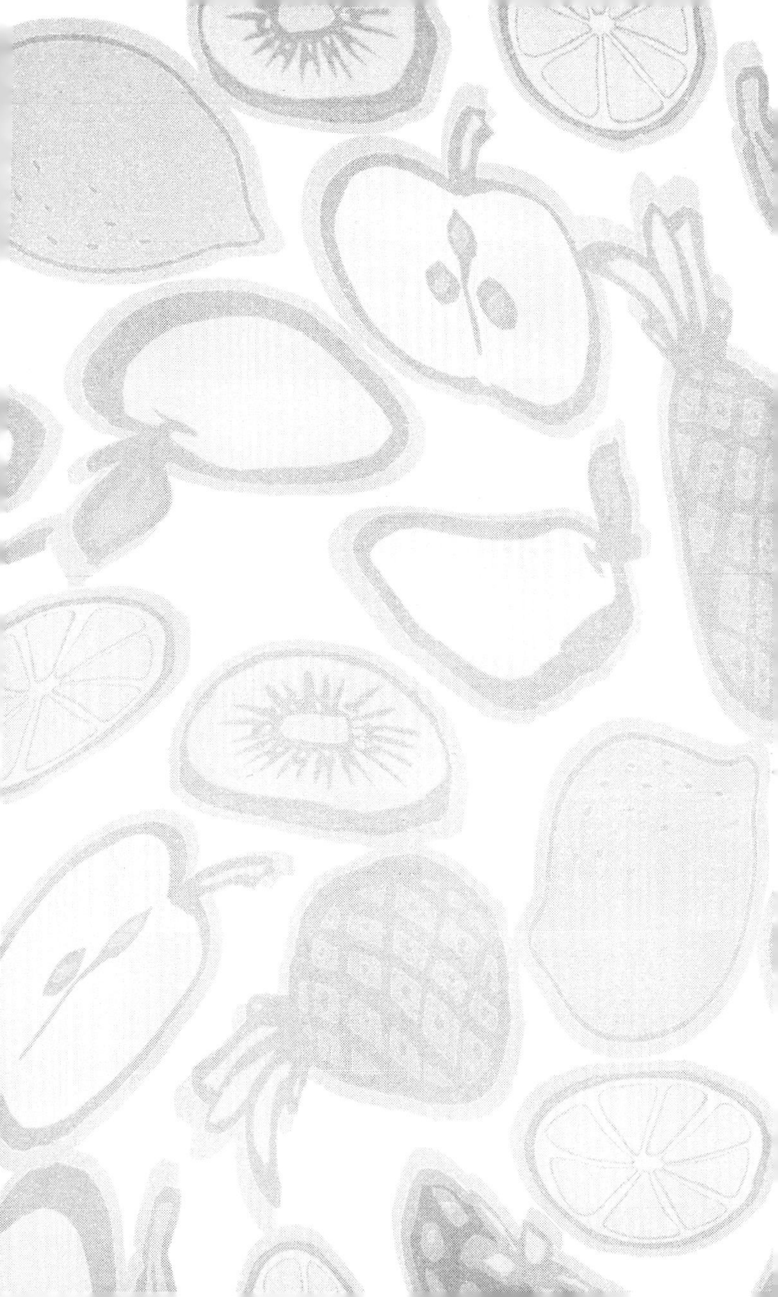

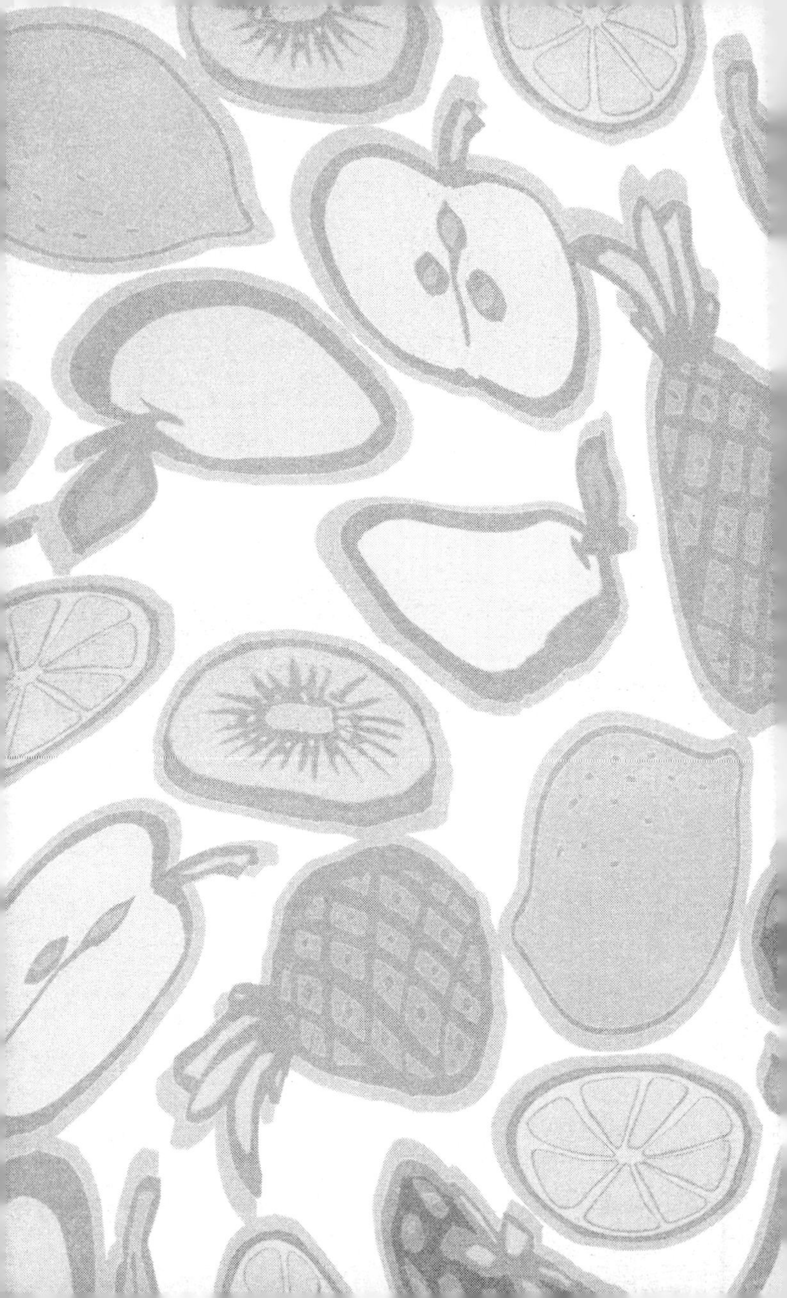

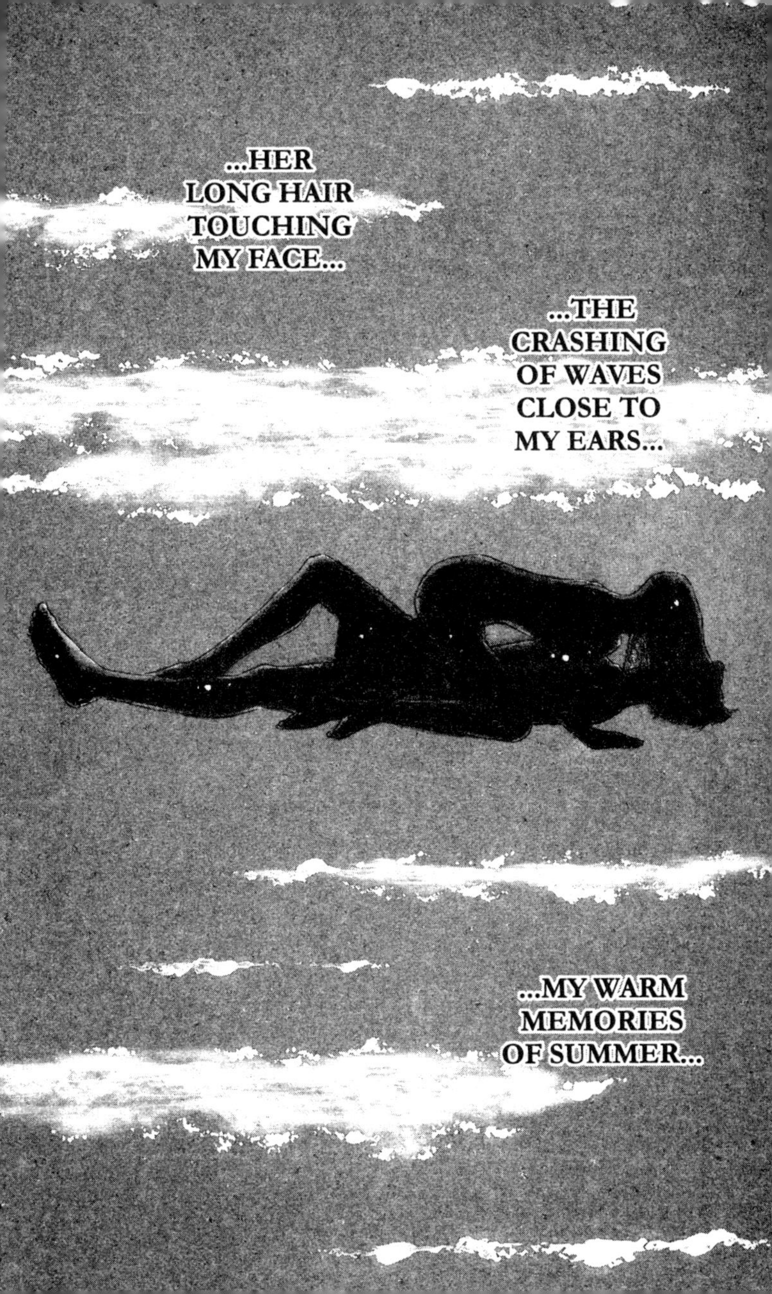
...HER LONG HAIR TOUCHING MY FACE...
...THE CRASHING OF WAVES CLOSE TO MY EARS...
...MY WARM MEMORIES OF SUMMER...

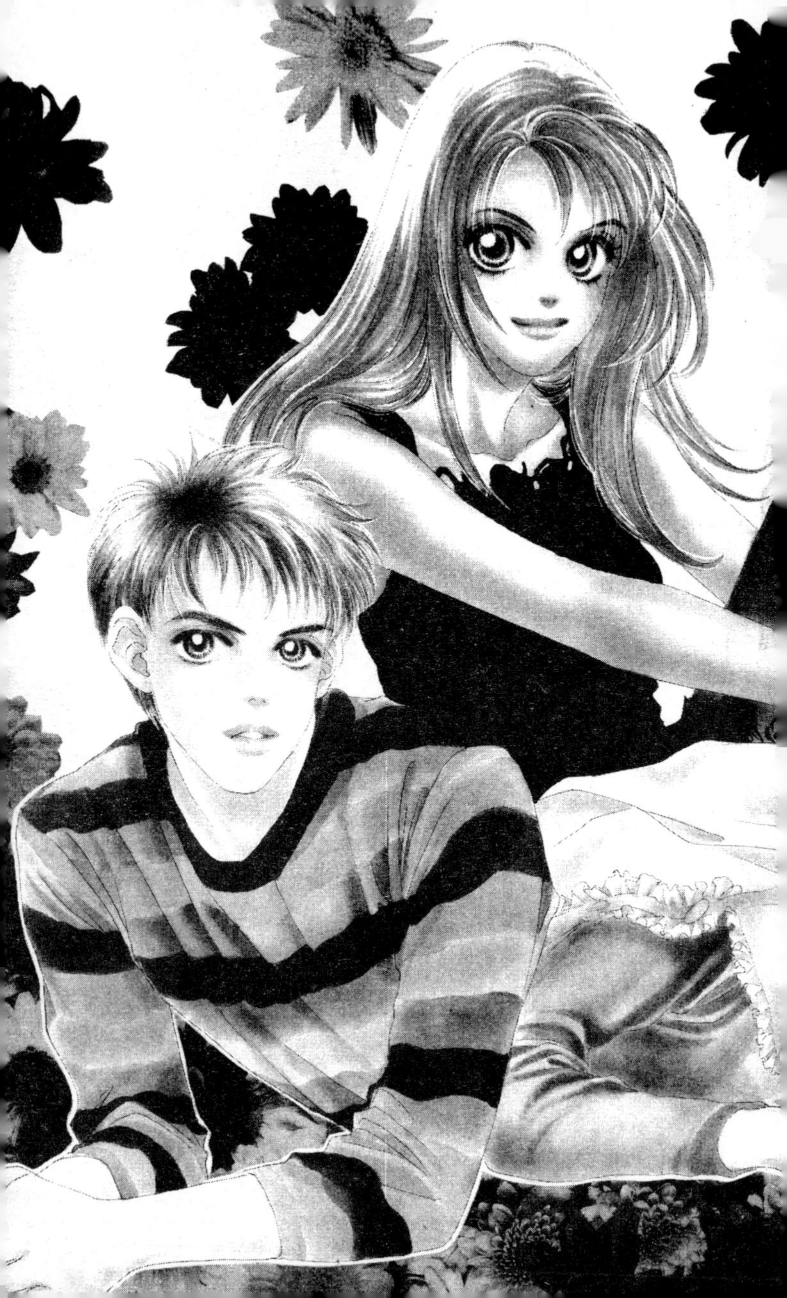

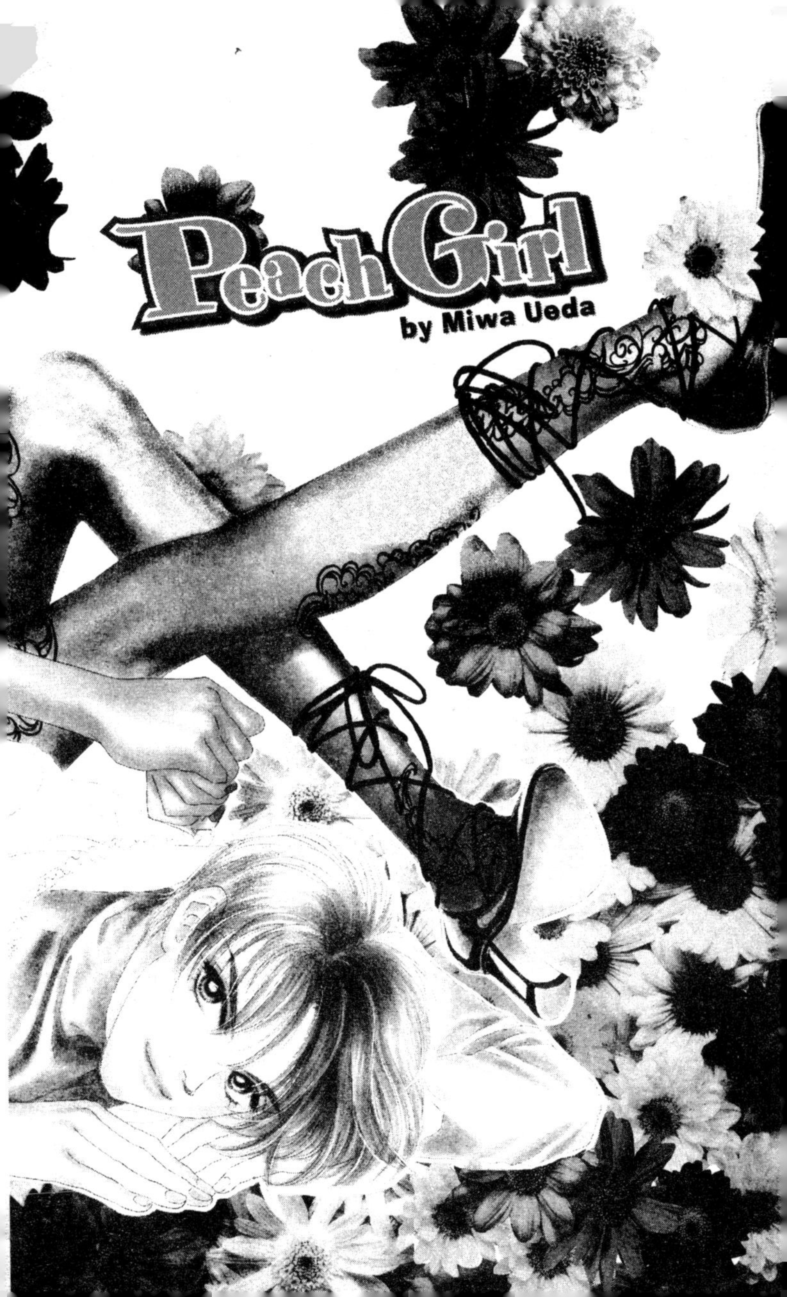
Peach Girl
by Miwa Ueda

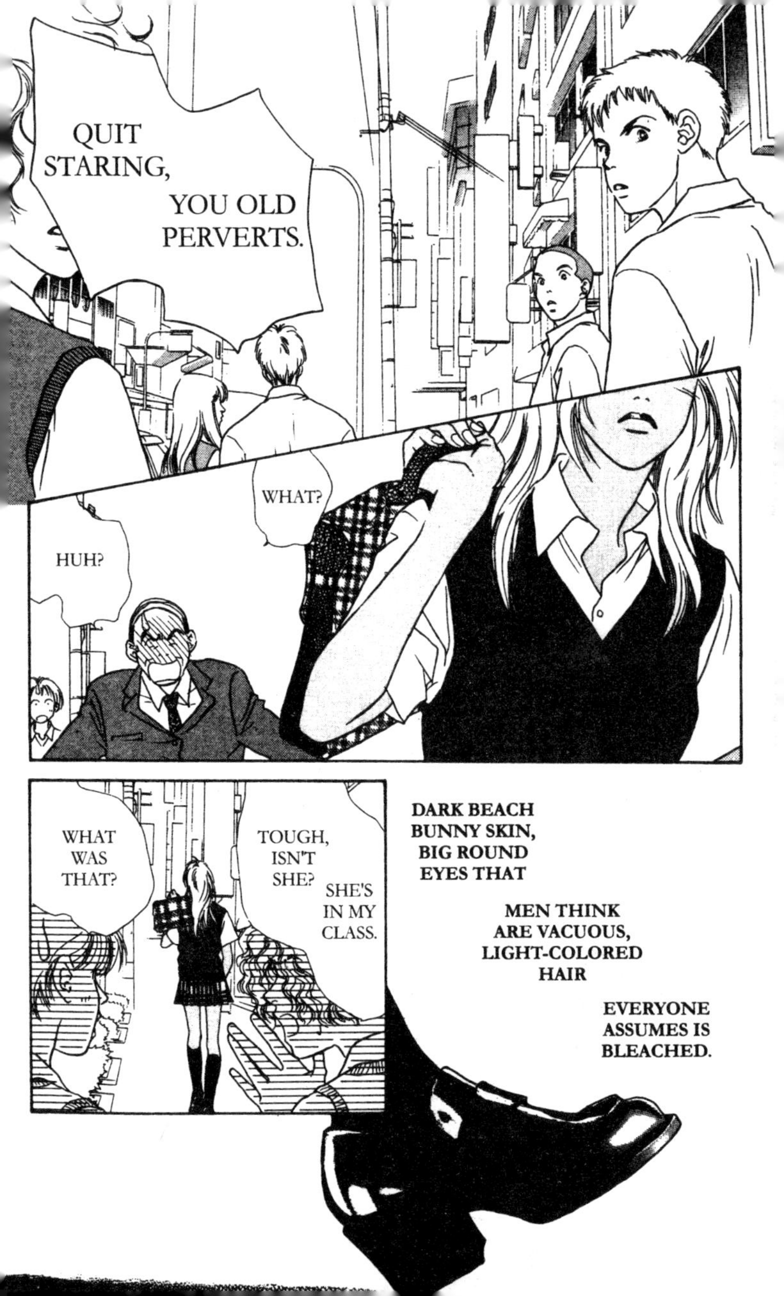
QUIT STARING, YOU OLD PERVERTS.
HUH?
WHAT?
WHAT WAS THAT?
TOUGH, ISN'T SHE?
SHE'S IN MY CLASS.
DARK BEACH BUNNY SKIN, BIG ROUND EYES THAT
MEN THINK ARE VACUOUS, LIGHT-COLORED HAIR
EVERYONE ASSUMES IS BLEACHED.

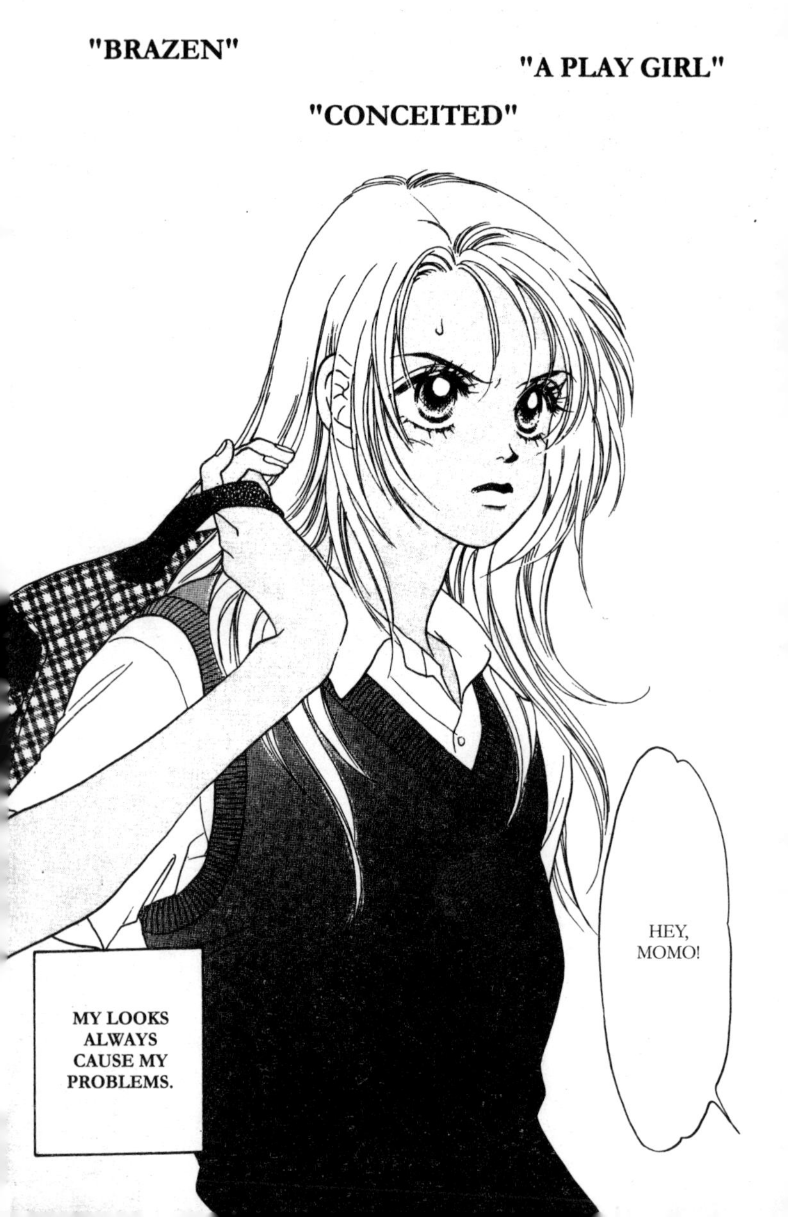
"BRAZEN"
"A PLAY GIRL"
"CONCEITED"
MY LOOKS ALWAYS CAUSE MY PROBLEMS.
HEY, MOMO!

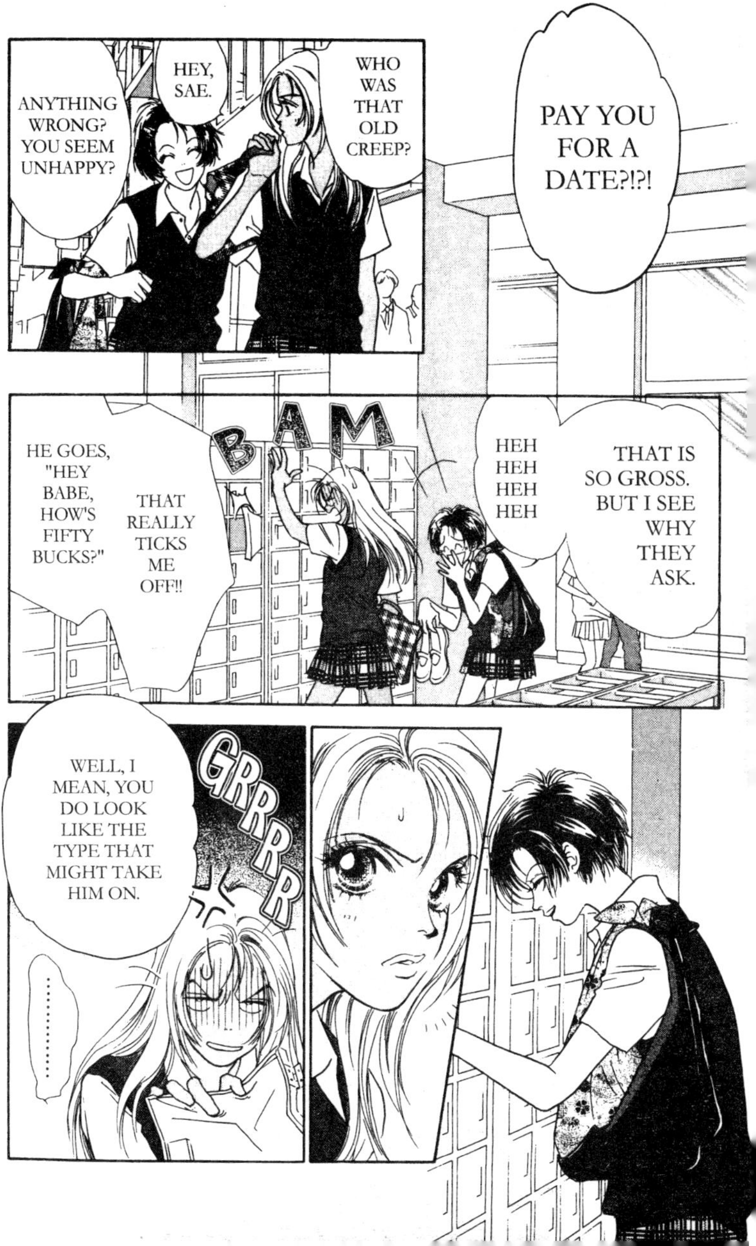
ANYTHING WRONG? YOU SEEM UNHAPPY?
HEY, SAE.
WHO WAS THAT OLD CREEP?
PAY YOU FOR A DATE?!?!
HE GOES, "HEY BABE, HOW'S FIFTY BUCKS?"
THAT REALLY TICKS ME OFF!!
BAM
HEH HEH HEH HEH
THAT IS SO GROSS. BUT I SEE WHY THEY ASK.
WELL, I MEAN, YOU DO LOOK LIKE THE TYPE THAT MIGHT TAKE HIM ON.
GRRRR
....

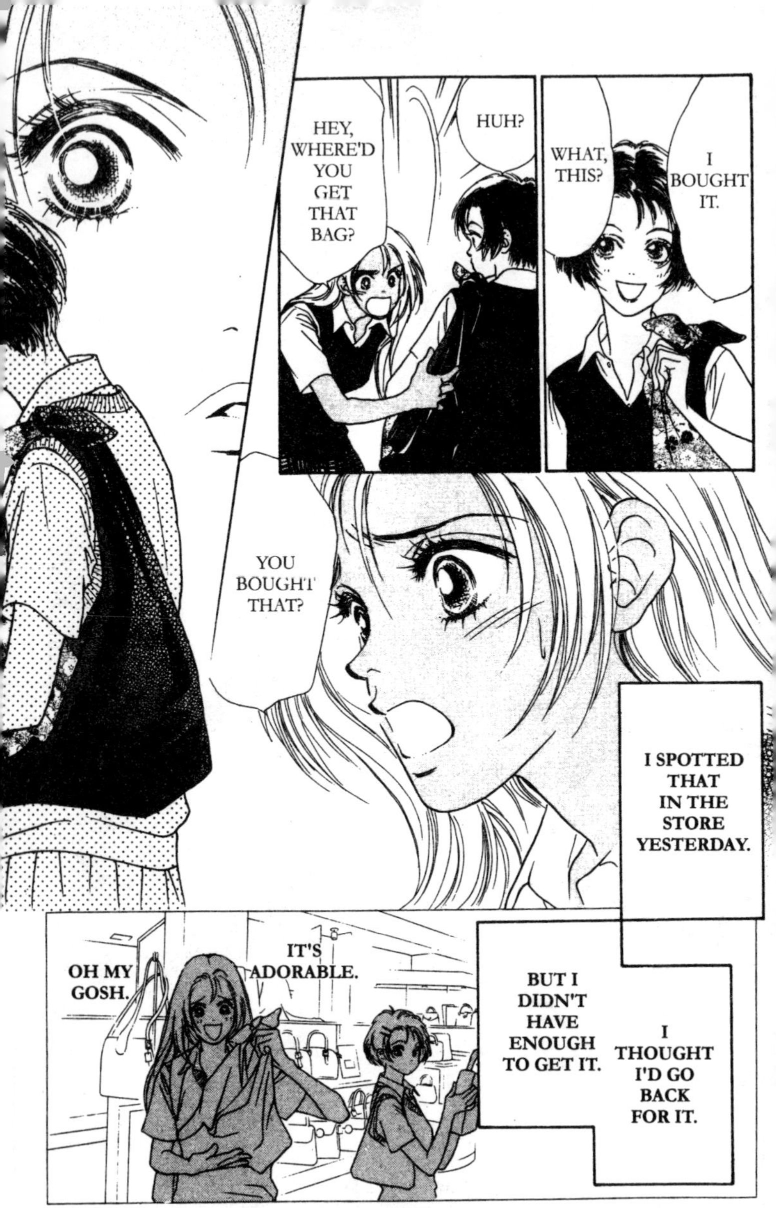
HEY, WHERE'D YOU GET THAT BAG?
HUH?
WHAT, THIS?
I BOUGHT IT.
YOU BOUGHT THAT?
I SPOTTED THAT IN THE STORE YESTERDAY.
OH MY GOSH.
IT'S ADORABLE.
BUT I DIDN'T HAVE ENOUGH TO GET IT.
I THOUGHT I'D GO BACK FOR IT.

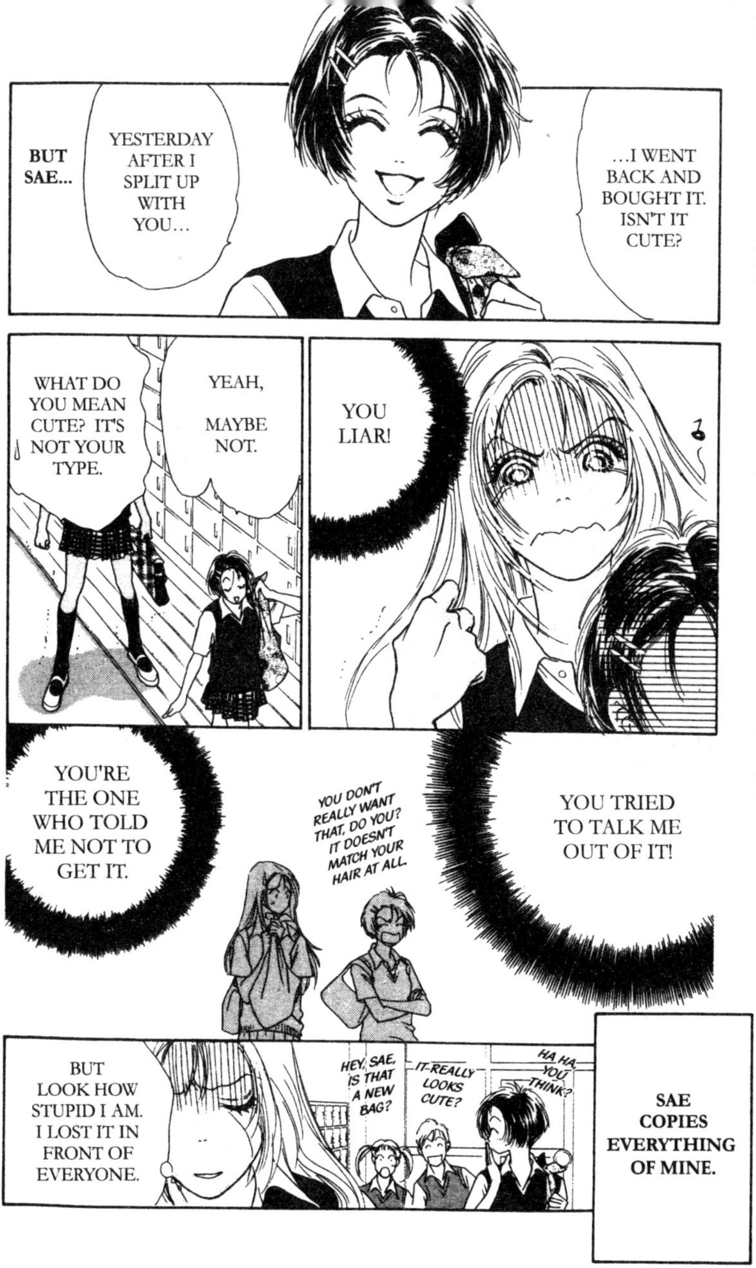
BUT SAE...
YESTERDAY AFTER I SPLIT UP WITH YOU...
...I WENT BACK AND BOUGHT IT. ISN'T IT CUTE?
WHAT DO YOU MEAN CUTE? IT'S NOT YOUR TYPE.
YEAH, MAYBE NOT.
YOU LIAR!
YOU'RE THE ONE WHO TOLD ME NOT TO GET IT.
YOU DON'T REALLY WANT THAT, DO YOU? IT DOESN'T MATCH YOUR HAIR AT ALL.
YOU TRIED TO TALK ME OUT OF IT!
BUT LOOK HOW STUPID I AM. I LOST IT IN FRONT OF EVERYONE.
HEY, SAE, IS THAT A NEW BAG?
IT REALLY LOOKS CUTE?
HA HA, YOU THINK?
SAE COPIES EVERYTHING OF MINE.

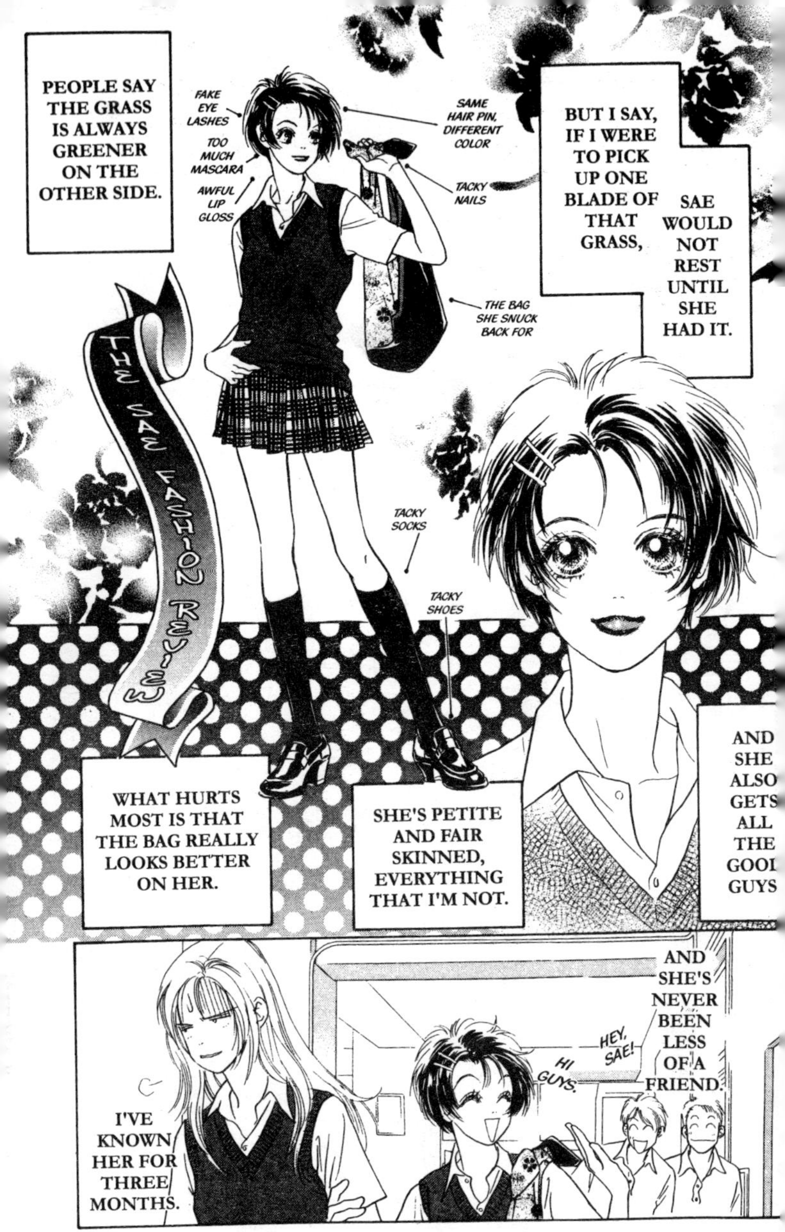
PEOPLE SAY THE GRASS IS ALWAYS GREENER ON THE OTHER SIDE.
FAKE EYE LASHES
TOO MUCH MASCARA
AWFUL LIP GLOSS
SAME HAIR PIN, DIFFERENT COLOR
TACKY NAILS
THE BAG SHE SNUCK BACK FOR
BUT I SAY, IF I WERE TO PICK UP ONE BLADE OF THAT GRASS,
SAE WOULD NOT REST UNTIL SHE HAD IT.
THE SAE FASHION REVIEW
TACKY SOCKS
TACKY SHOES
WHAT HURTS MOST IS THAT THE BAG REALLY LOOKS BETTER ON HER.
SHE'S PETITE AND FAIR SKINNED, EVERYTHING THAT I'M NOT.
AND SHE ALSO GETS ALL THE GOOD GUYS
I'VE KNOWN HER FOR THREE MONTHS.
HI GUYS.
HEY, SAE!
AND SHE'S NEVER BEEN LESS OF A FRIEND.

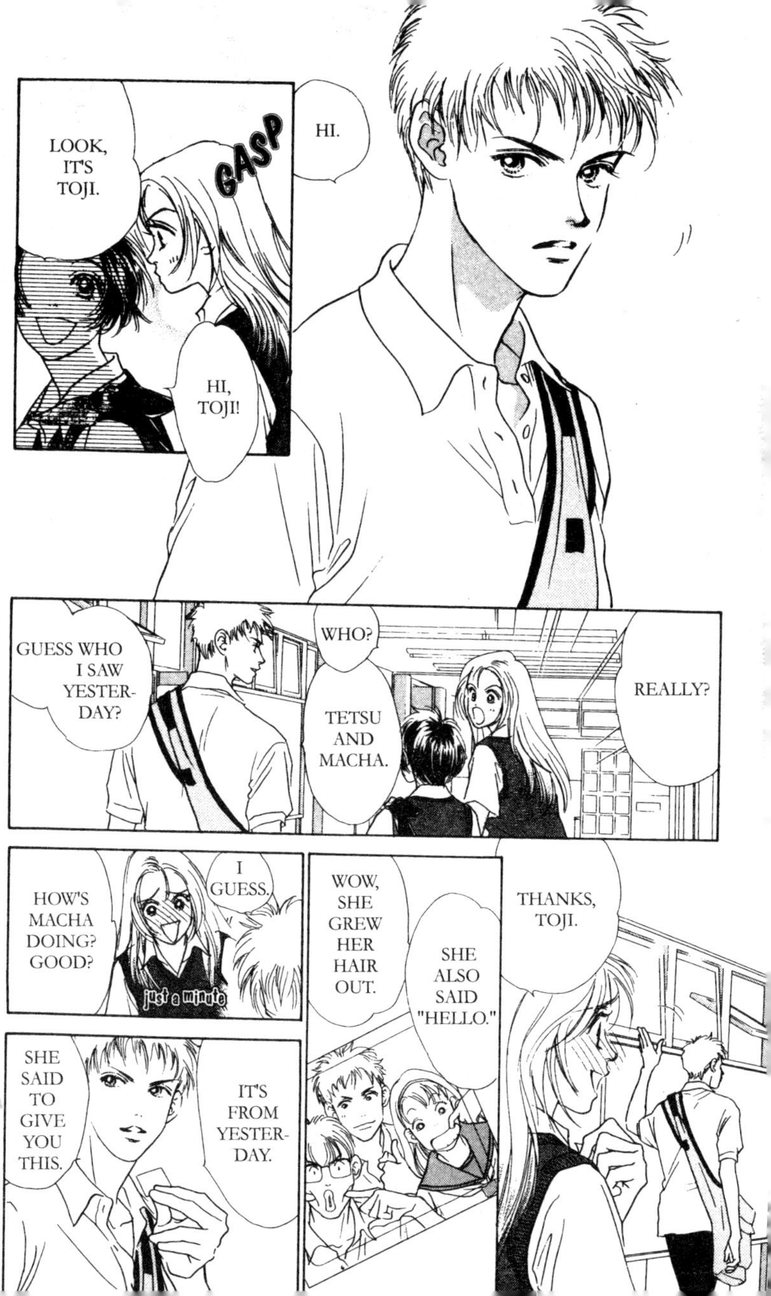
LOOK, IT'S TOJI.
GASP
HI, TOJI!
HI.
GUESS WHO I SAW YESTER-DAY?
WHO?
TETSU AND MACHA.
REALLY?
HOW'S MACHA DOING? GOOD?
I GUESS.
just a minute
SHE SAID TO GIVE YOU THIS.
IT'S FROM YESTER-DAY.
WOW, SHE GREW HER HAIR OUT.
SHE ALSO SAID "HELLO."
THANKS, TOJI.

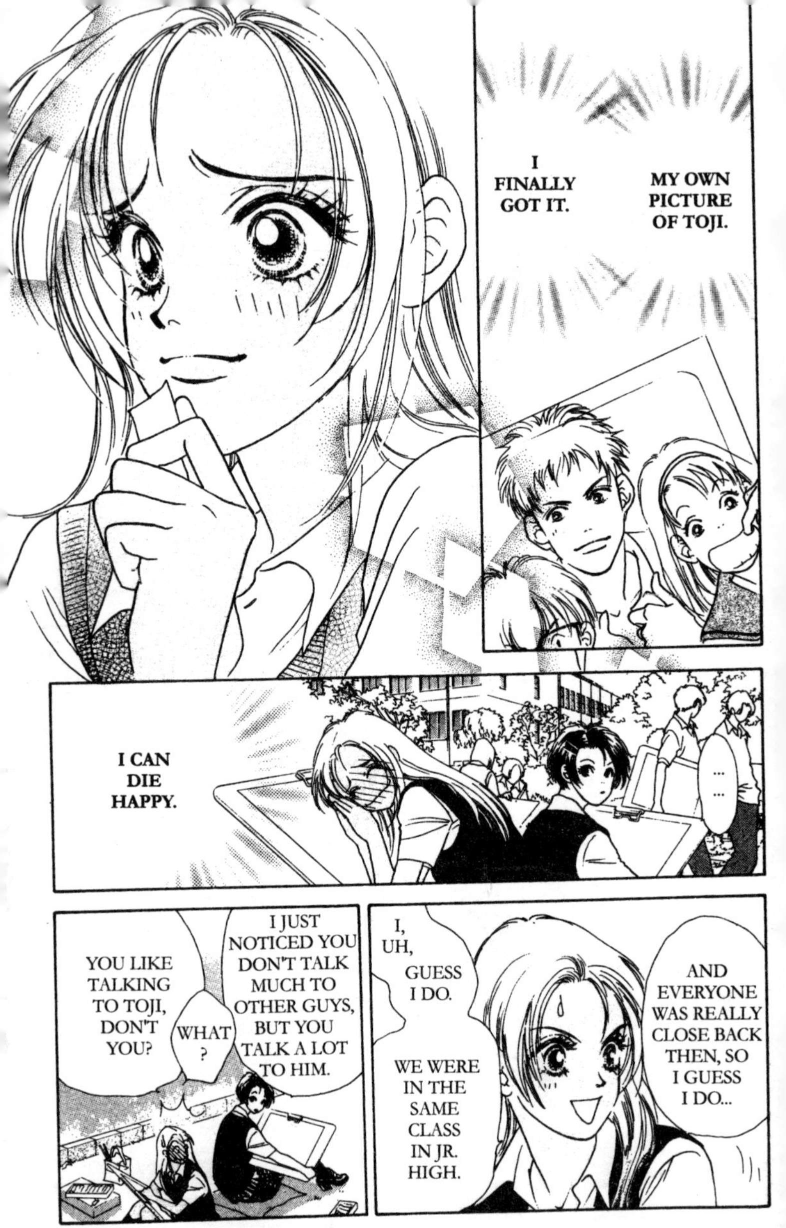
I FINALLY GOT IT.
MY OWN PICTURE OF TOJI.
I CAN DIE HAPPY.
... ...
YOU LIKE TALKING TO TOJI, DON'T YOU?
WHAT?
I JUST NOTICED YOU DON'T TALK MUCH TO OTHER GUYS, BUT YOU TALK A LOT TO HIM.
I, UH, GUESS I DO.
WE WERE IN THE SAME CLASS IN JR. HIGH.
AND EVERYONE WAS REALLY CLOSE BACK THEN, SO I GUESS I DO...

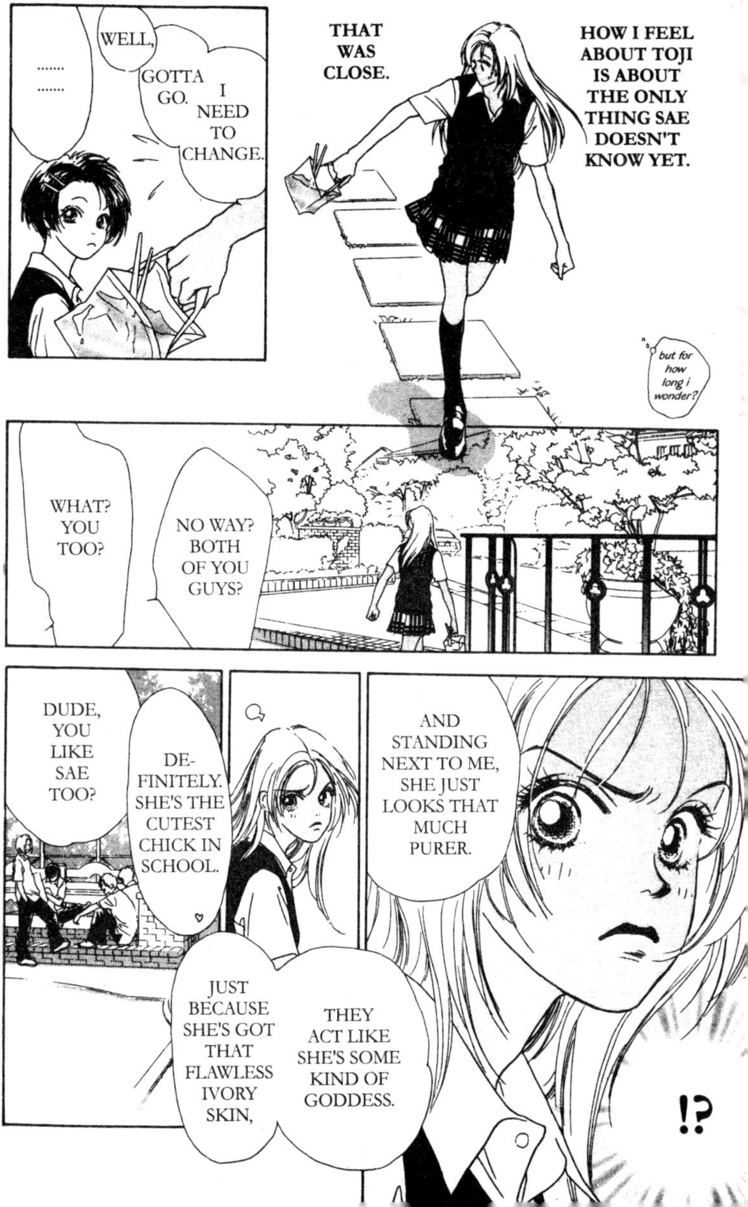

....
....
WELL,
GOTTA GO.
I NEED TO CHANGE.
THAT WAS CLOSE.
HOW I FEEL ABOUT TOJI IS ABOUT THE ONLY THING SAE DOESN'T KNOW YET.
but for how long i wonder?
WHAT? YOU TOO?
NO WAY? BOTH OF YOU GUYS?
DUDE, YOU LIKE SAE TOO?
DE-FINITELY. SHE'S THE CUTEST CHICK IN SCHOOL.
JUST BECAUSE SHE'S GOT THAT FLAWLESS IVORY SKIN,
THEY ACT LIKE SHE'S SOME KIND OF GODDESS.
AND STANDING NEXT TO ME, SHE JUST LOOKS THAT MUCH PURER.
!?

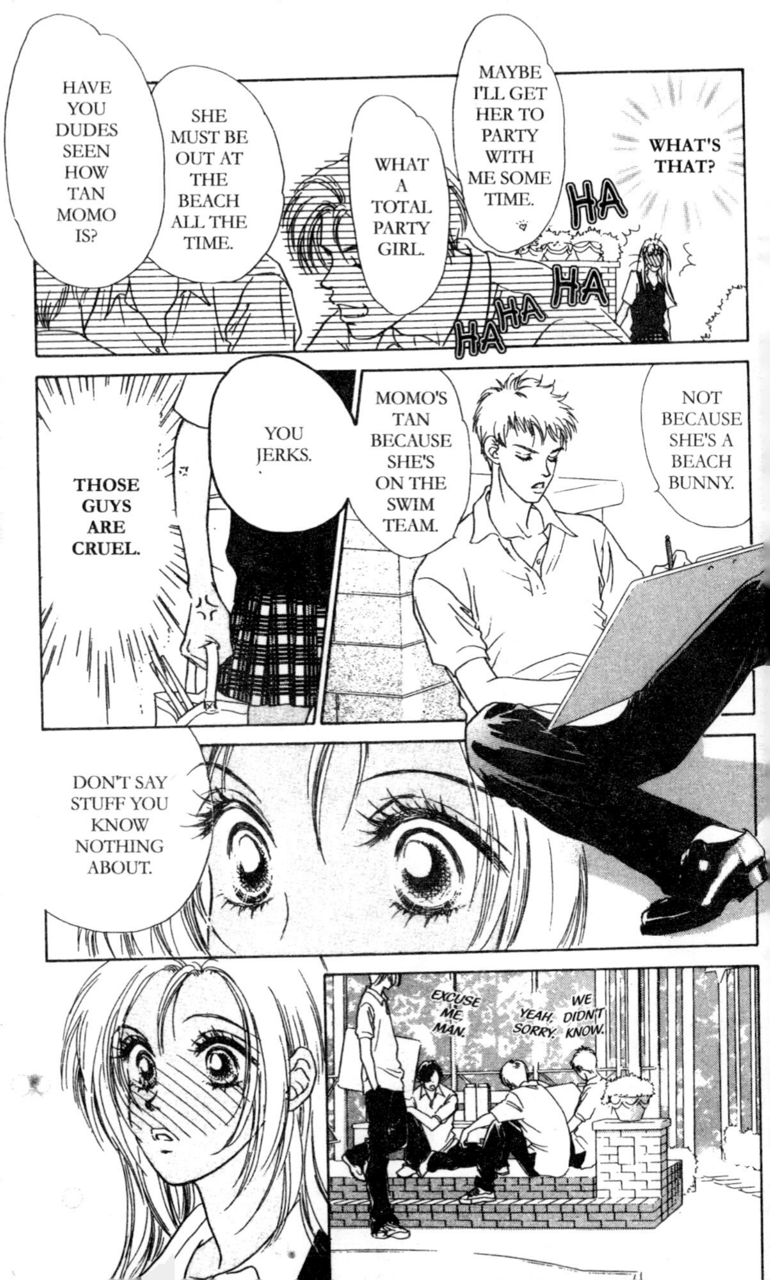
HAVE YOU DUDES SEEN HOW TAN MOMO IS?
SHE MUST BE OUT AT THE BEACH ALL THE TIME.
WHAT A TOTAL PARTY GIRL.
MAYBE I'LL GET HER TO PARTY WITH ME SOME TIME.
HA HA HA HA
WHAT'S THAT?
THOSE GUYS ARE CRUEL.
YOU JERKS.
MOMO'S TAN BECAUSE SHE'S ON THE SWIM TEAM.
NOT BECAUSE SHE'S A BEACH BUNNY.
DON'T SAY STUFF YOU KNOW NOTHING ABOUT.
EXCUSE ME, MAN.
YEAH, SORRY.
WE DIDN'T KNOW.

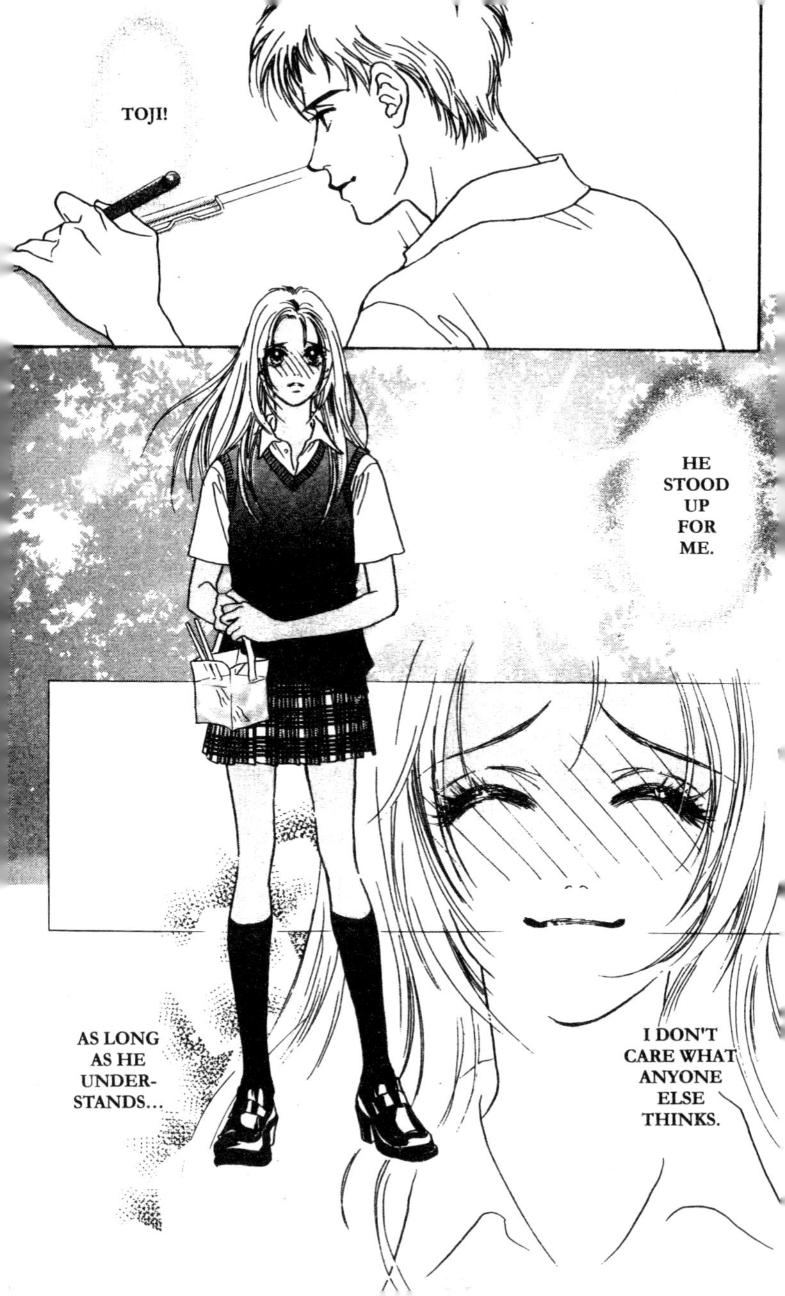
TOJI!
HE STOOD UP FOR ME.
AS LONG AS HE UNDER-STANDS...
I DON'T CARE WHAT ANYONE ELSE THINKS.

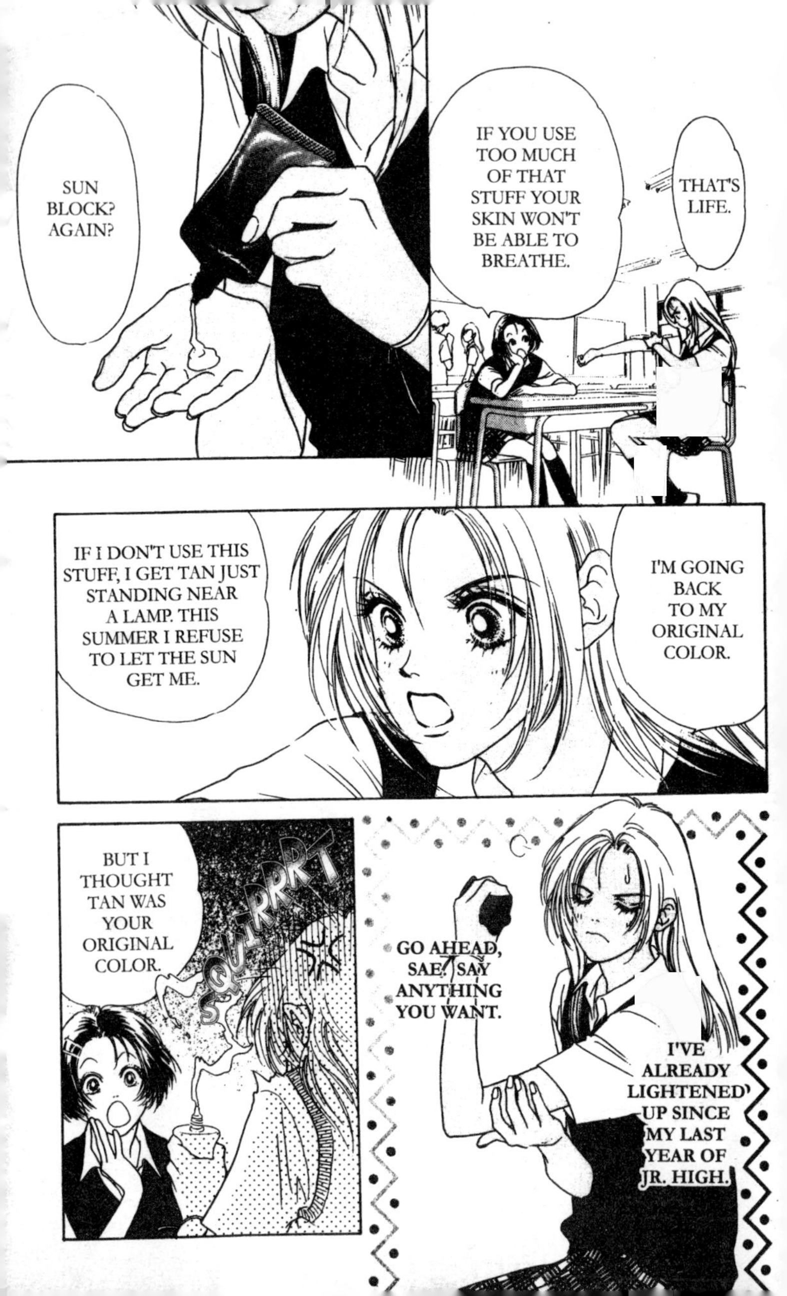
SUN BLOCK? AGAIN?
IF YOU USE TOO MUCH OF THAT STUFF YOUR SKIN WON'T BE ABLE TO BREATHE.
THAT'S LIFE.
IF I DON'T USE THIS STUFF, I GET TAN JUST STANDING NEAR A LAMP. THIS SUMMER I REFUSE TO LET THE SUN GET ME.
I'M GOING BACK TO MY ORIGINAL COLOR.
BUT I THOUGHT TAN WAS YOUR ORIGINAL COLOR.
SQUIRRRT
GO AHEAD, SAE. SAY ANYTHING YOU WANT.
I'VE ALREADY LIGHTENED UP SINCE MY LAST YEAR OF JR. HIGH.

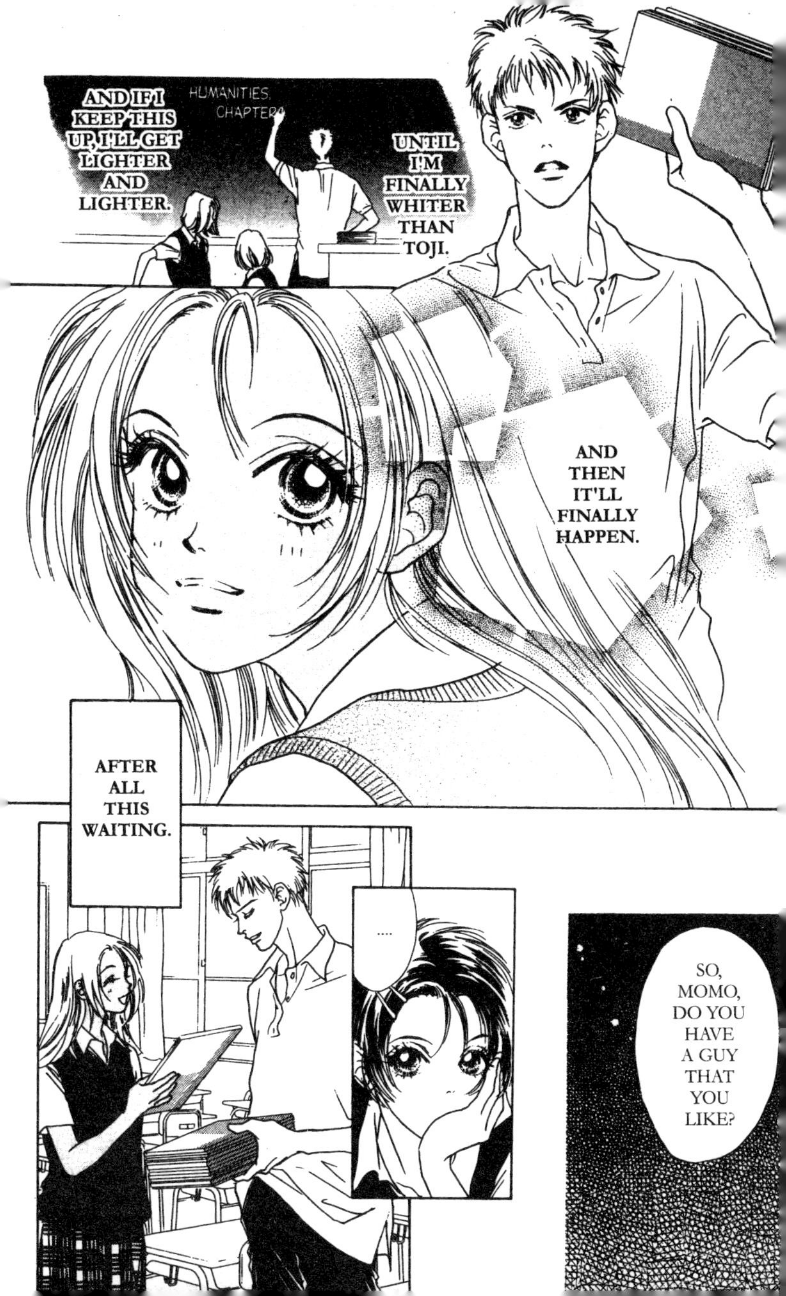
HUMANITIES, CHAPTER 2
AND IF I KEEP THIS UP, I'LL GET LIGHTER AND LIGHTER.
UNTIL I'M FINALLY WHITER THAN TOJI.
AND THEN IT'LL FINALLY HAPPEN.
AFTER ALL THIS WAITING.
....
SO, MOMO, DO YOU HAVE A GUY THAT YOU LIKE?

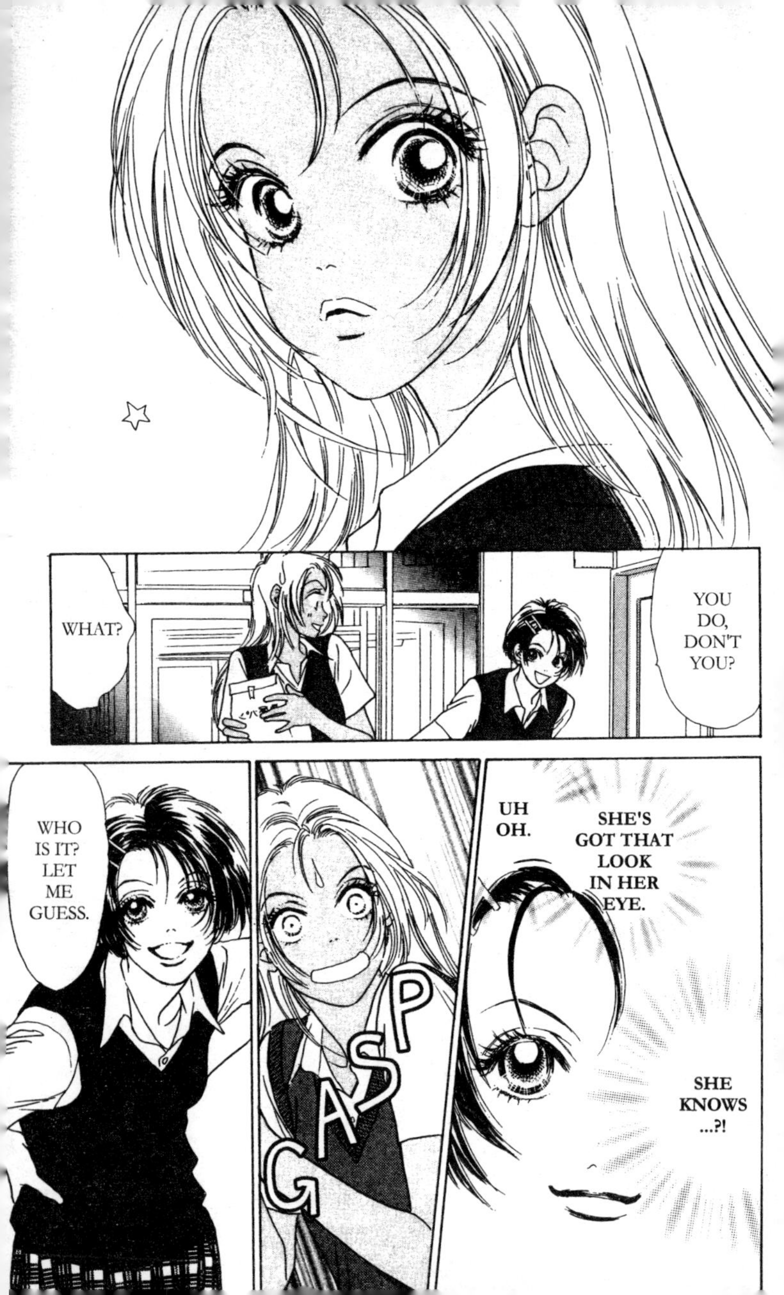
WHAT?
YOU DO, DON'T YOU?
WHO IS IT? LET ME GUESS.
GASP
UH OH.
SHE'S GOT THAT LOOK IN HER EYE.
SHE KNOWS ...?!

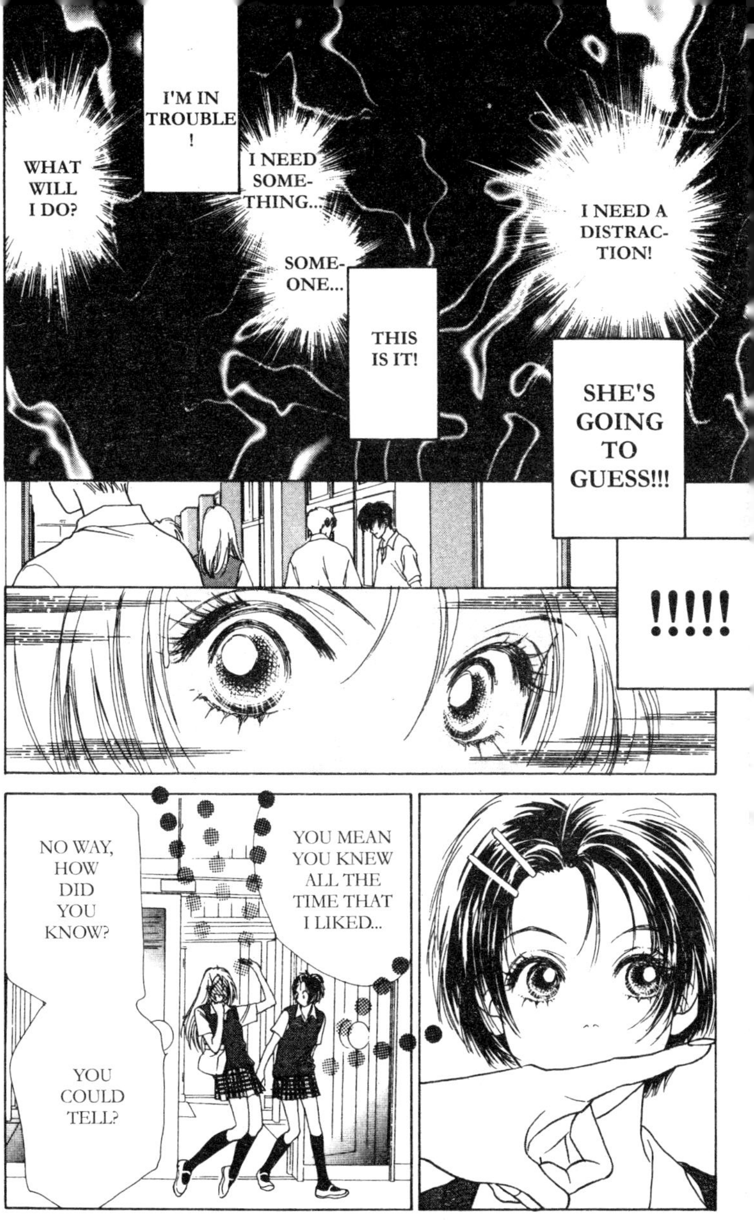
I'M IN TROUBLE!
WHAT WILL I DO?
I NEED SOMETHING...
I NEED A DISTRACTION!
SOMEONE...
THIS IS IT!
SHE'S GOING TO GUESS!!!
!!!!!
NO WAY, HOW DID YOU KNOW?
YOU COULD TELL?
YOU MEAN YOU KNEW ALL THE TIME THAT I LIKED...

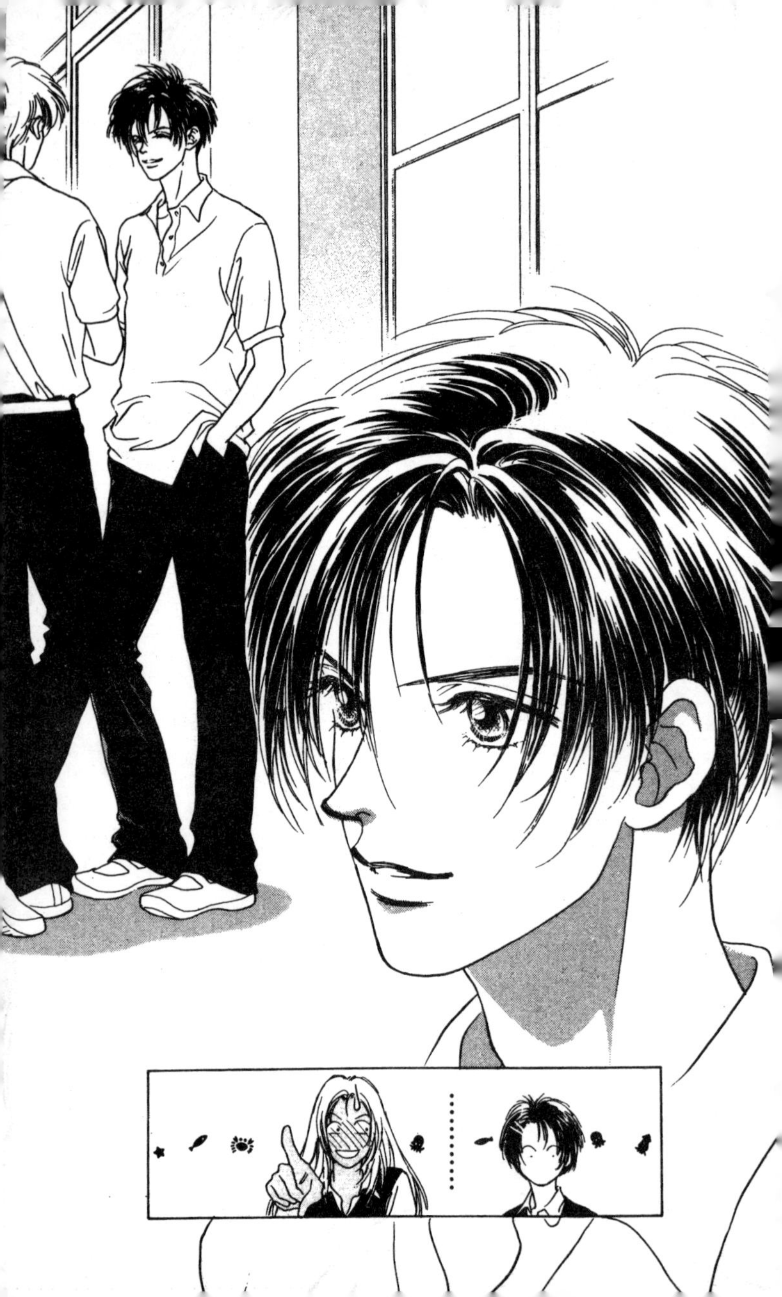

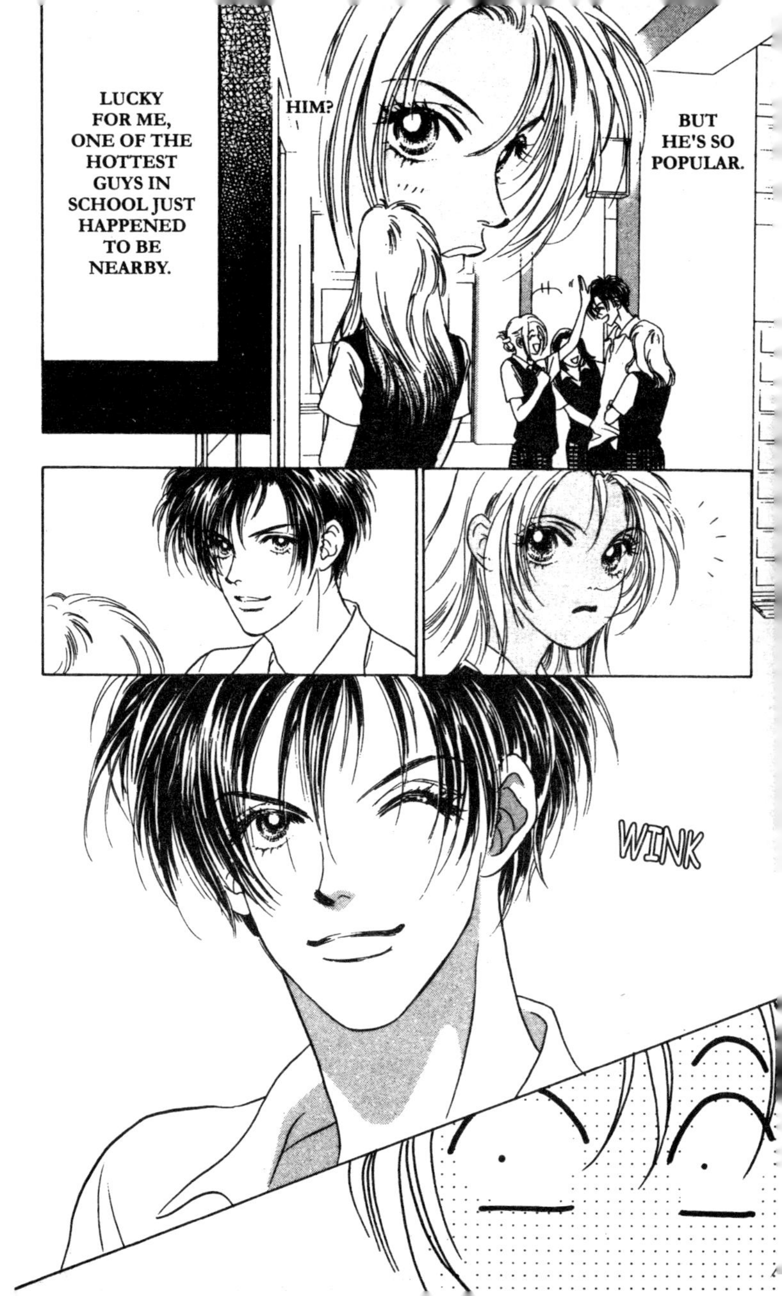
LUCKY FOR ME, ONE OF THE HOTTEST GUYS IN SCHOOL JUST HAPPENED TO BE NEARBY.
HIM?
BUT HE'S SO POPULAR.
WINK

I...

HE JUST...

GULP

THAT WAS THE FIRST TIME A GUY EVER WINKED AT ME.

I WAS IN SHOCK.

THE GUY WAS KILEY OKAYASU. HE NEVER EVEN LOOKED MY WAY BEFORE.

TALK ABOUT CONCEITED.

THE KIND OF FACE THAT SHOULD BE MODELING SOMETHING.

IT'S EASY TO SEE WHY THE GIRLS MAKE SUCH A FUSS.

EVEN THOUGH TOJI'S A HUNDRED TIMES COOLER.

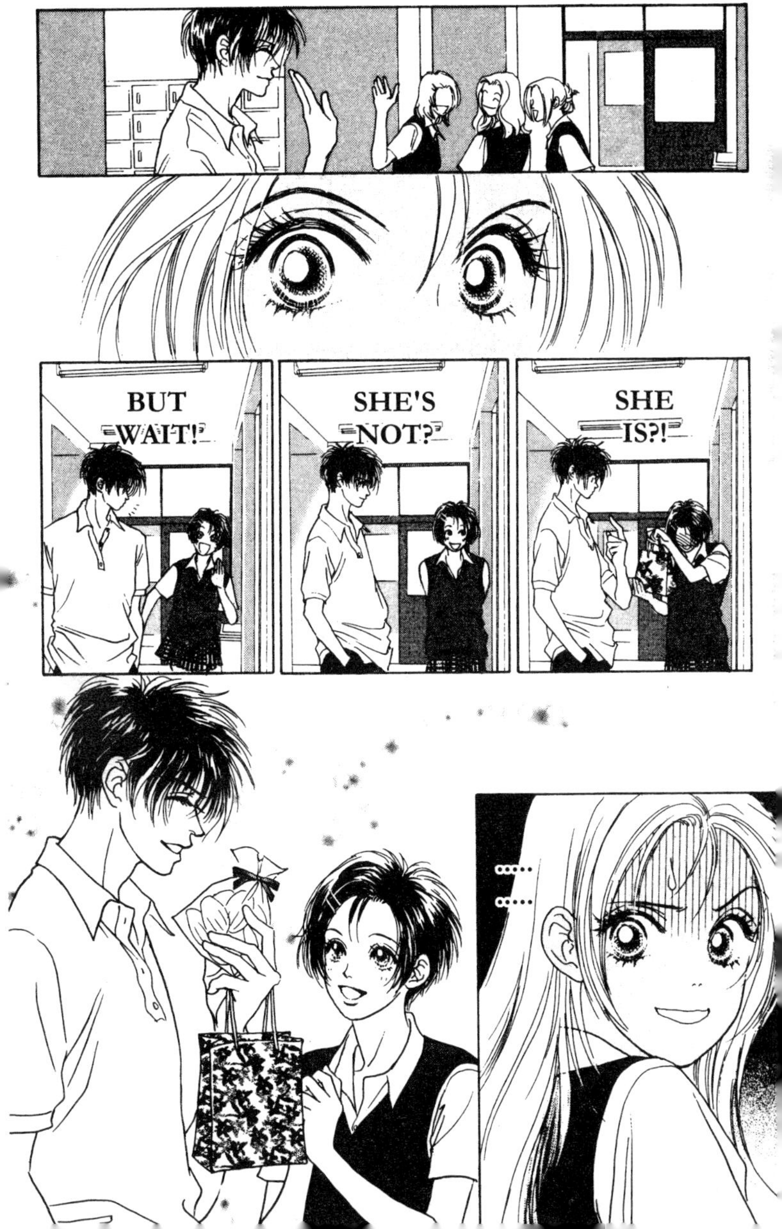

BUT WAIT!
SHE'S NOT?
SHE IS?!
......
......

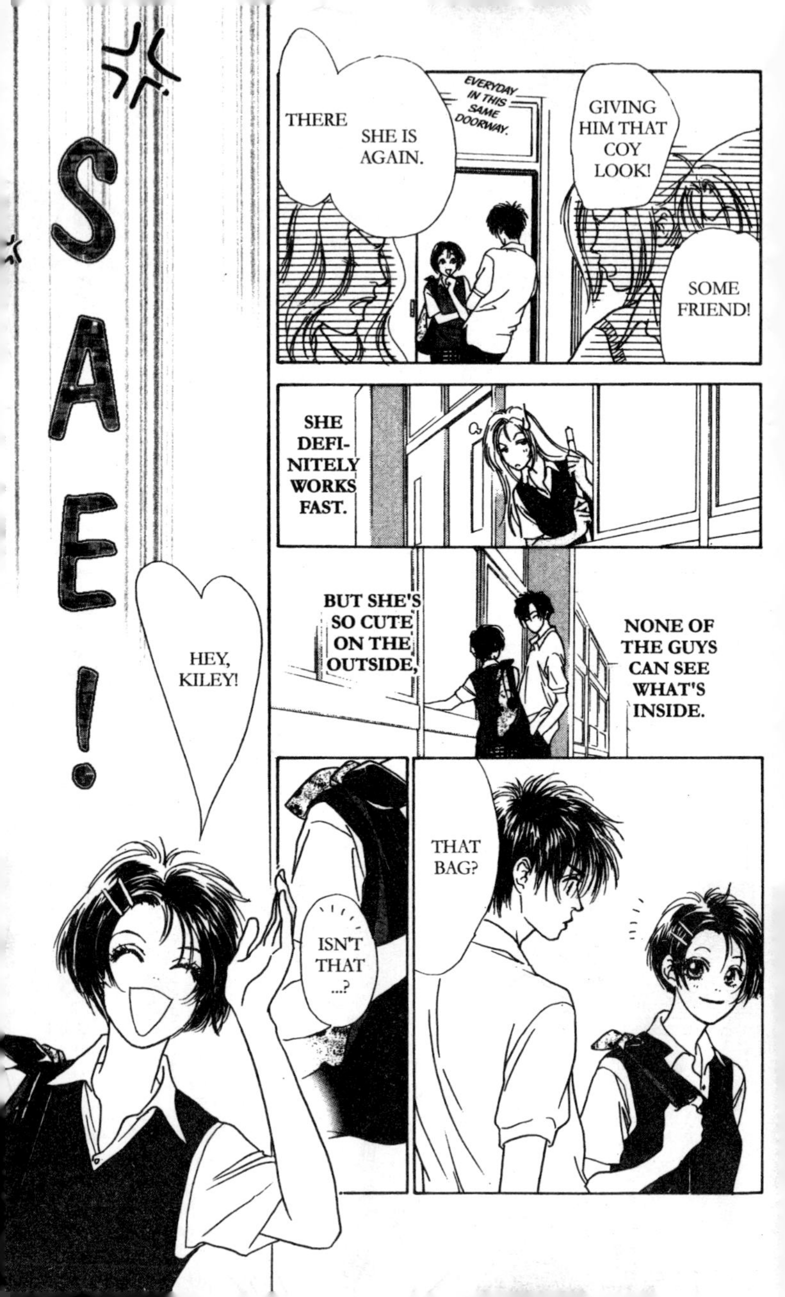
SAE!
HEY, KILEY!
THERE SHE IS AGAIN.
EVERYDAY IN THIS SAME DOORWAY.
GIVING HIM THAT COY LOOK!
SOME FRIEND!
SHE DEFI-NITELY WORKS FAST.
BUT SHE'S SO CUTE ON THE OUTSIDE,
NONE OF THE GUYS CAN SEE WHAT'S INSIDE.
ISN'T THAT ...?
THAT BAG?

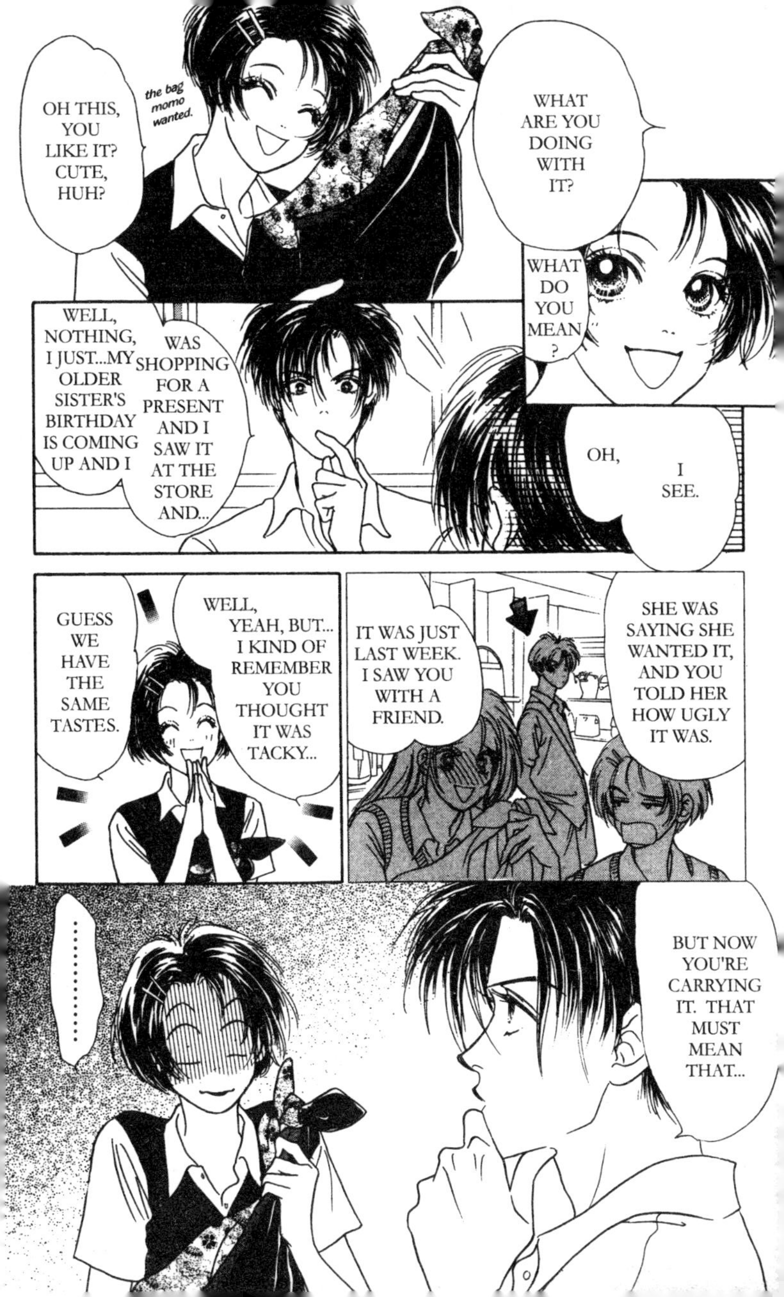
OH THIS, YOU LIKE IT? CUTE, HUH?
the bag momo wanted.
WHAT ARE YOU DOING WITH IT?
WHAT DO YOU MEAN?
WELL, NOTHING, I JUST...MY OLDER SISTER'S BIRTHDAY IS COMING UP AND I
WAS SHOPPING FOR A PRESENT AND I SAW IT AT THE STORE AND...
OH,
I SEE.
GUESS WE HAVE THE SAME TASTES.
WELL, YEAH, BUT... I KIND OF REMEMBER YOU THOUGHT IT WAS TACKY...
IT WAS JUST LAST WEEK. I SAW YOU WITH A FRIEND.
SHE WAS SAYING SHE WANTED IT, AND YOU TOLD HER HOW UGLY IT WAS.
....
BUT NOW YOU'RE CARRYING IT. THAT MUST MEAN THAT...

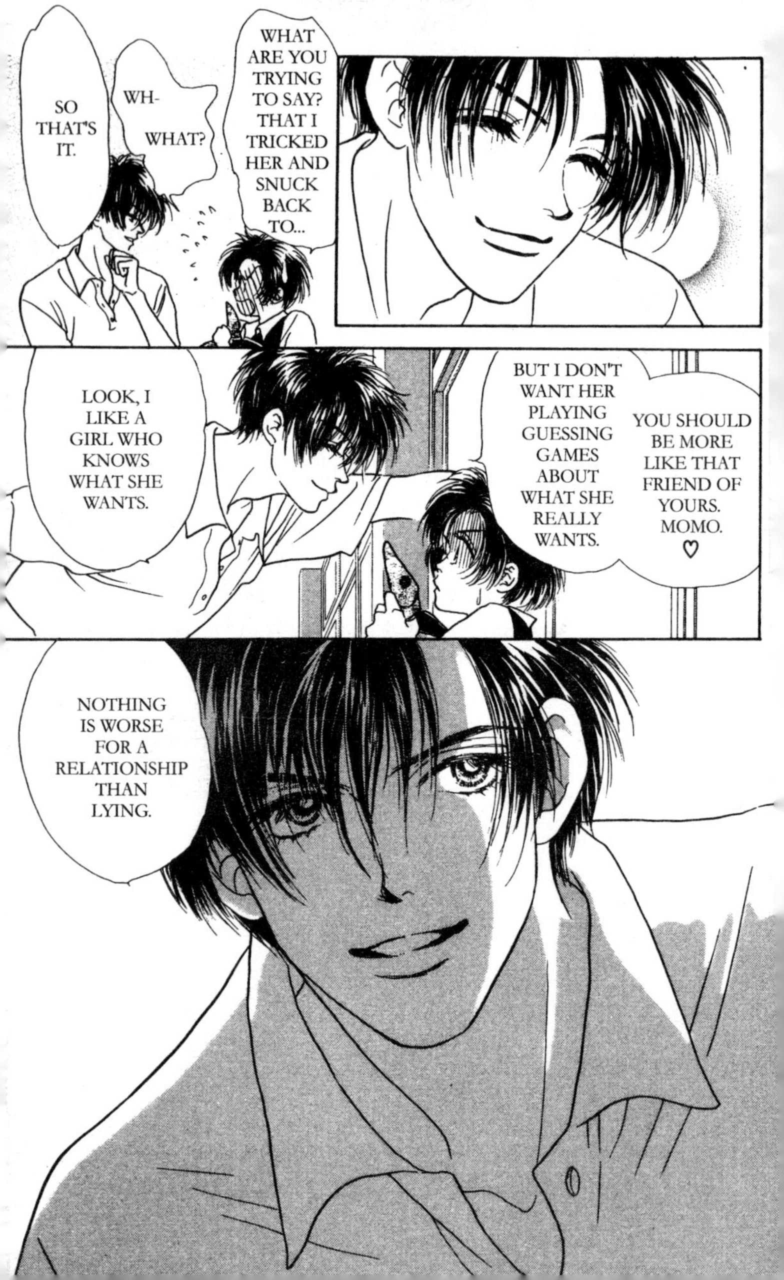
SO THAT'S IT.
WH- WHAT?
WHAT ARE YOU TRYING TO SAY? THAT I TRICKED HER AND SNUCK BACK TO...
LOOK, I LIKE A GIRL WHO KNOWS WHAT SHE WANTS.
BUT I DON'T WANT HER PLAYING GUESSING GAMES ABOUT WHAT SHE REALLY WANTS.
YOU SHOULD BE MORE LIKE THAT FRIEND OF YOURS. MOMO. ♡
NOTHING IS WORSE FOR A RELATIONSHIP THAN LYING.

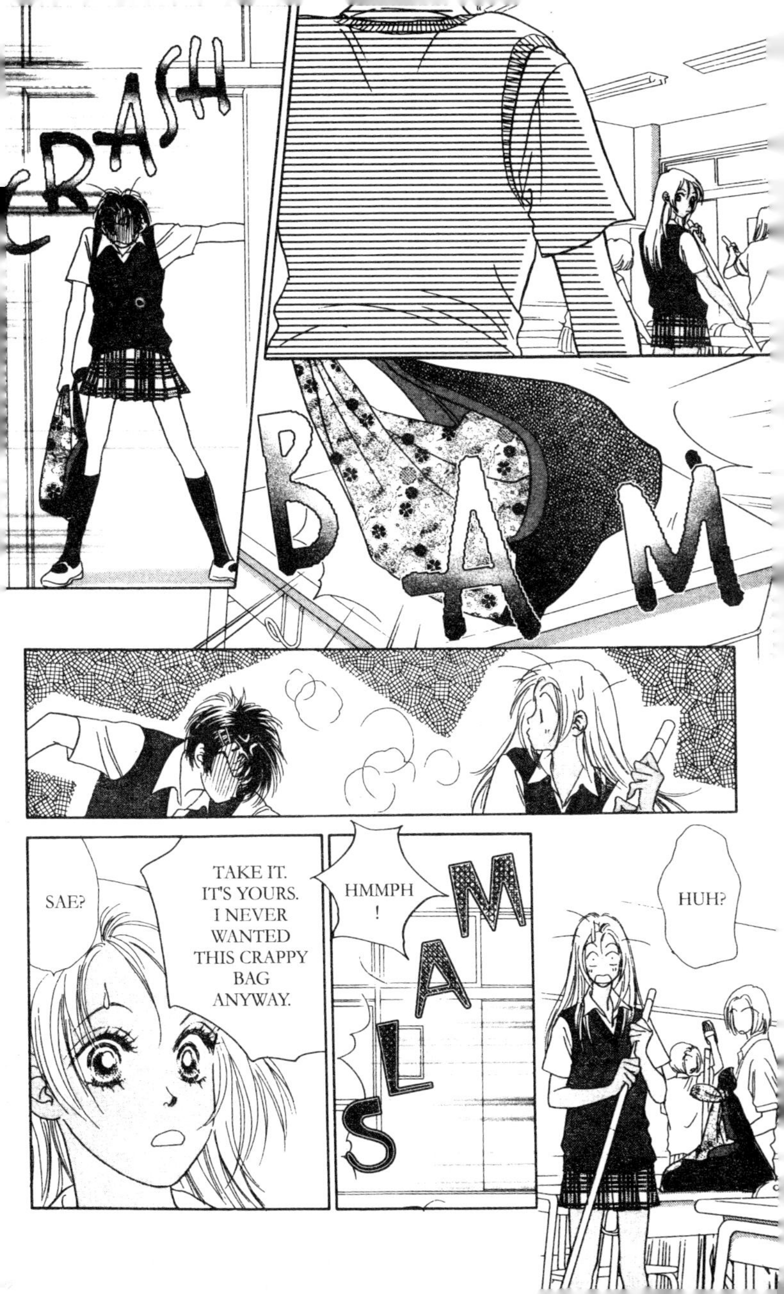
CRASH
BAM
SAE?
TAKE IT. IT'S YOURS. I NEVER WANTED THIS CRAPPY BAG ANYWAY.
HMMPH!
SLAM
HUH?

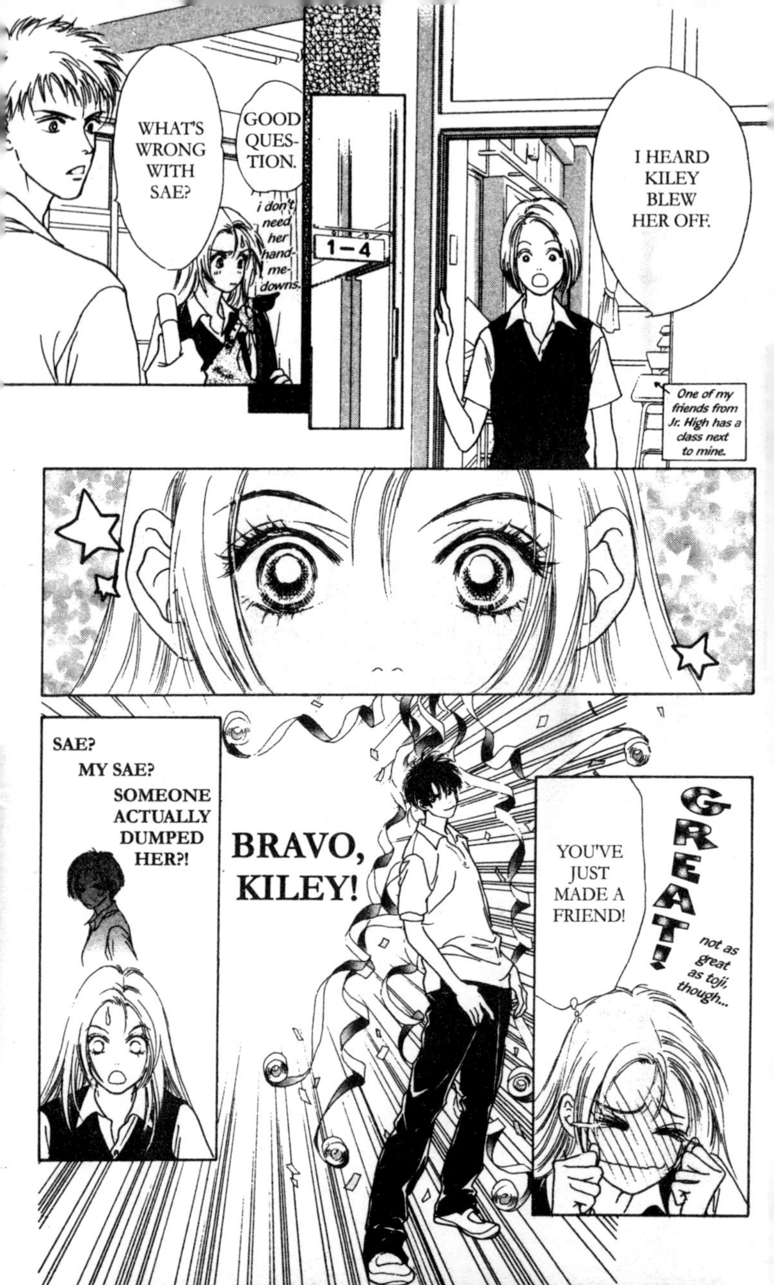
WHAT'S WRONG WITH SAE?
GOOD QUES-TION.
i don't need her hand-me-downs.
1-4
I HEARD KILEY BLEW HER OFF.
One of my friends from Jr. High has a class next to mine.
SAE? MY SAE? SOMEONE ACTUALLY DUMPED HER?!
BRAVO, KILEY!
YOU'VE JUST MADE A FRIEND!
GREAT!
not as great as toji, though...

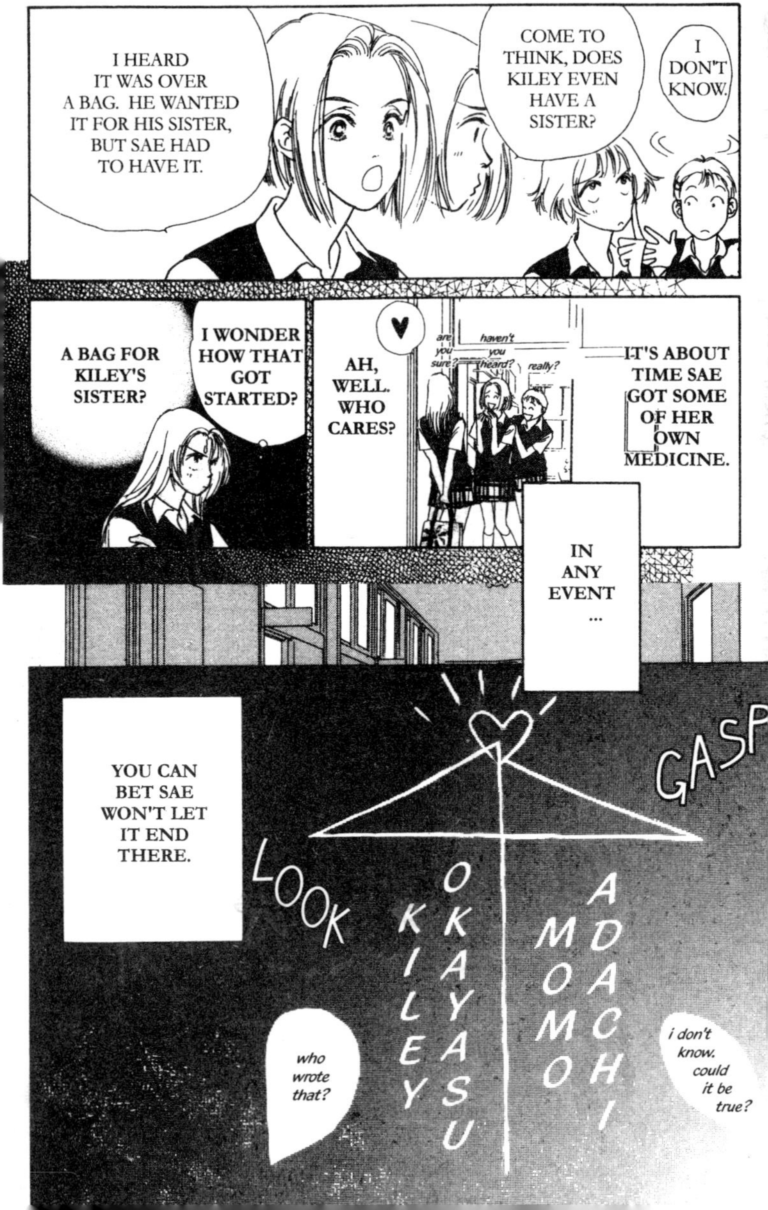
I HEARD IT WAS OVER A BAG. HE WANTED IT FOR HIS SISTER, BUT SAE HAD TO HAVE IT.
COME TO THINK, DOES KILEY EVEN HAVE A SISTER?
I DON'T KNOW.
A BAG FOR KILEY'S SISTER?
I WONDER HOW THAT GOT STARTED?
AH, WELL. WHO CARES?
are you sure?
haven't you heard?
really?
IT'S ABOUT TIME SAE GOT SOME OF HER OWN MEDICINE.
IN ANY EVENT ...
YOU CAN BET SAE WON'T LET IT END THERE.
LOOK
KILEY
OKAYASU
MOMO
ADACHI
GASP
who wrote that?
i don't know. could it be true?

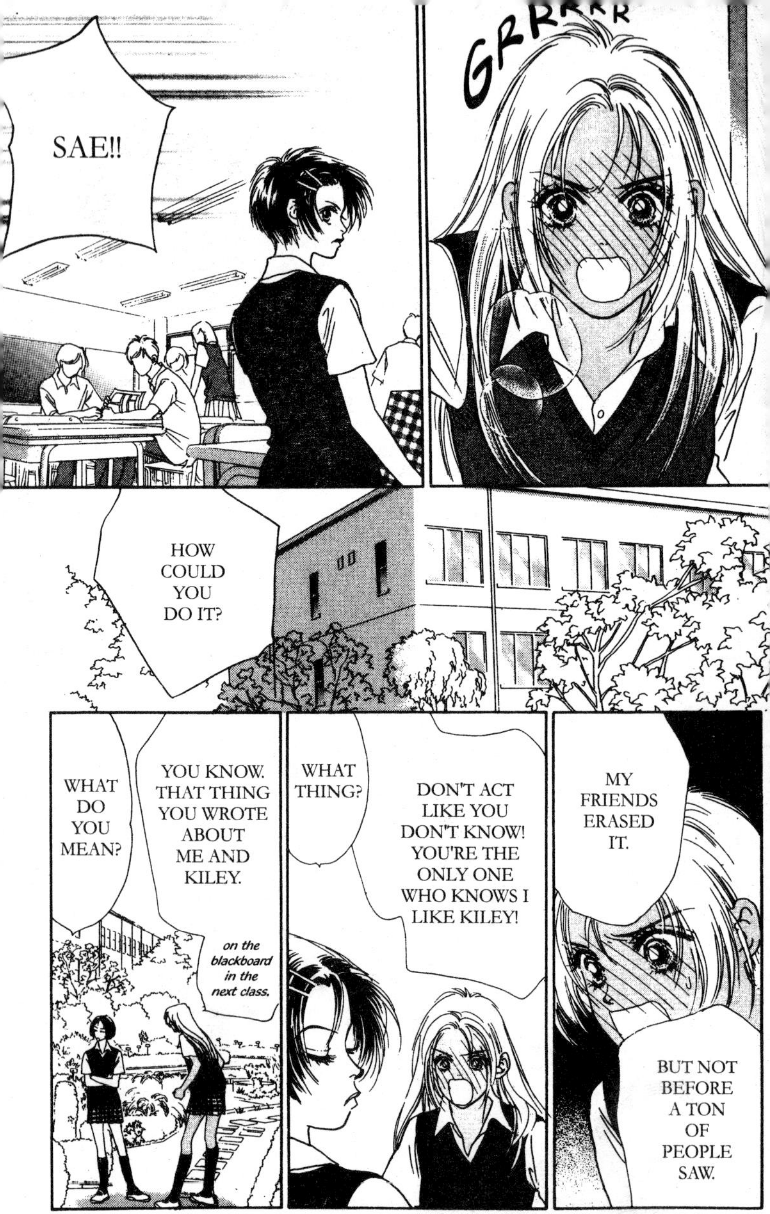
SAE!!
GRRRRR
HOW COULD YOU DO IT?
WHAT DO YOU MEAN?
YOU KNOW. THAT THING YOU WROTE ABOUT ME AND KILEY.
on the blackboard in the next class.
WHAT THING?
DON'T ACT LIKE YOU DON'T KNOW! YOU'RE THE ONLY ONE WHO KNOWS I LIKE KILEY!
MY FRIENDS ERASED IT.
BUT NOT BEFORE A TON OF PEOPLE SAW.

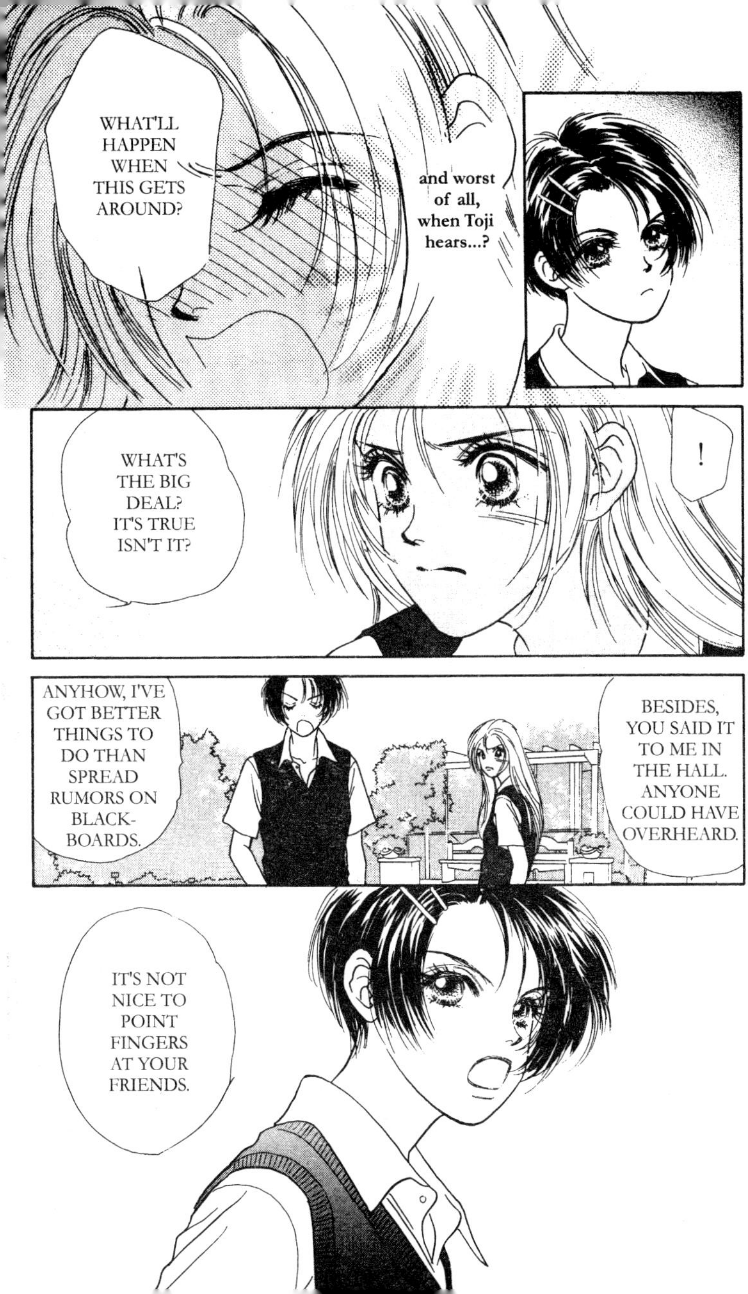
WHAT'LL HAPPEN WHEN THIS GETS AROUND?
and worst of all, when Toji hears...?
WHAT'S THE BIG DEAL? IT'S TRUE ISN'T IT?
!
ANYHOW, I'VE GOT BETTER THINGS TO DO THAN SPREAD RUMORS ON BLACK-BOARDS.
BESIDES, YOU SAID IT TO ME IN THE HALL. ANYONE COULD HAVE OVERHEARD.
IT'S NOT NICE TO POINT FINGERS AT YOUR FRIENDS.

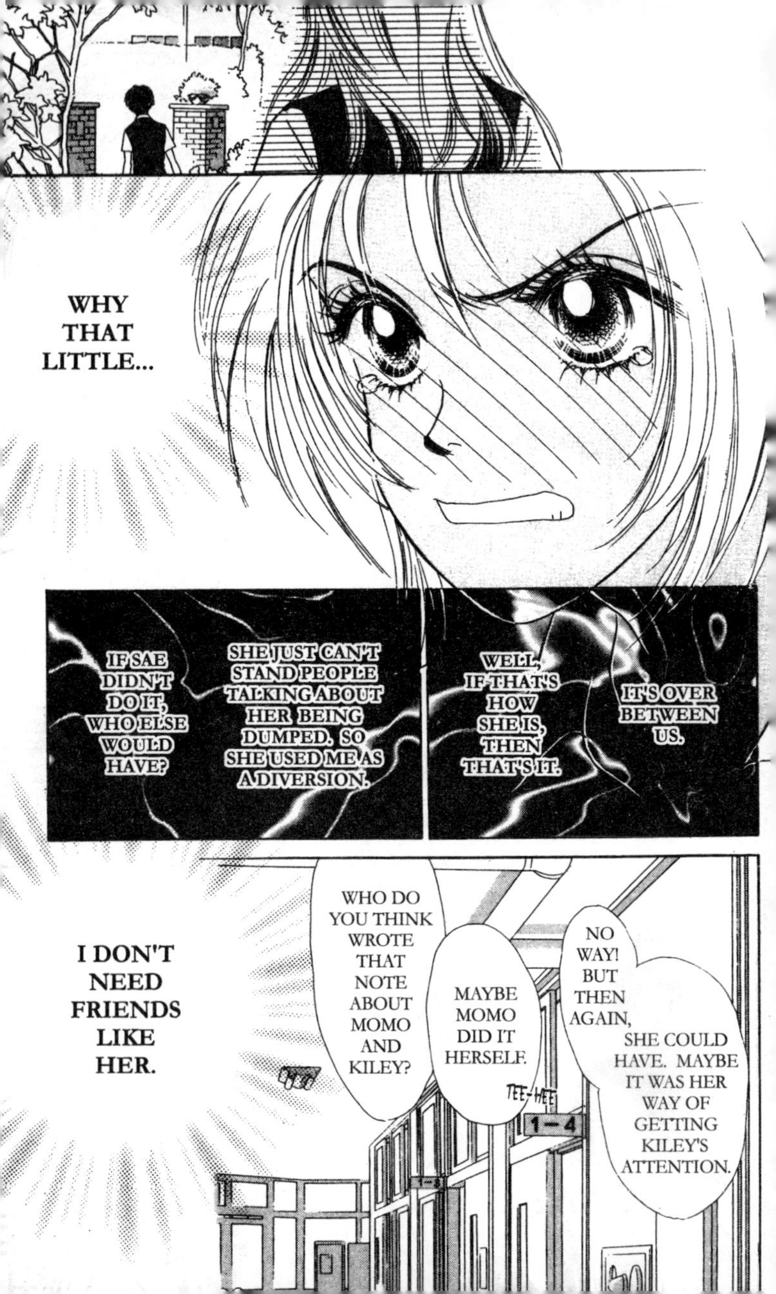
WHY THAT LITTLE...
IF SAE DIDN'T DO IT, WHO ELSE WOULD HAVE?
SHE JUST CAN'T STAND PEOPLE TALKING ABOUT HER BEING DUMPED. SO SHE USED ME AS A DIVERSION.
WELL, IF THAT'S HOW SHE IS, THEN THAT'S IT.
IT'S OVER BETWEEN US.
I DON'T NEED FRIENDS LIKE HER.
WHO DO YOU THINK WROTE THAT NOTE ABOUT MOMO AND KILEY?
MAYBE MOMO DID IT HERSELF.
TEE-HEE
NO WAY! BUT THEN AGAIN,
SHE COULD HAVE. MAYBE IT WAS HER WAY OF GETTING KILEY'S ATTENTION.
1-4

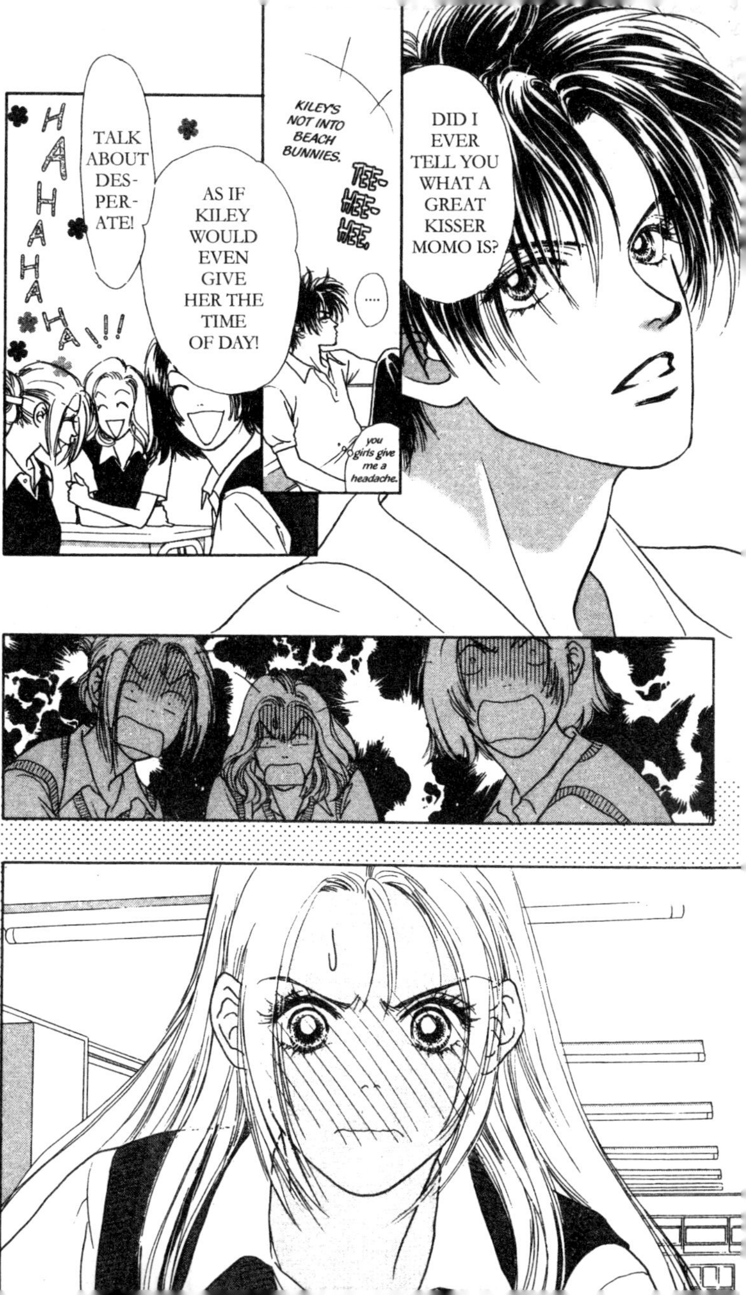
HAHAHAHAHA!!!
TALK ABOUT DES-PER-ATE!
AS IF KILEY WOULD EVEN GIVE HER THE TIME OF DAY!
KILEY'S NOT INTO BEACH BUNNIES.
TEE-HEE-HEE.
....
you girls give me a headache.
DID I EVER TELL YOU WHAT A GREAT KISSER MOMO IS?

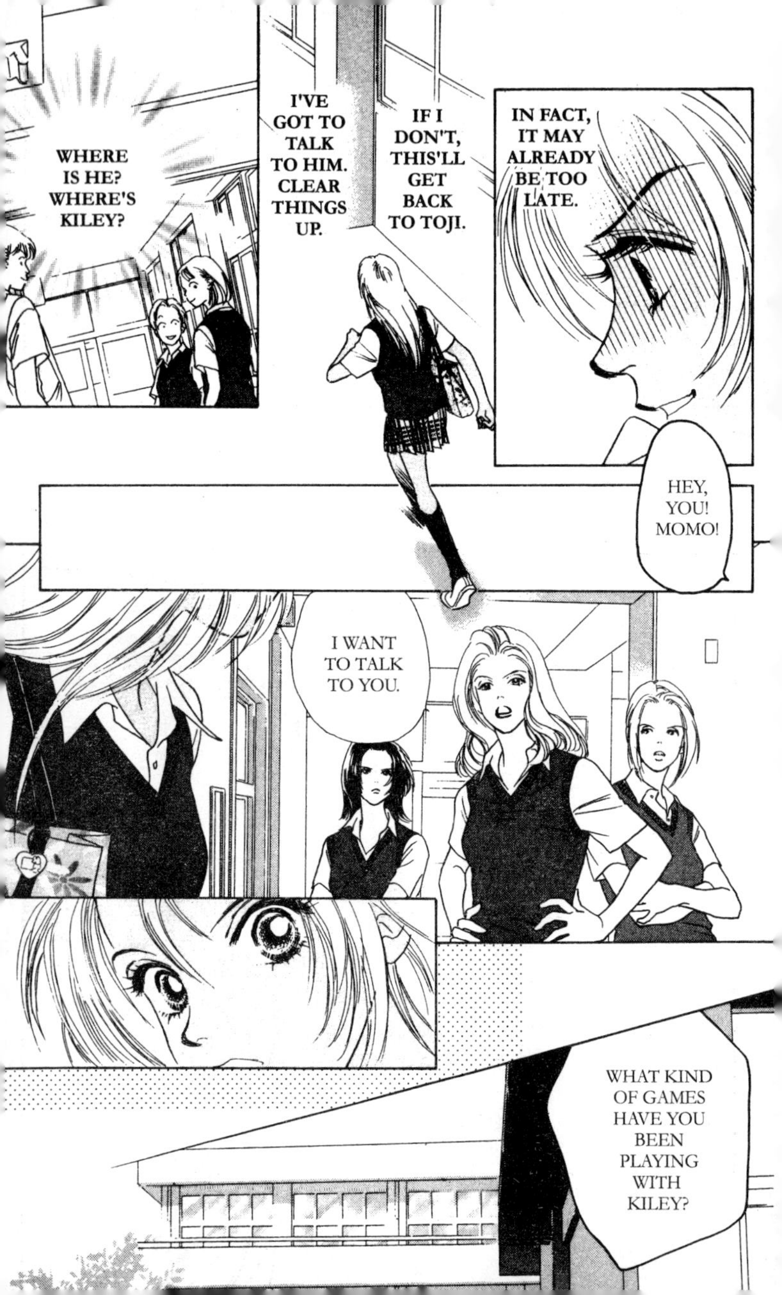
WHERE IS HE? WHERE'S KILEY?
I'VE GOT TO TALK TO HIM. CLEAR THINGS UP.
IF I DON'T, THIS'LL GET BACK TO TOJI.
IN FACT, IT MAY ALREADY BE TOO LATE.
HEY, YOU! MOMO!
I WANT TO TALK TO YOU.
WHAT KIND OF GAMES HAVE YOU BEEN PLAYING WITH KILEY?

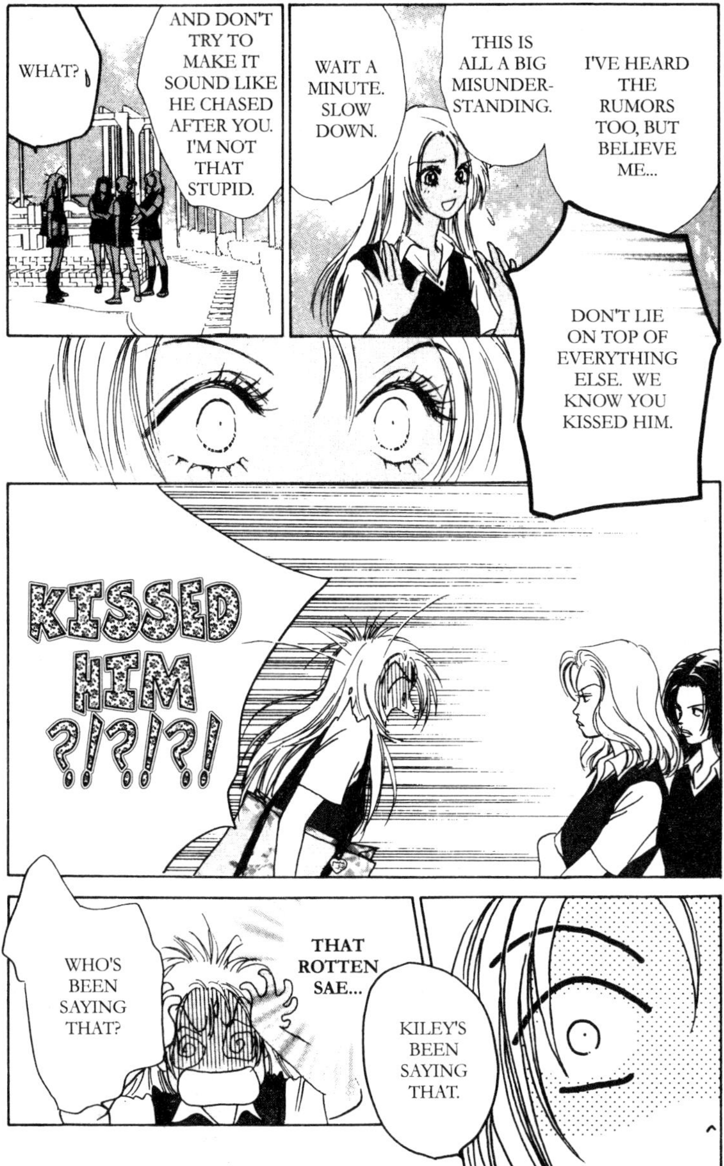
WHAT?
AND DON'T TRY TO MAKE IT SOUND LIKE HE CHASED AFTER YOU. I'M NOT THAT STUPID.
WAIT A MINUTE. SLOW DOWN.
THIS IS ALL A BIG MISUNDER-STANDING.
I'VE HEARD THE RUMORS TOO, BUT BELIEVE ME...
DON'T LIE ON TOP OF EVERYTHING ELSE. WE KNOW YOU KISSED HIM.
KISSED HIM ?!?!?!
WHO'S BEEN SAYING THAT?
THAT ROTTEN SAE...
KILEY'S BEEN SAYING THAT.

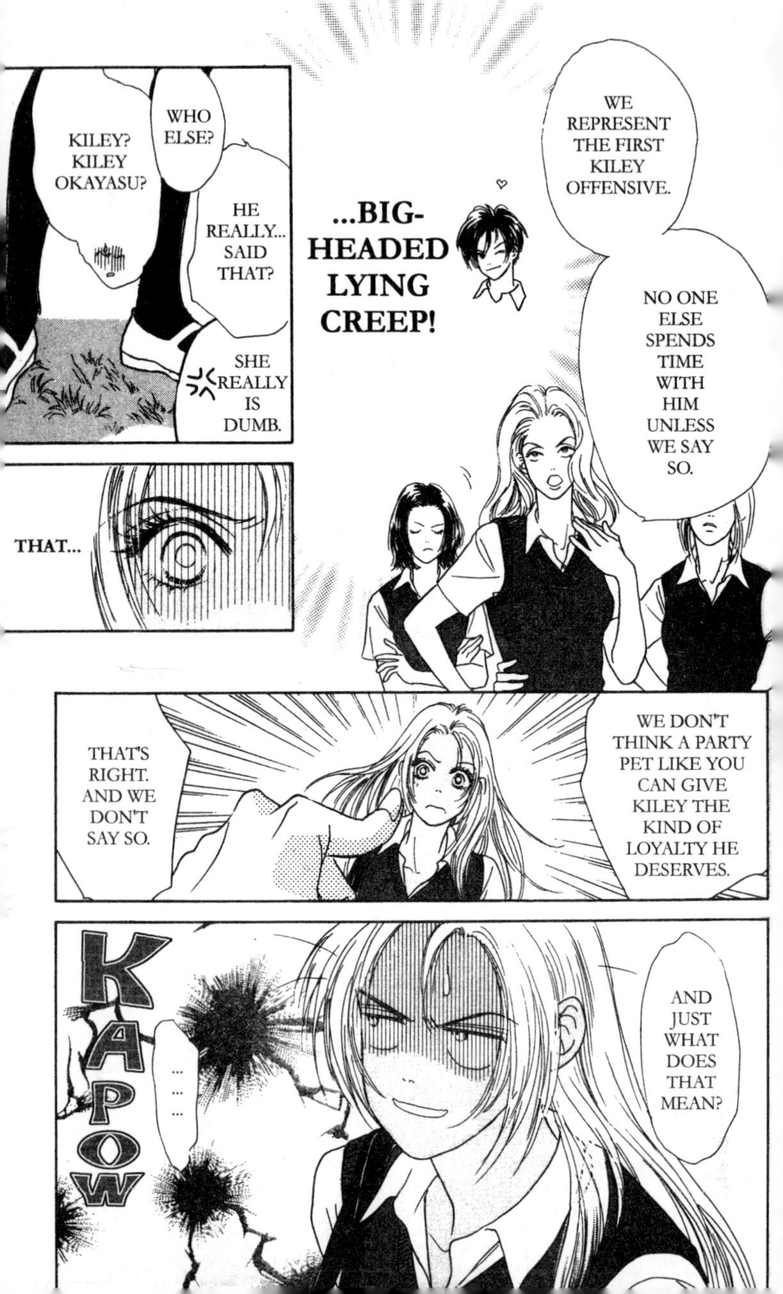
KILEY? KILEY OKAYASU?
WHO ELSE?
HE REALLY... SAID THAT?
SHE REALLY IS DUMB.
THAT...
WE REPRESENT THE FIRST KILEY OFFENSIVE.
...BIG-HEADED LYING CREEP!
NO ONE ELSE SPENDS TIME WITH HIM UNLESS WE SAY SO.
THAT'S RIGHT. AND WE DON'T SAY SO.
WE DON'T THINK A PARTY PET LIKE YOU CAN GIVE KILEY THE KIND OF LOYALTY HE DESERVES.
KAPOW
... ...
AND JUST WHAT DOES THAT MEAN?

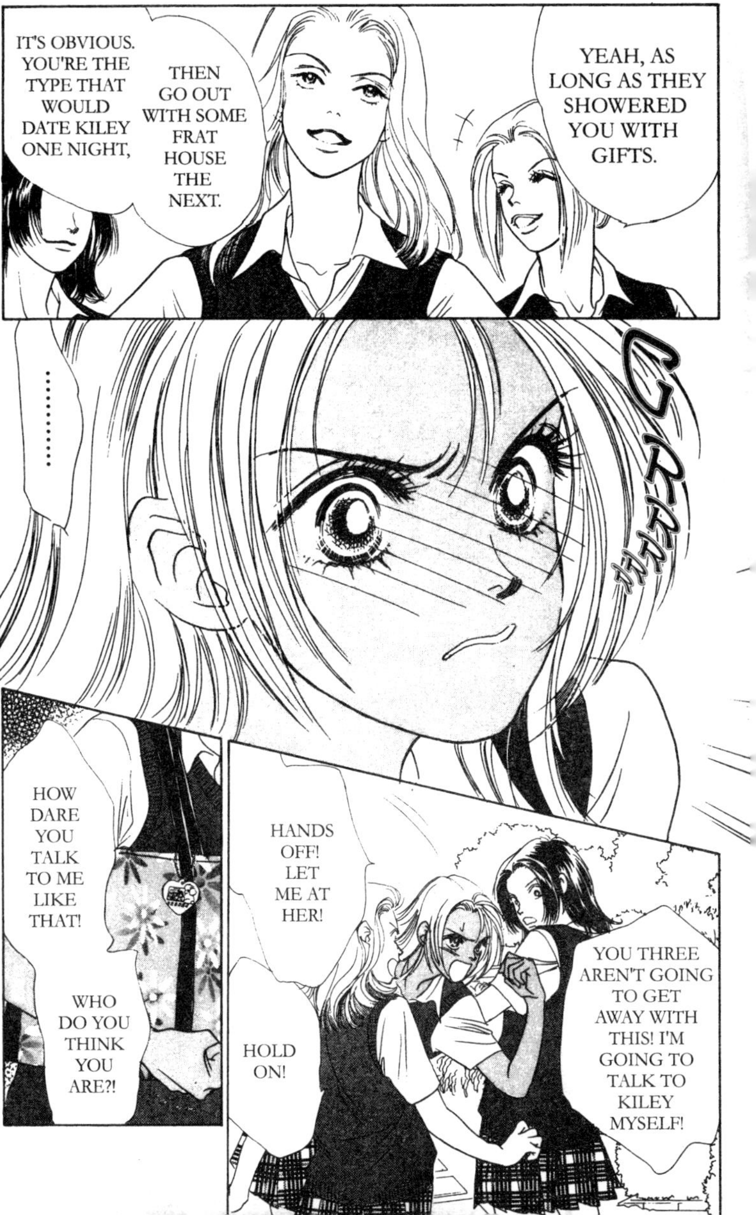
IT'S OBVIOUS. YOU'RE THE TYPE THAT WOULD DATE KILEY ONE NIGHT,
THEN GO OUT WITH SOME FRAT HOUSE THE NEXT.
YEAH, AS LONG AS THEY SHOWERED YOU WITH GIFTS.
....
GRRRR
HOW DARE YOU TALK TO ME LIKE THAT!
WHO DO YOU THINK YOU ARE?!
HANDS OFF! LET ME AT HER!
HOLD ON!
YOU THREE AREN'T GOING TO GET AWAY WITH THIS! I'M GOING TO TALK TO KILEY MYSELF!

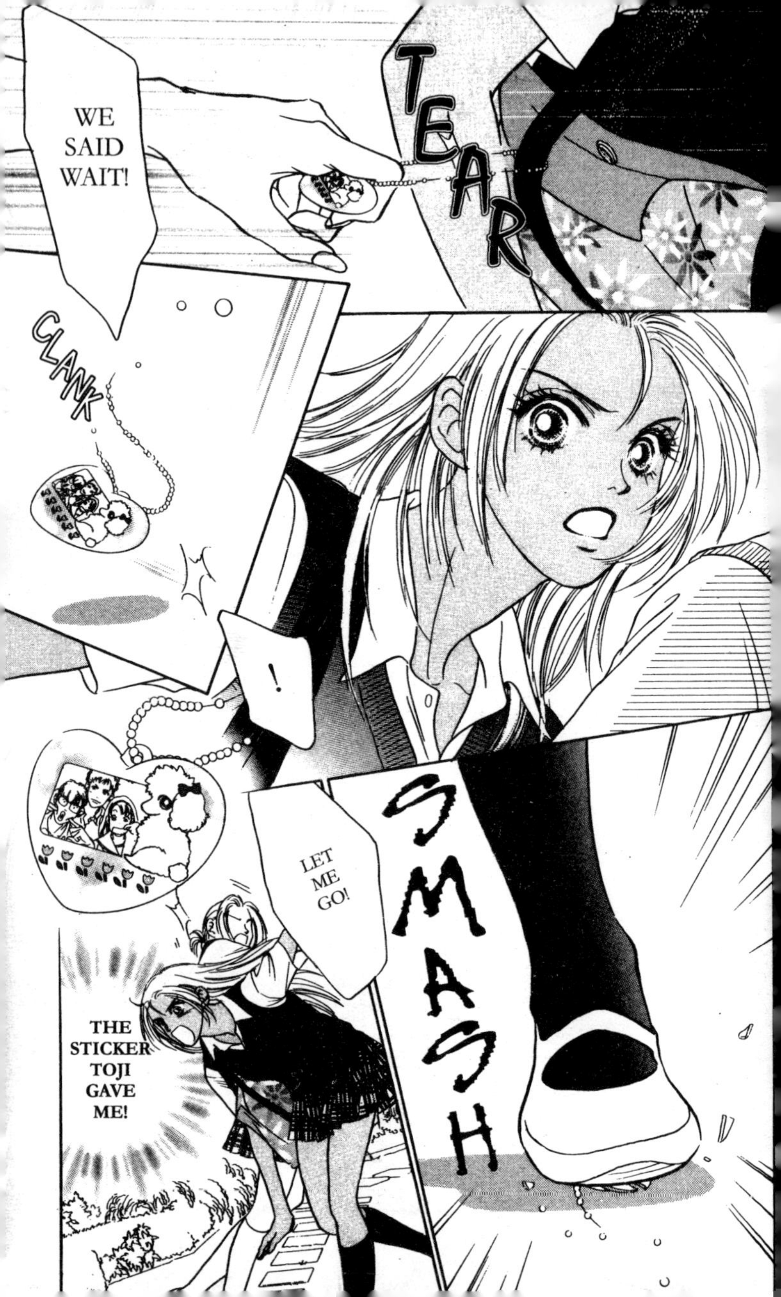
WE SAID WAIT!
TEAR
CLANK
!
LET ME GO!
SMASH
THE STICKER TOJI GAVE ME!

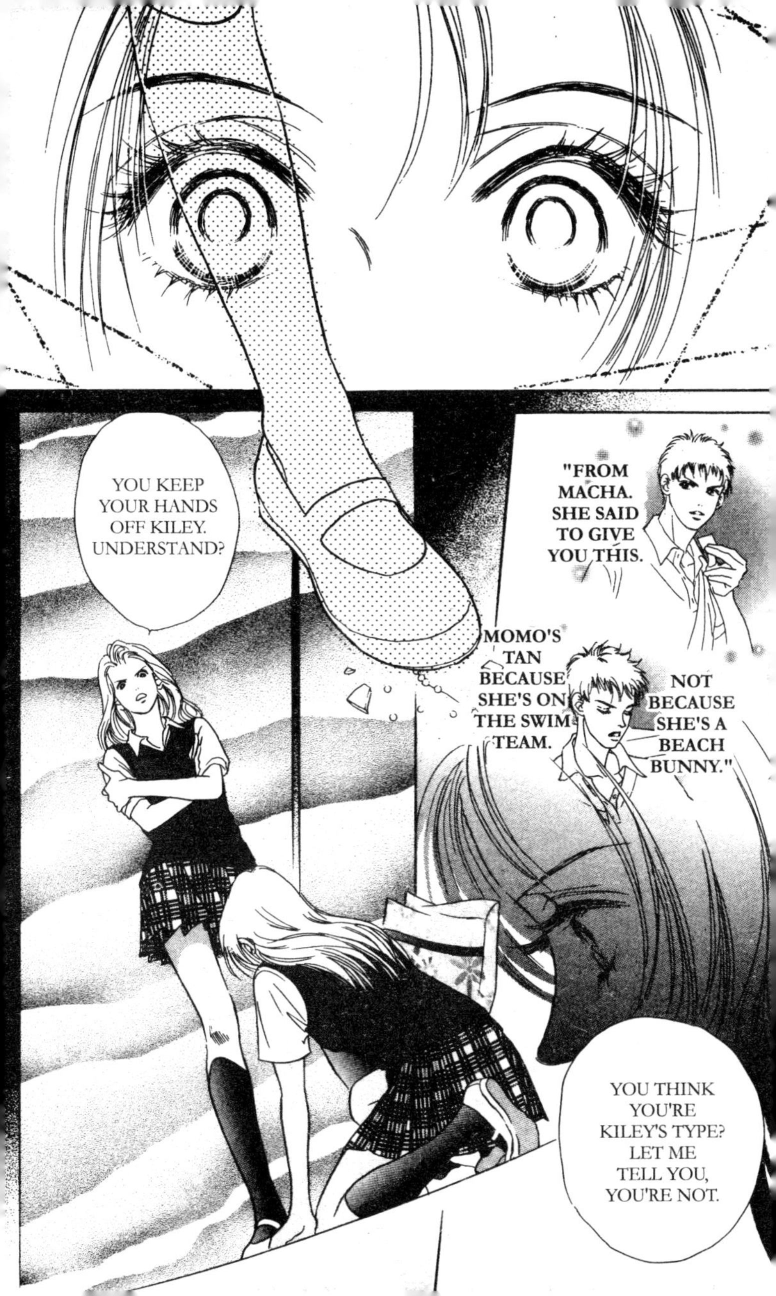
YOU KEEP YOUR HANDS OFF KILEY. UNDERSTAND?
"FROM MACHA. SHE SAID TO GIVE YOU THIS.
MOMO'S TAN BECAUSE SHE'S ON THE SWIM TEAM.
NOT BECAUSE SHE'S A BEACH BUNNY."
YOU THINK YOU'RE KILEY'S TYPE? LET ME TELL YOU, YOU'RE NOT.

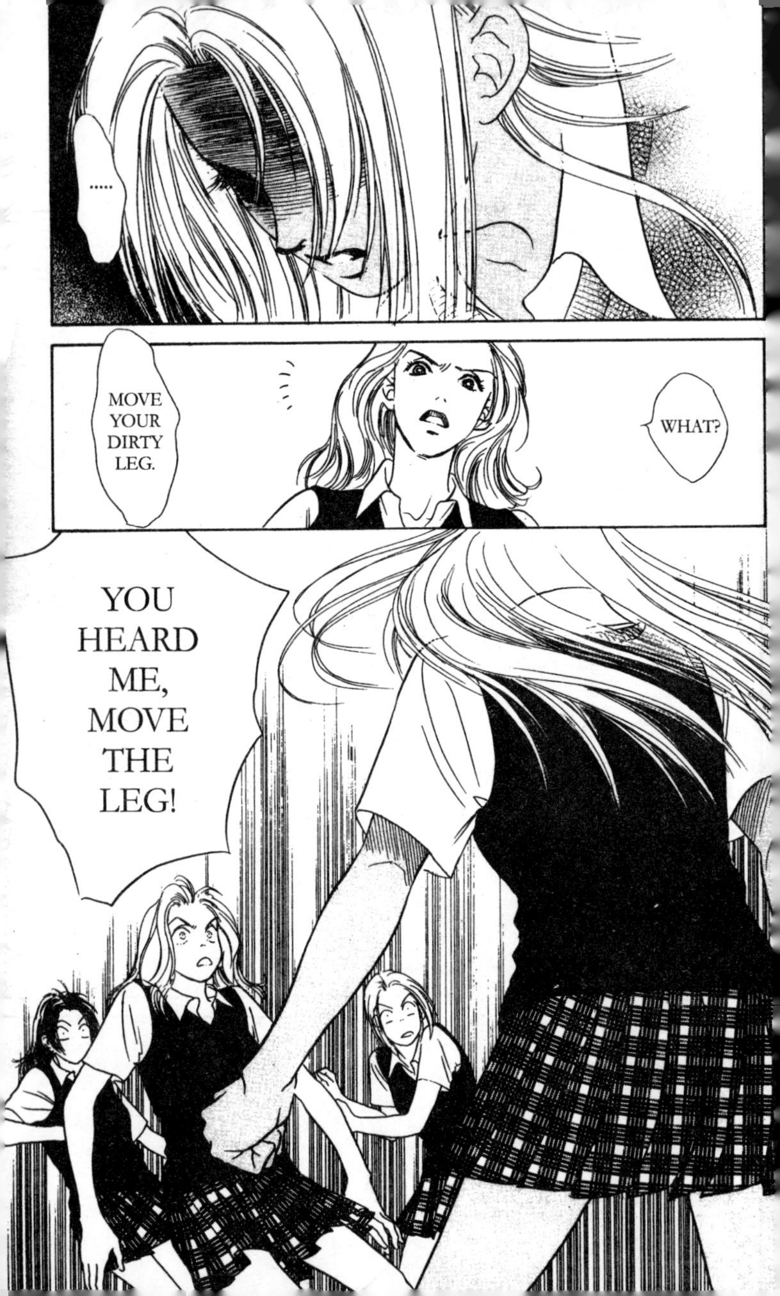
.....
MOVE YOUR DIRTY LEG.
WHAT?
YOU HEARD ME, MOVE THE LEG!

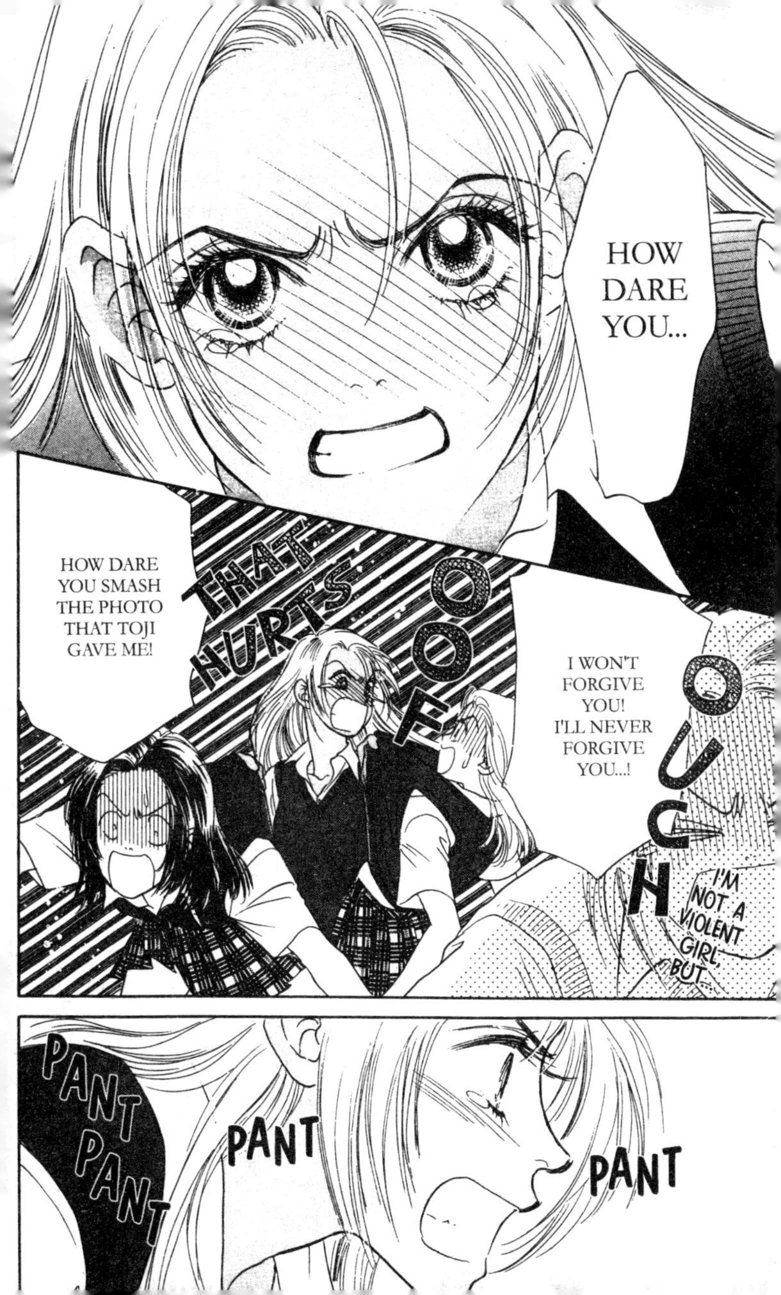
HOW DARE YOU...
HOW DARE YOU SMASH THE PHOTO THAT TOJI GAVE ME!
THAT HURTS
OOOF
I WON'T FORGIVE YOU! I'LL NEVER FORGIVE YOU...!
OUCH
I'M NOT A VIOLENT GIRL, BUT...
PANT PANT PANT
PANT
PANT

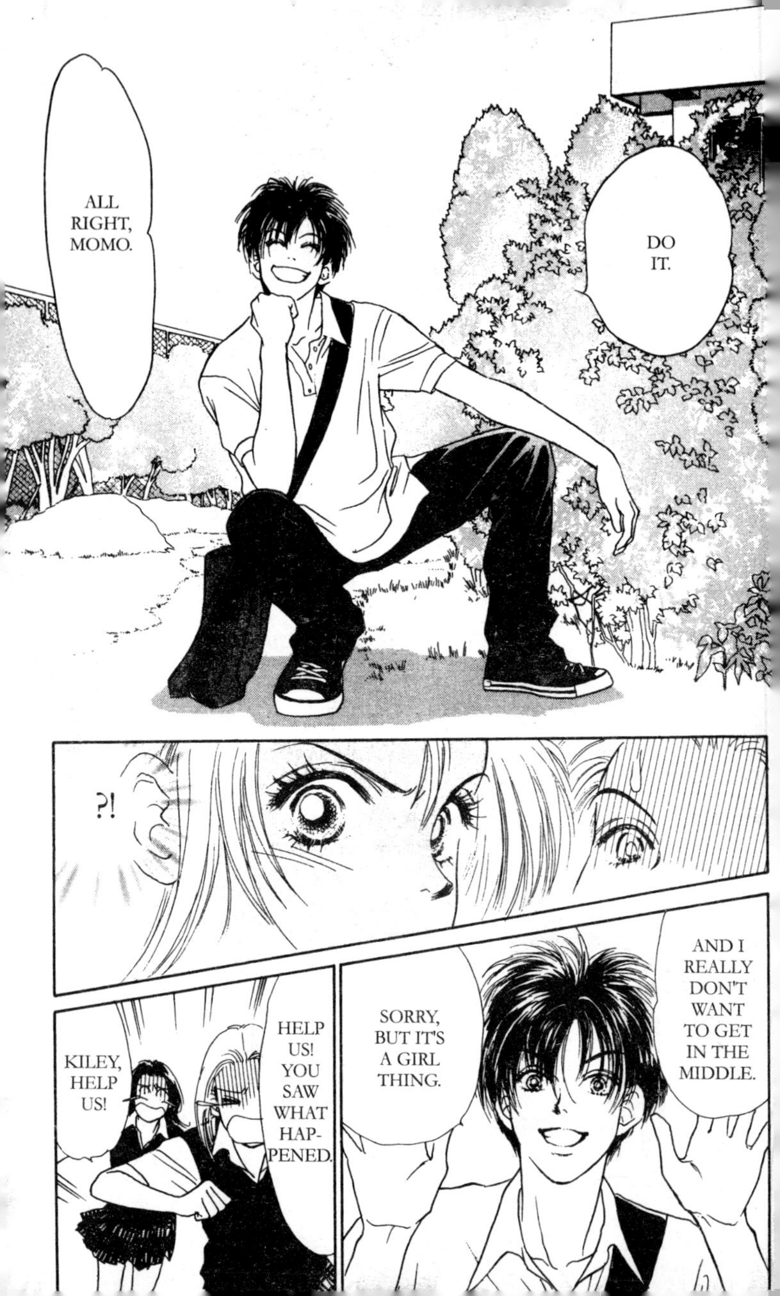
ALL RIGHT, MOMO.
DO IT.
?!
KILEY, HELP US!
HELP US! YOU SAW WHAT HAP-PENED.
SORRY, BUT IT'S A GIRL THING.
AND I REALLY DON'T WANT TO GET IN THE MIDDLE.

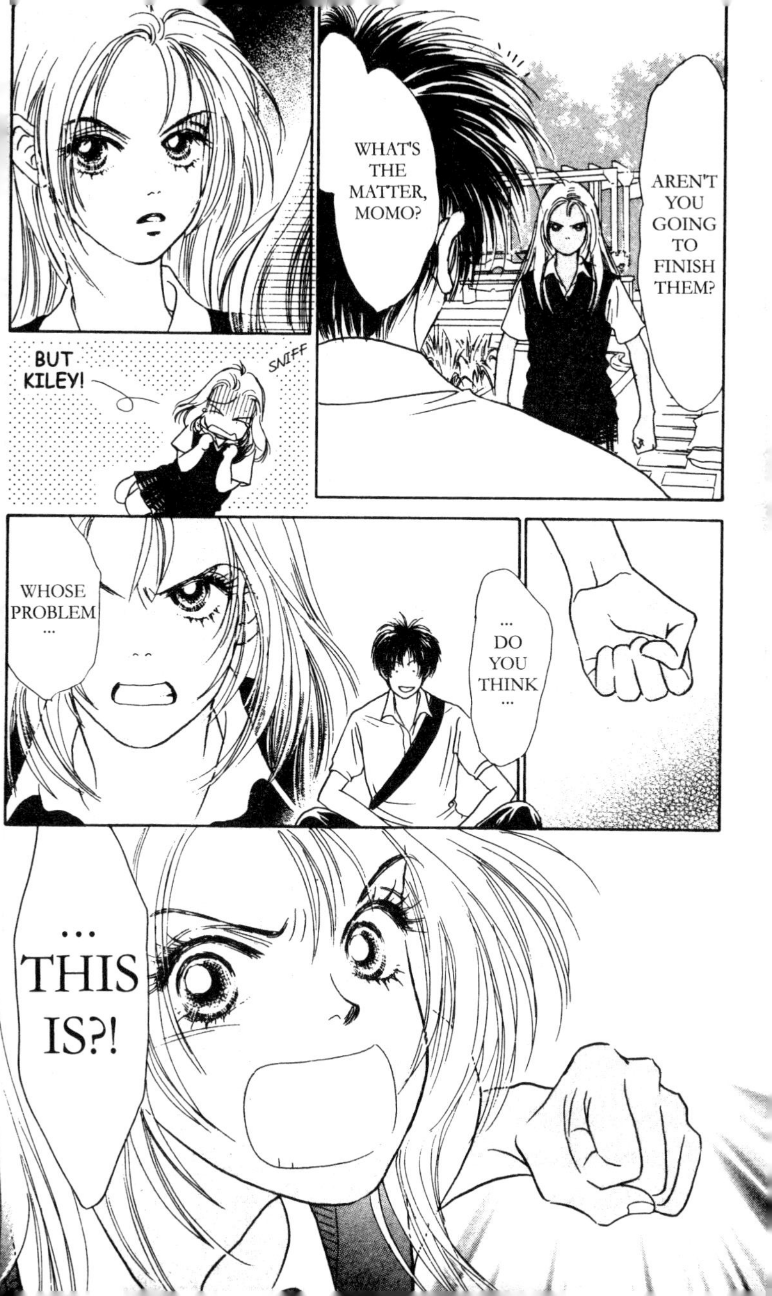
BUT KILEY!
SNIFF
WHAT'S THE MATTER, MOMO?
AREN'T YOU GOING TO FINISH THEM?
WHOSE PROBLEM ...
... DO YOU THINK ...
... THIS IS?!

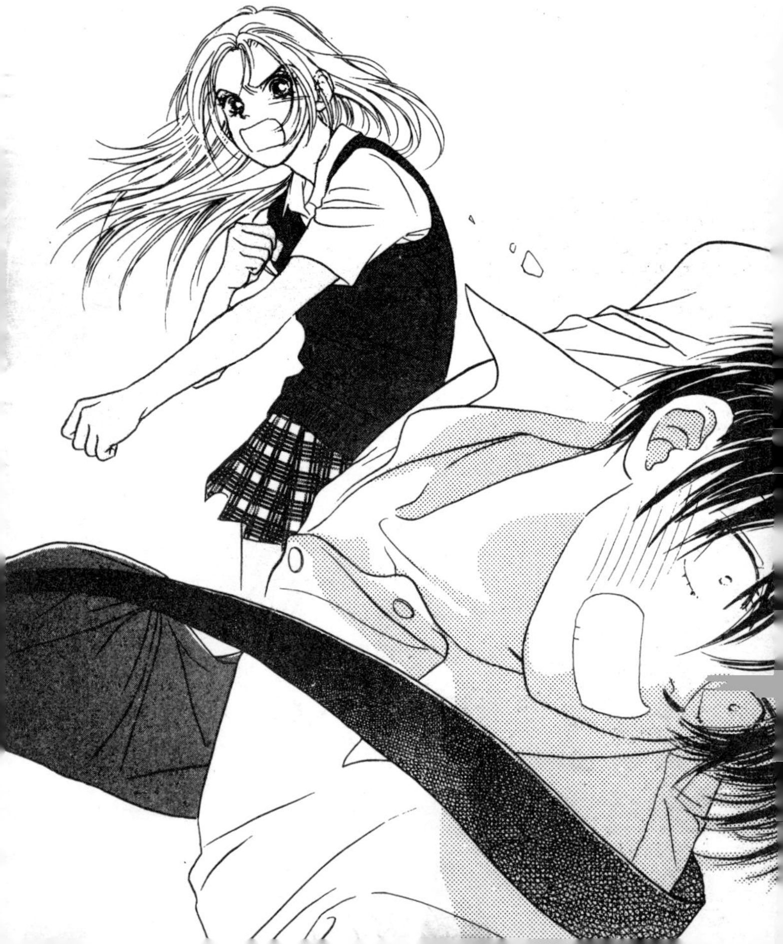

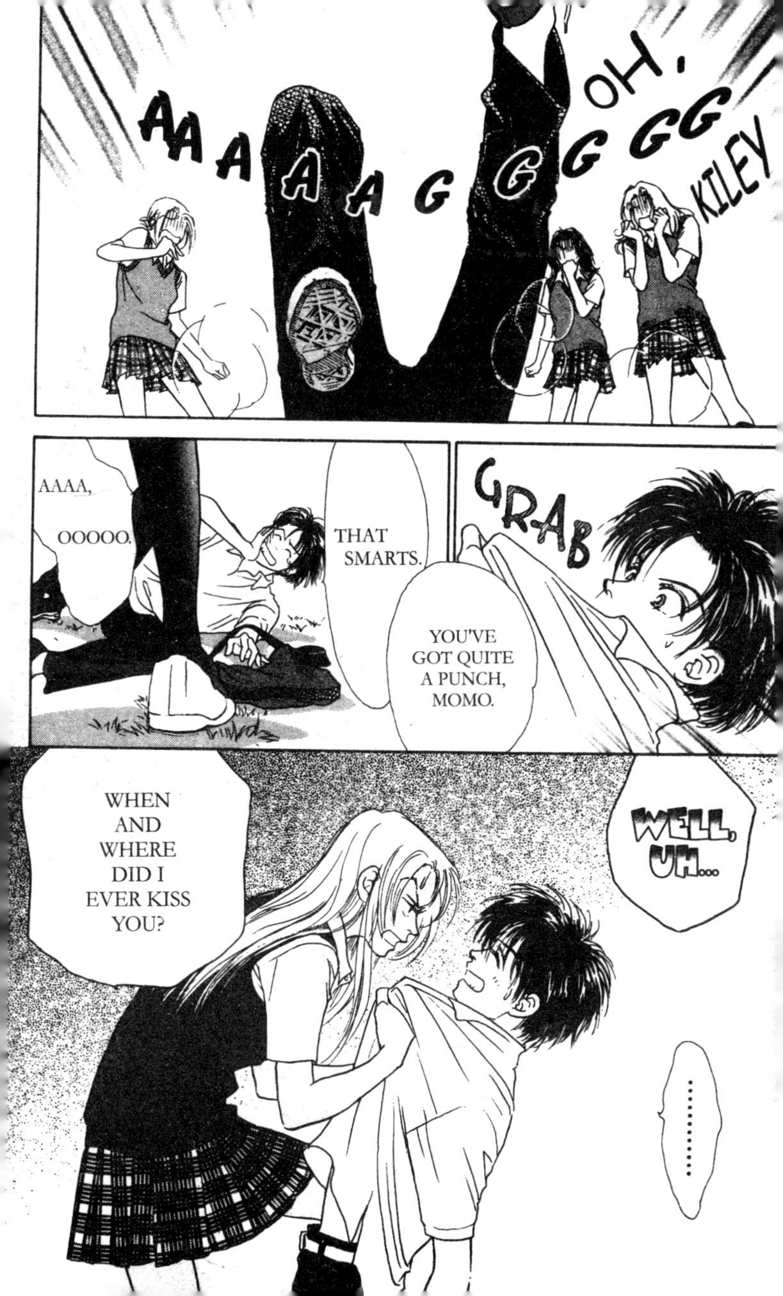
AAAAAAGGGGGG
OH, KILEY
AAAA,
OOOOO.
THAT SMARTS.
YOU'VE GOT QUITE A PUNCH, MOMO.
GRAB
WHEN AND WHERE DID I EVER KISS YOU?
WELL, UH...
....

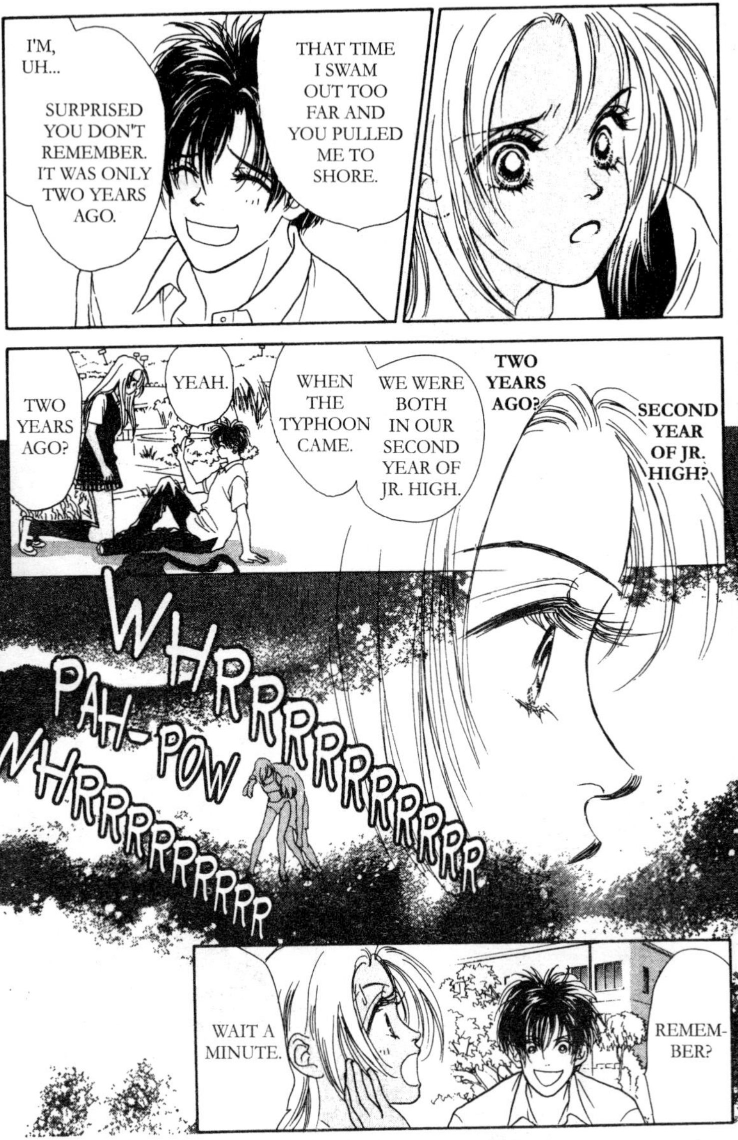
I'M, UH...
SURPRISED YOU DON'T REMEMBER. IT WAS ONLY TWO YEARS AGO.
THAT TIME I SWAM OUT TOO FAR AND YOU PULLED ME TO SHORE.
TWO YEARS AGO?
YEAH.
WHEN THE TYPHOON CAME.
WE WERE BOTH IN OUR SECOND YEAR OF JR. HIGH.
TWO YEARS AGO?
SECOND YEAR OF JR. HIGH?
WHRRRRRRRRRRR
PAH-POW
WHRRRRRRRRRRR
WAIT A MINUTE.
REMEMBER?

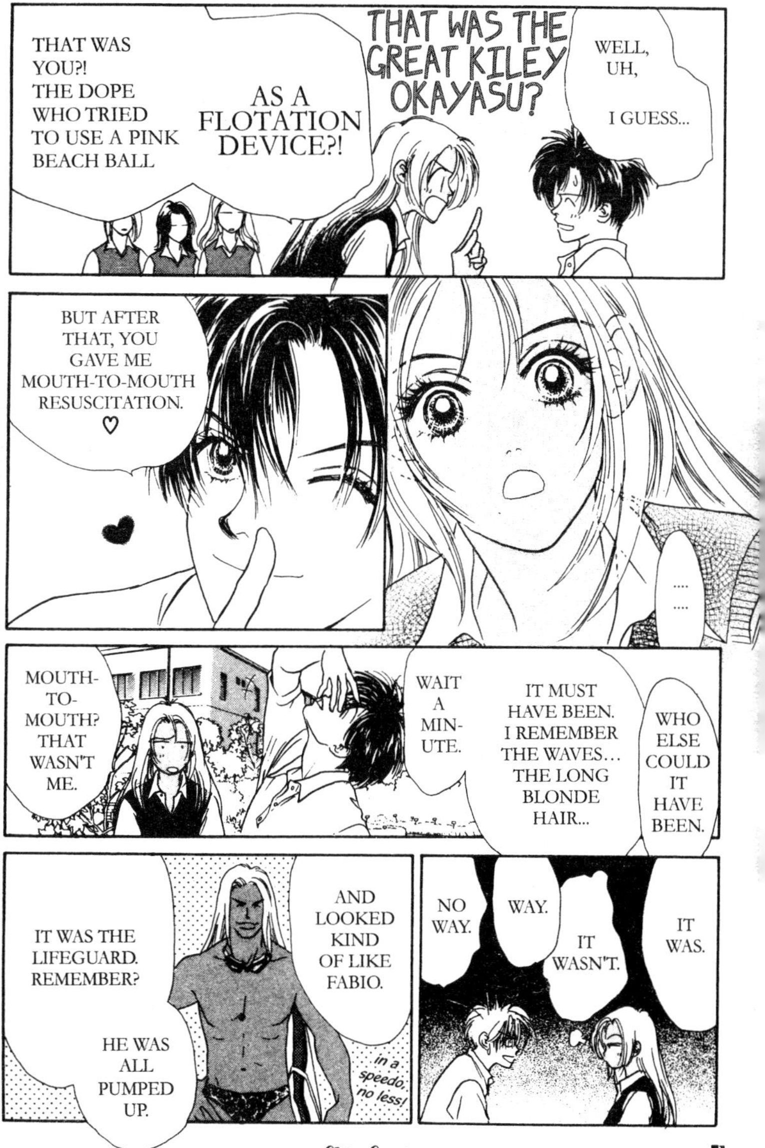
THAT WAS YOU?! THE DOPE WHO TRIED TO USE A PINK BEACH BALL
AS A FLOTATION DEVICE?!
THAT WAS THE GREAT KILEY OKAYASU?
WELL, UH,
I GUESS...
BUT AFTER THAT, YOU GAVE ME MOUTH-TO-MOUTH RESUSCITATION. ♡
....
....
MOUTH-TO-MOUTH? THAT WASN'T ME.
WAIT A MIN-UTE.
IT MUST HAVE BEEN. I REMEMBER THE WAVES… THE LONG BLONDE HAIR...
WHO ELSE COULD IT HAVE BEEN.
IT WAS THE LIFEGUARD. REMEMBER?
AND LOOKED KIND OF LIKE FABIO.
HE WAS ALL PUMPED UP.
in a speedo, no less!
NO WAY.
WAY.
IT WASN'T.
IT WAS.

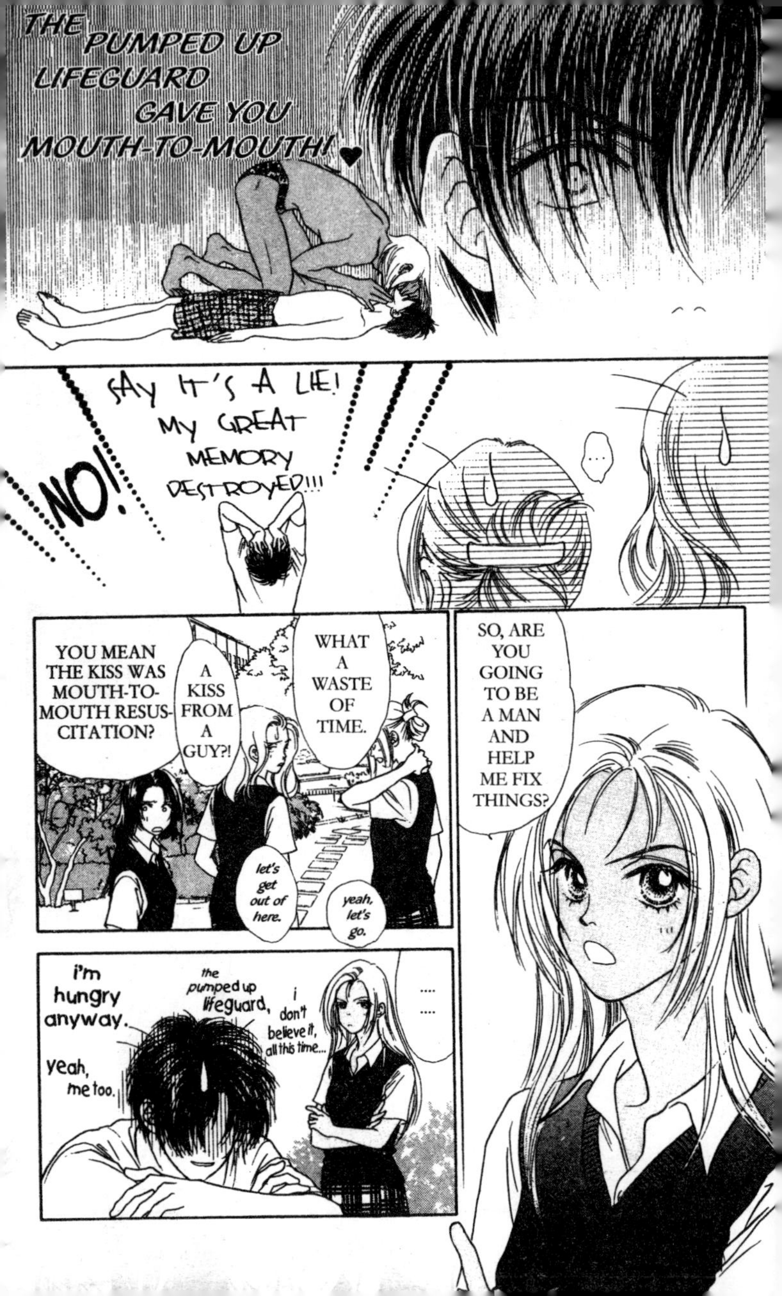
THE PUMPED UP LIFEGUARD GAVE YOU MOUTH-TO-MOUTH!
NO!
SAY IT'S A LIE! MY GREAT MEMORY DESTROYED!!!
...
YOU MEAN THE KISS WAS MOUTH-TO-MOUTH RESUSCITATION?
A KISS FROM A GUY?!
WHAT A WASTE OF TIME.
let's get out of here.
yeah, let's go.
i'm hungry anyway.
yeah, me too.
the pumped up lifeguard,
i don't believe it, all this time...
....
....
SO, ARE YOU GOING TO BE A MAN AND HELP ME FIX THINGS?

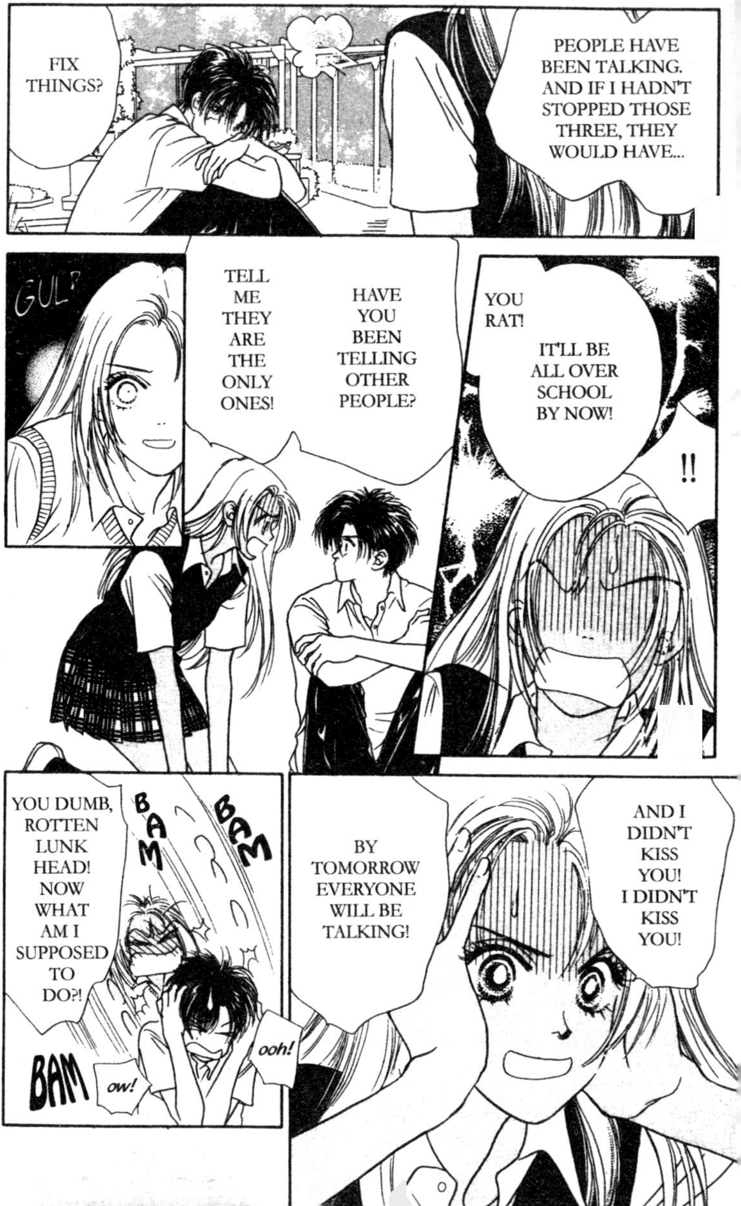
FIX THINGS?
PEOPLE HAVE BEEN TALKING. AND IF I HADN'T STOPPED THOSE THREE, THEY WOULD HAVE...
GUL?
TELL ME THEY ARE THE ONLY ONES!
HAVE YOU BEEN TELLING OTHER PEOPLE?
YOU RAT!
IT'LL BE ALL OVER SCHOOL BY NOW!
!!
YOU DUMB, ROTTEN LUNK HEAD! NOW WHAT AM I SUPPOSED TO DO?!
BAM
BAM
BAM
ow!
ooh!
BY TOMORROW EVERYONE WILL BE TALKING!
AND I DIDN'T KISS YOU! I DIDN'T KISS YOU!

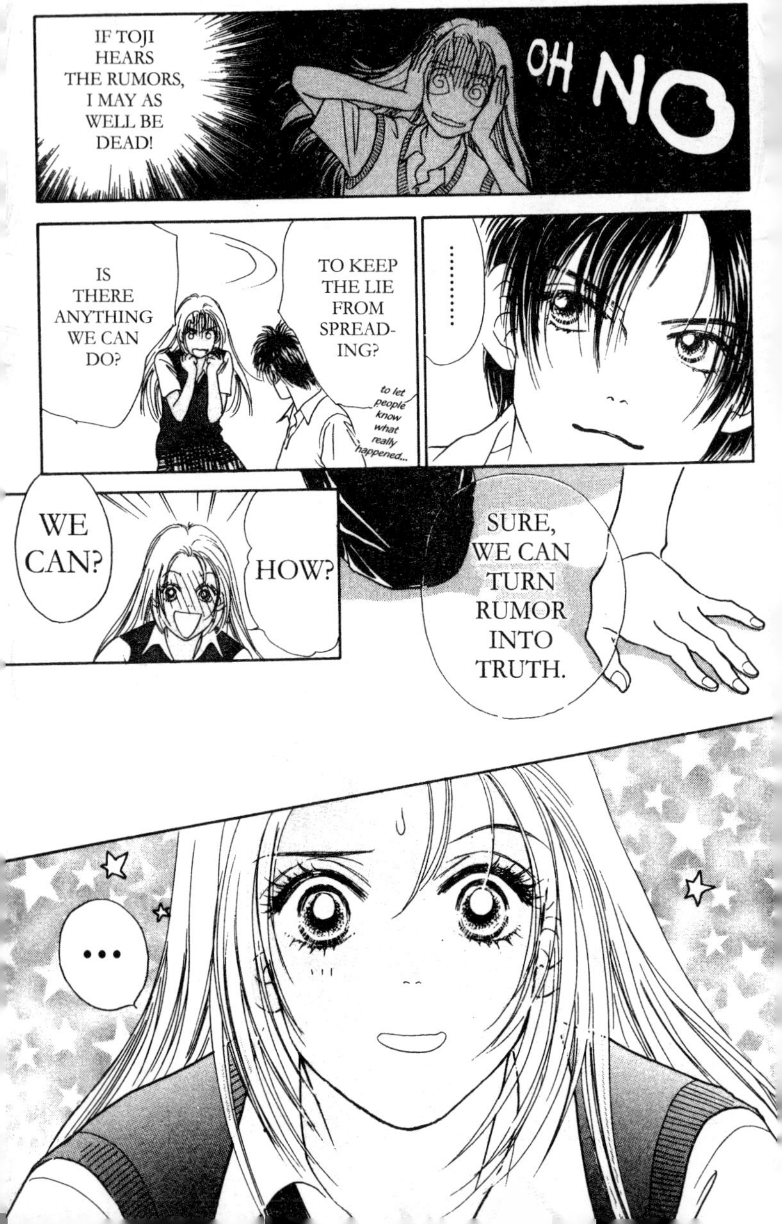
IF TOJI HEARS THE RUMORS, I MAY AS WELL BE DEAD!
OH NO
IS THERE ANYTHING WE CAN DO?
TO KEEP THE LIE FROM SPREAD-ING?
to let people know what really happened...
....
WE CAN?
HOW?
SURE, WE CAN TURN RUMOR INTO TRUTH.
...

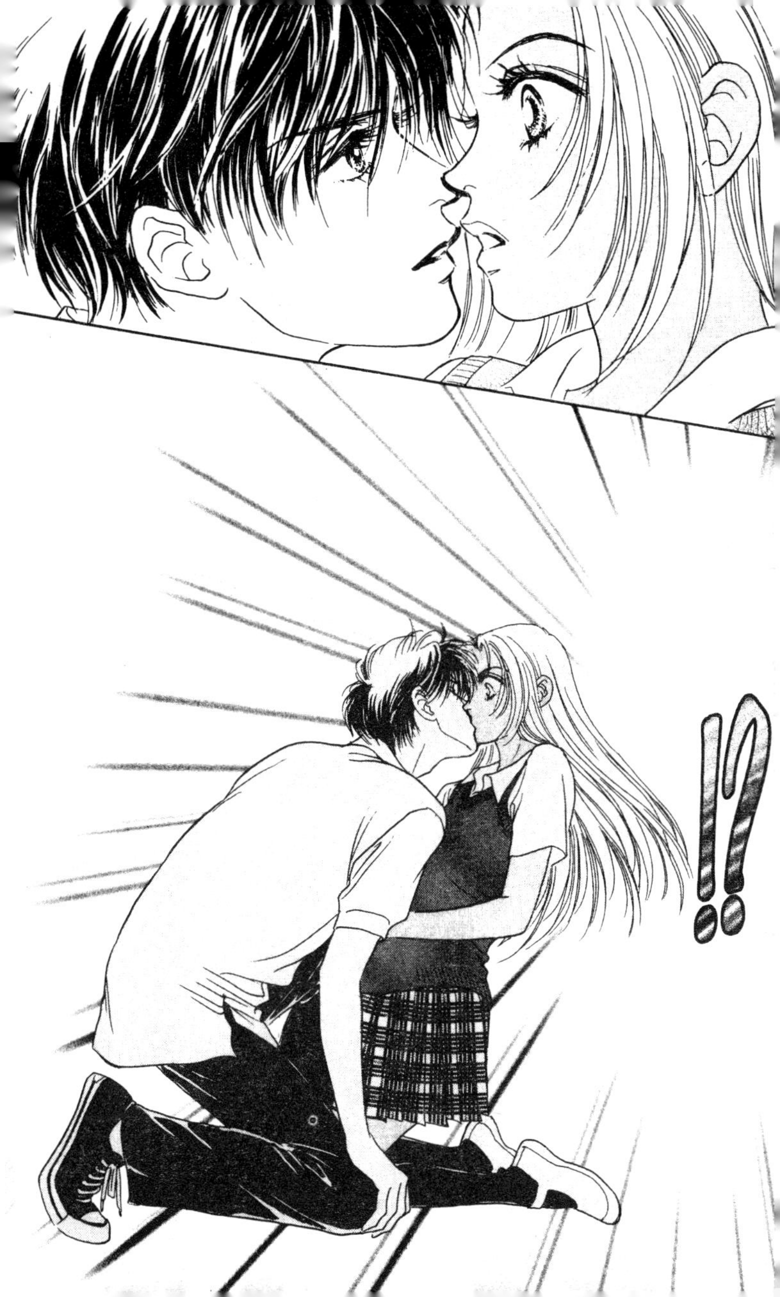
!?

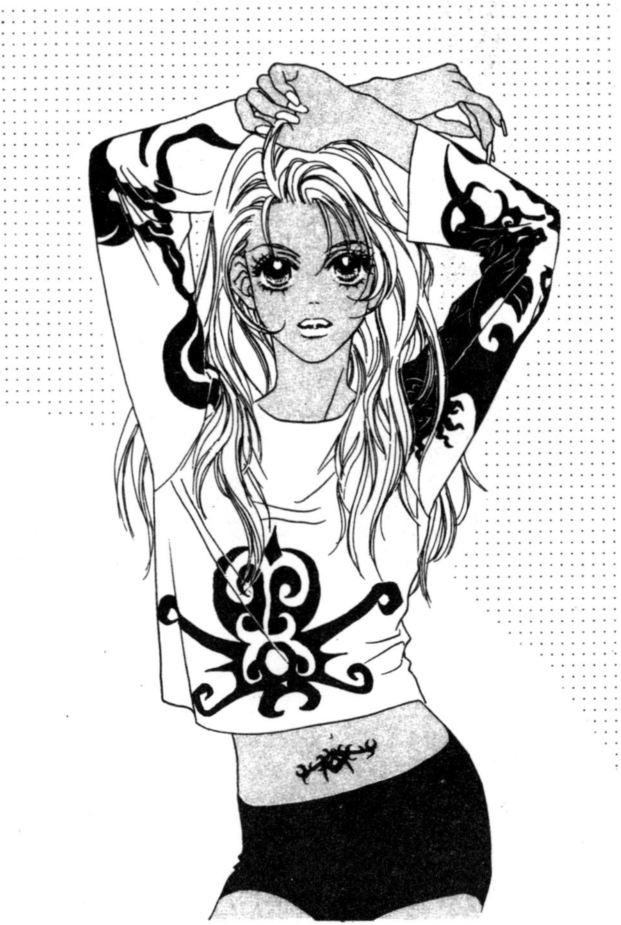

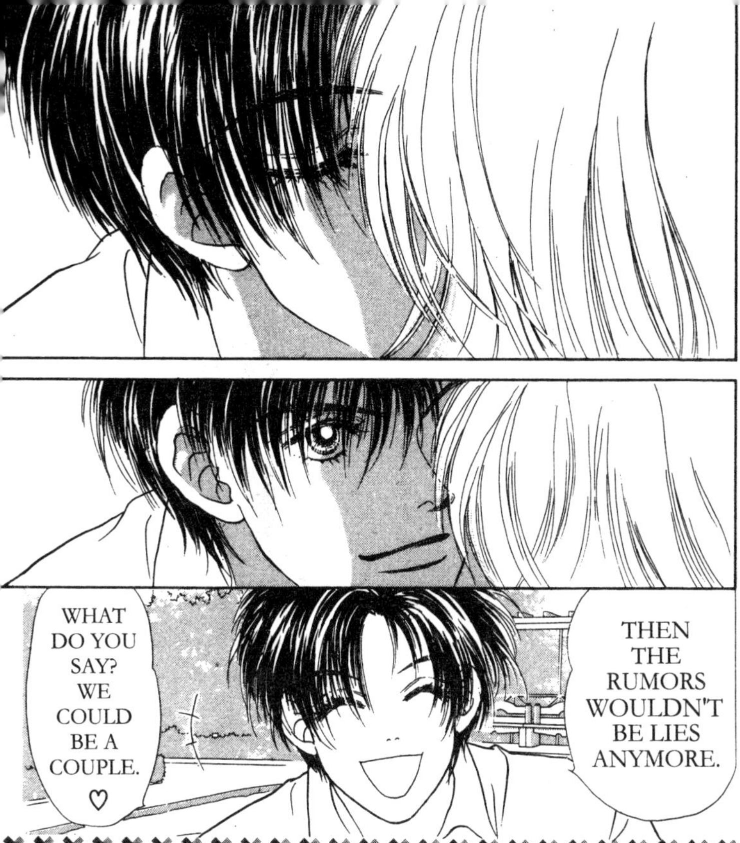
WHAT DO YOU SAY? WE COULD BE A COUPLE. ♡
THEN THE RUMORS WOULDN'T BE LIES ANYMORE.

PEACH CLUB CORNER

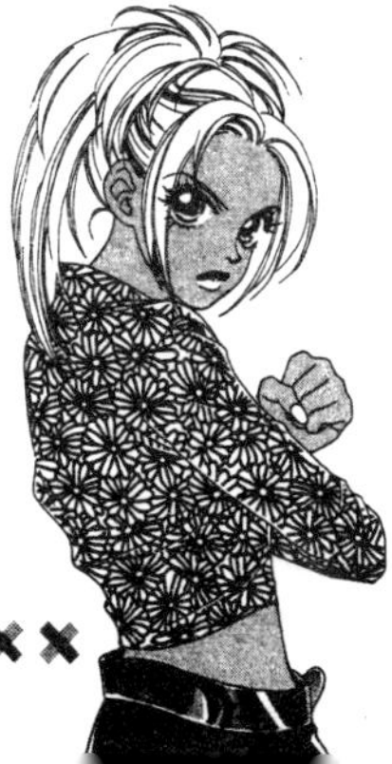

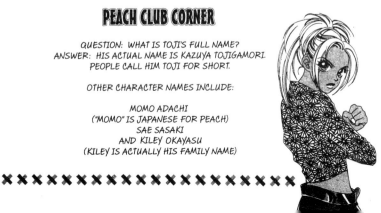

QUESTION: WHAT IS TOJI'S FULL NAME?
ANSWER: HIS ACTUAL NAME IS KAZUYA TOJIGAMORI.
PEOPLE CALL HIM TOJI FOR SHORT.

OTHER CHARACTER NAMES INCLUDE:

MOMO ADACHI
("MOMO" IS JAPANESE FOR PEACH)
SAE SASAKI
AND KILEY OKAYASU
(KILEY IS ACTUALLY HIS FAMILY NAME)

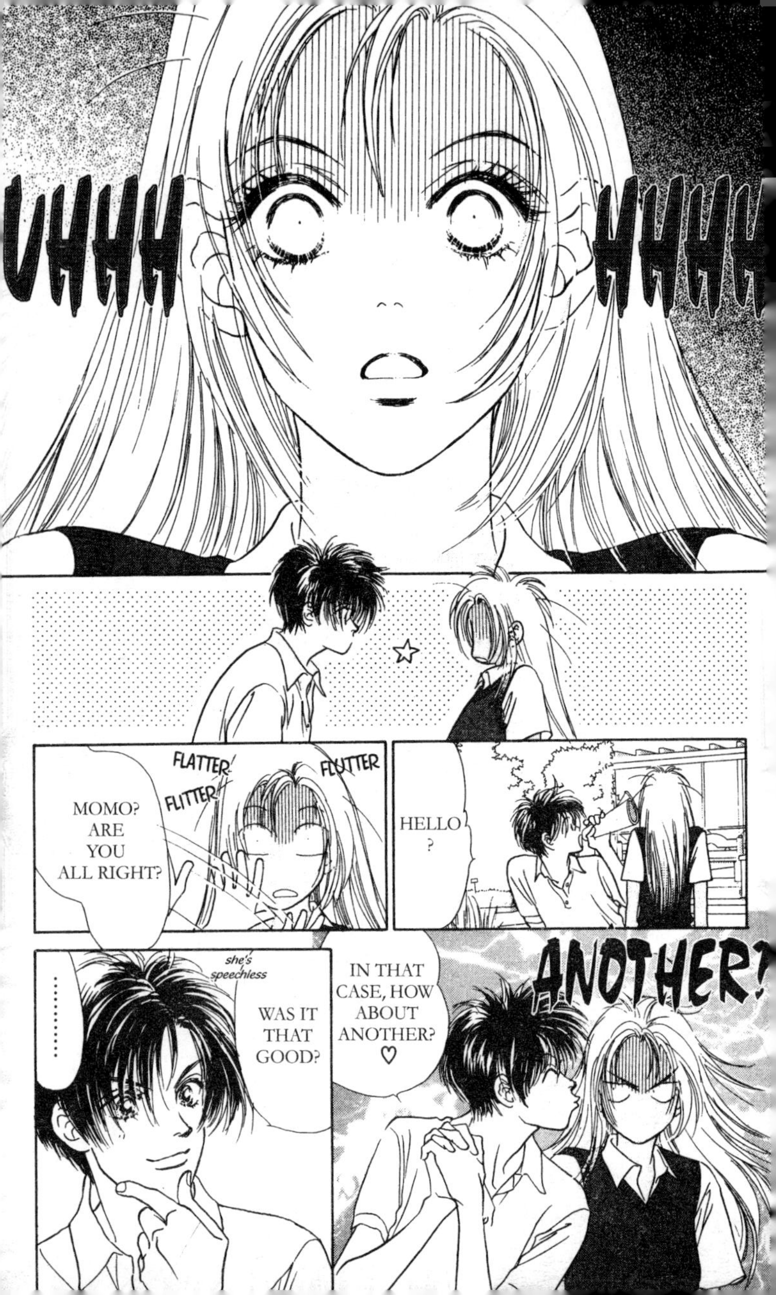
UHHH
HHHH
FLATTER
FLITTER
FLUTTER
MOMO? ARE YOU ALL RIGHT?
HELLO ?
....
she's speechless
WAS IT THAT GOOD?
IN THAT CASE, HOW ABOUT ANOTHER? ♡
ANOTHER?!

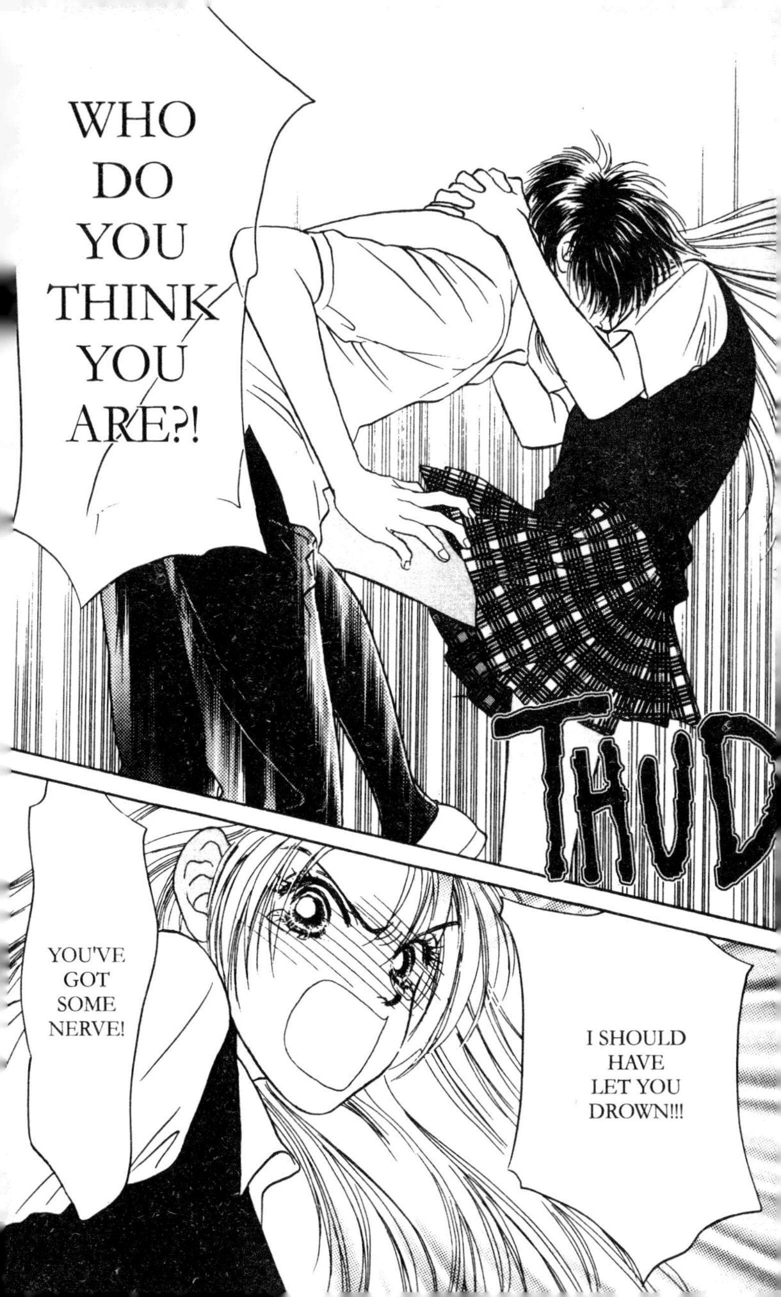
WHO DO YOU THINK YOU ARE?!
THUD
YOU'VE GOT SOME NERVE!
I SHOULD HAVE LET YOU DROWN!!!

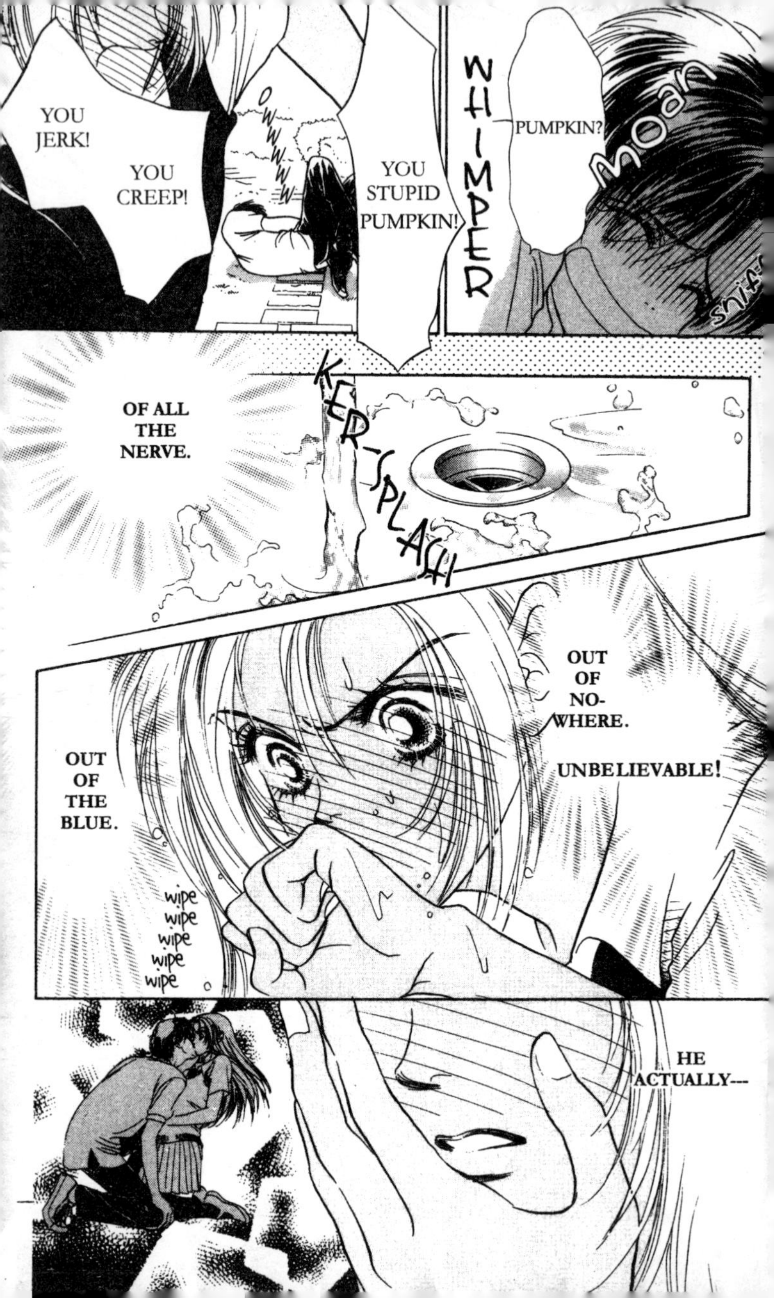

YOU JERK!
YOU CREEP!
OWWWWWW
YOU STUPID PUMPKIN!
WHIMPER
PUMPKIN?
moan
sniff
OF ALL THE NERVE.
KER-SPLASH
OUT OF THE BLUE.
wipe wipe wipe wipe wipe
OUT OF NO-WHERE.
UNBELIEVABLE!
HE ACTUALLY---

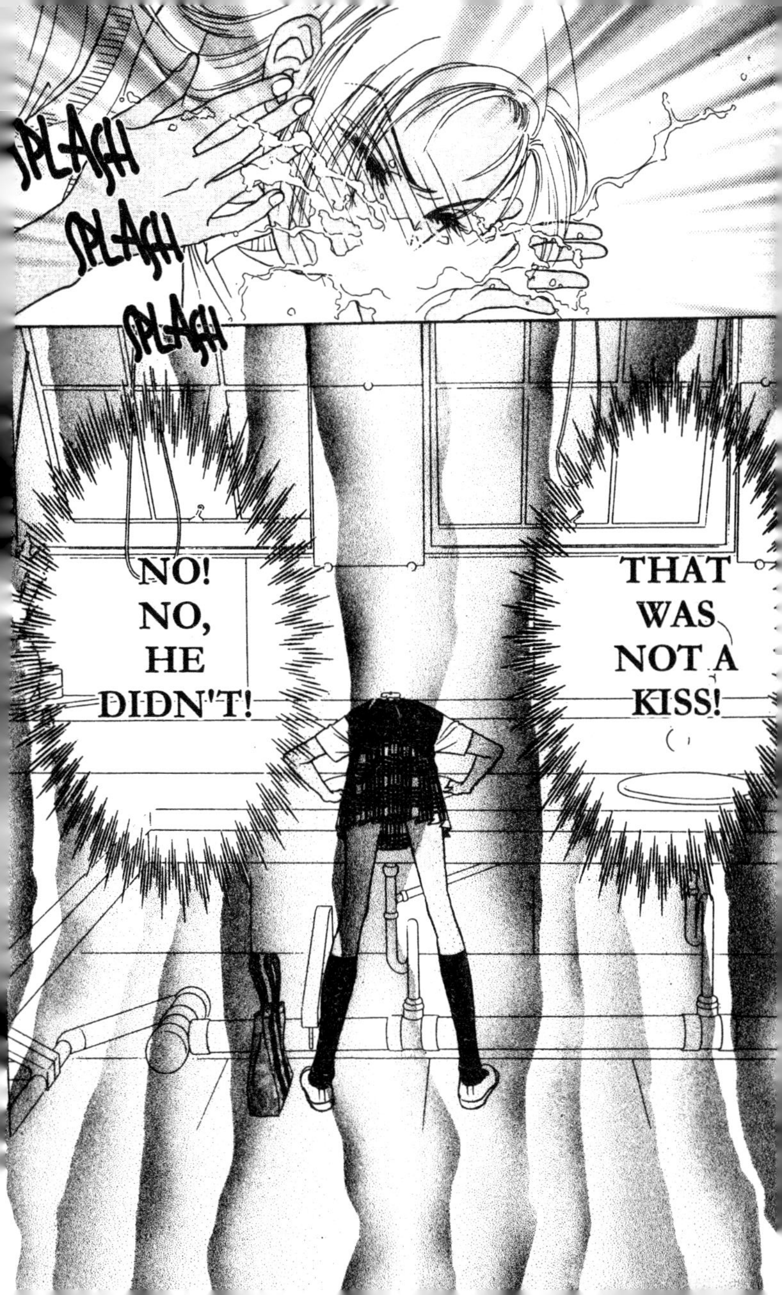
SPLASH
SPLASH
SPLASH
NO! NO, HE DIDN'T!
THAT WAS NOT A KISS!

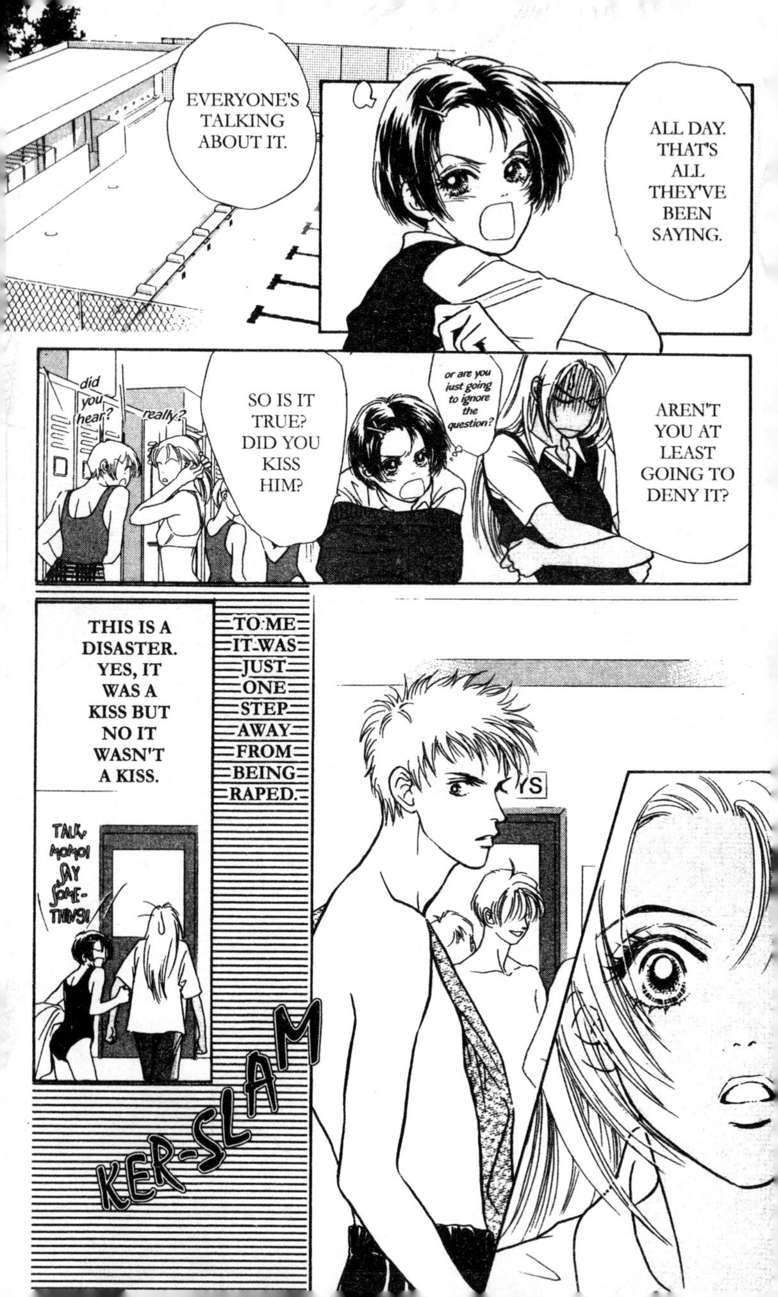
ALL DAY. THAT'S ALL THEY'VE BEEN SAYING.
EVERYONE'S TALKING ABOUT IT.
AREN'T YOU AT LEAST GOING TO DENY IT?
or are you just going to ignore the question?
SO IS IT TRUE? DID YOU KISS HIM?
really?
did you hear?
THIS IS A DISASTER. YES, IT WAS A KISS BUT NO IT WASN'T A KISS.
TO ME IT WAS JUST ONE STEP AWAY FROM BEING RAPED.
TALK, MOMO! SAY SOME-THING!
KER-SLAM

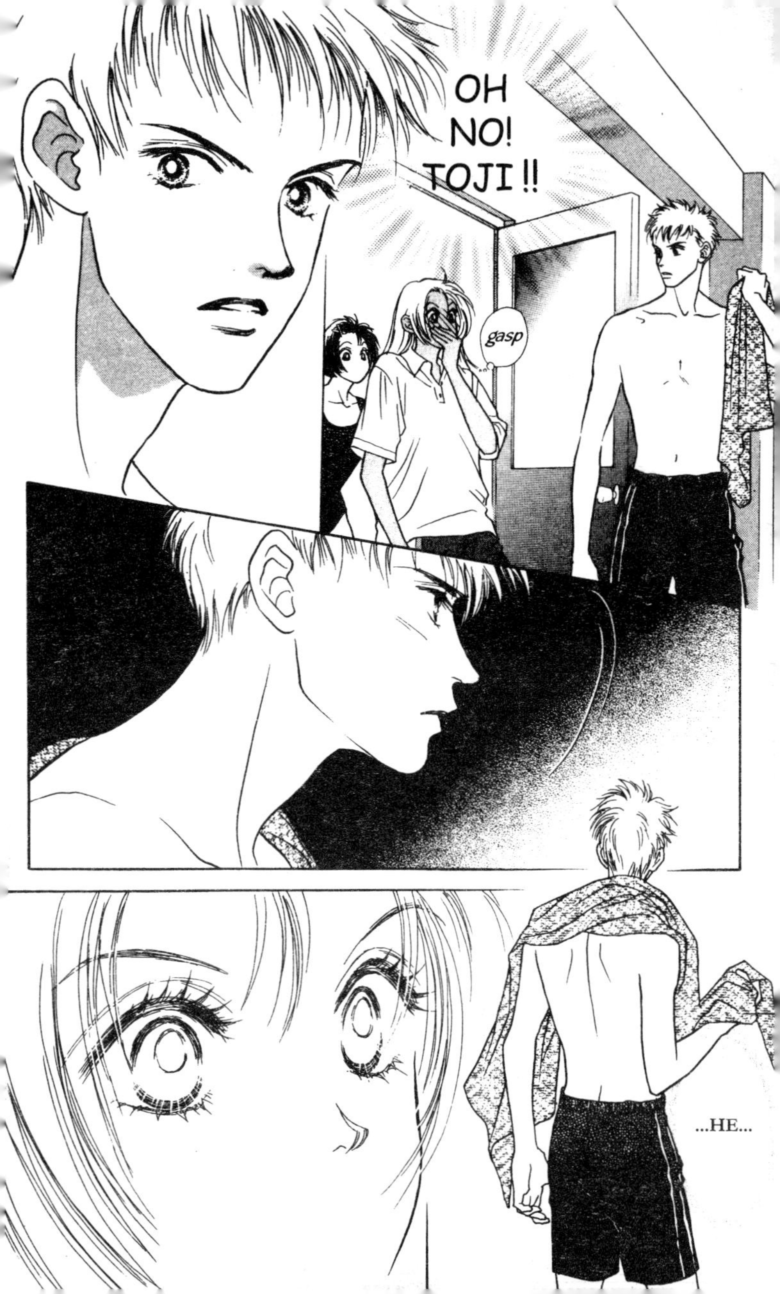
OH NO! TOJI!!
gasp
...HE...

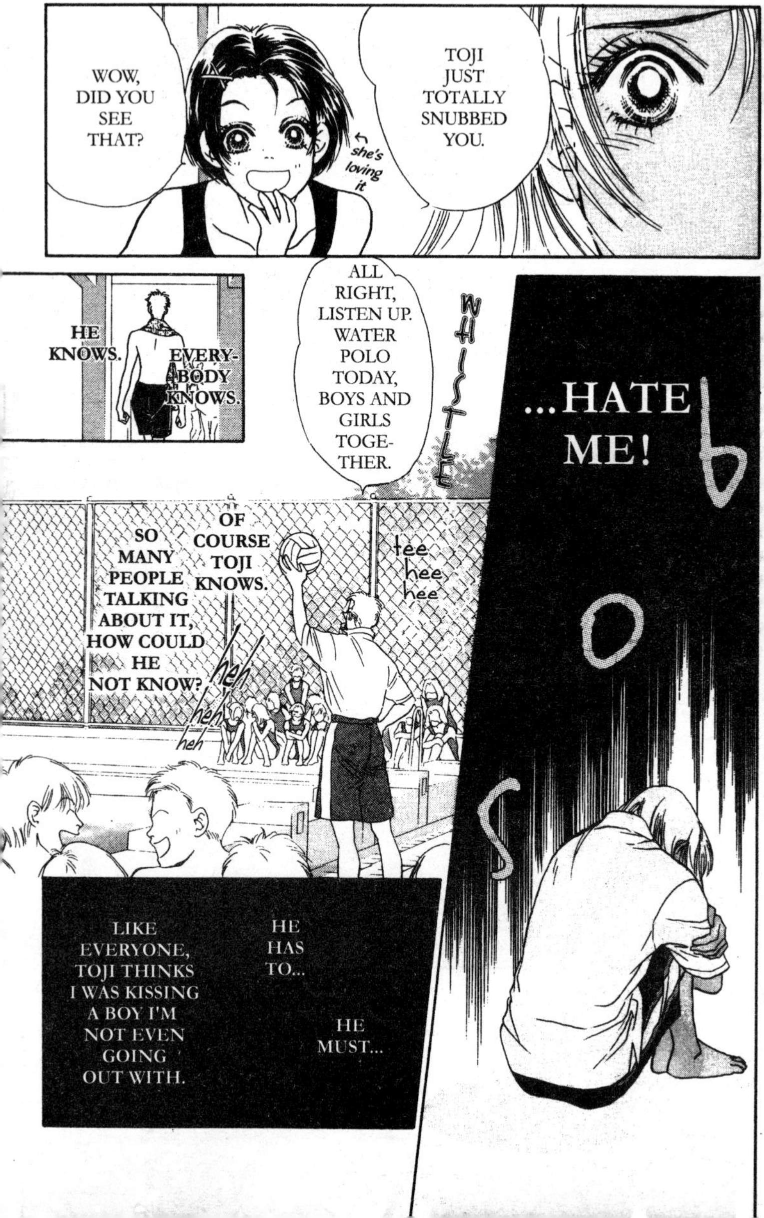
WOW, DID YOU SEE THAT?
she's loving it
TOJI JUST TOTALLY SNUBBED YOU.
HE KNOWS.
EVERY-BODY KNOWS.
ALL RIGHT, LISTEN UP. WATER POLO TODAY, BOYS AND GIRLS TOGE-THER.
WHISTLE
SO MANY PEOPLE TALKING ABOUT IT, HOW COULD HE NOT KNOW?
OF COURSE TOJI KNOWS.
heh heh heh
tee hee hee
LIKE EVERYONE, TOJI THINKS I WAS KISSING A BOY I'M NOT EVEN GOING OUT WITH.
HE HAS TO...
HE MUST...
...HATE ME!
SOB

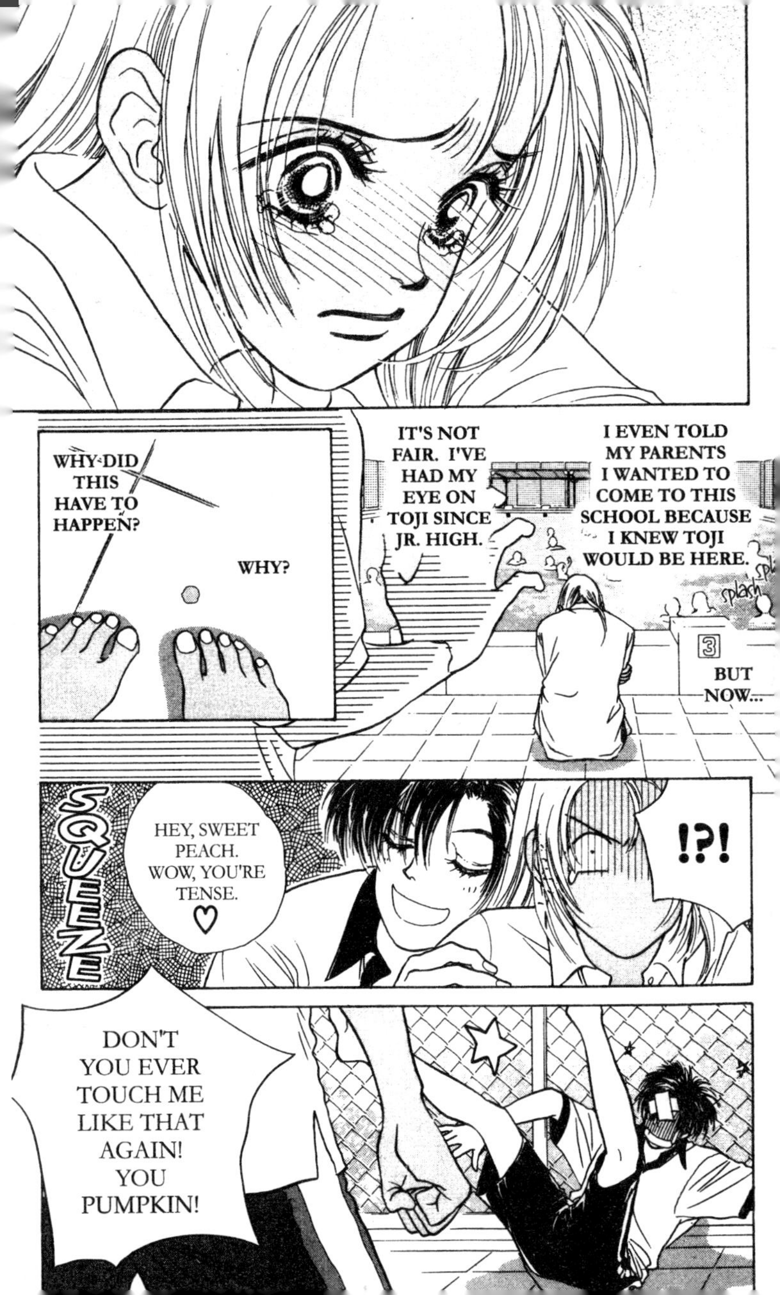
WHY DID THIS HAVE TO HAPPEN?
WHY?
IT'S NOT FAIR. I'VE HAD MY EYE ON TOJI SINCE JR. HIGH.
I EVEN TOLD MY PARENTS I WANTED TO COME TO THIS SCHOOL BECAUSE I KNEW TOJI WOULD BE HERE.
splash
BUT NOW...
SQUEEZE
HEY, SWEET PEACH. WOW, YOU'RE TENSE. ♡
!?!
DON'T YOU EVER TOUCH ME LIKE THAT AGAIN! YOU PUMPKIN!

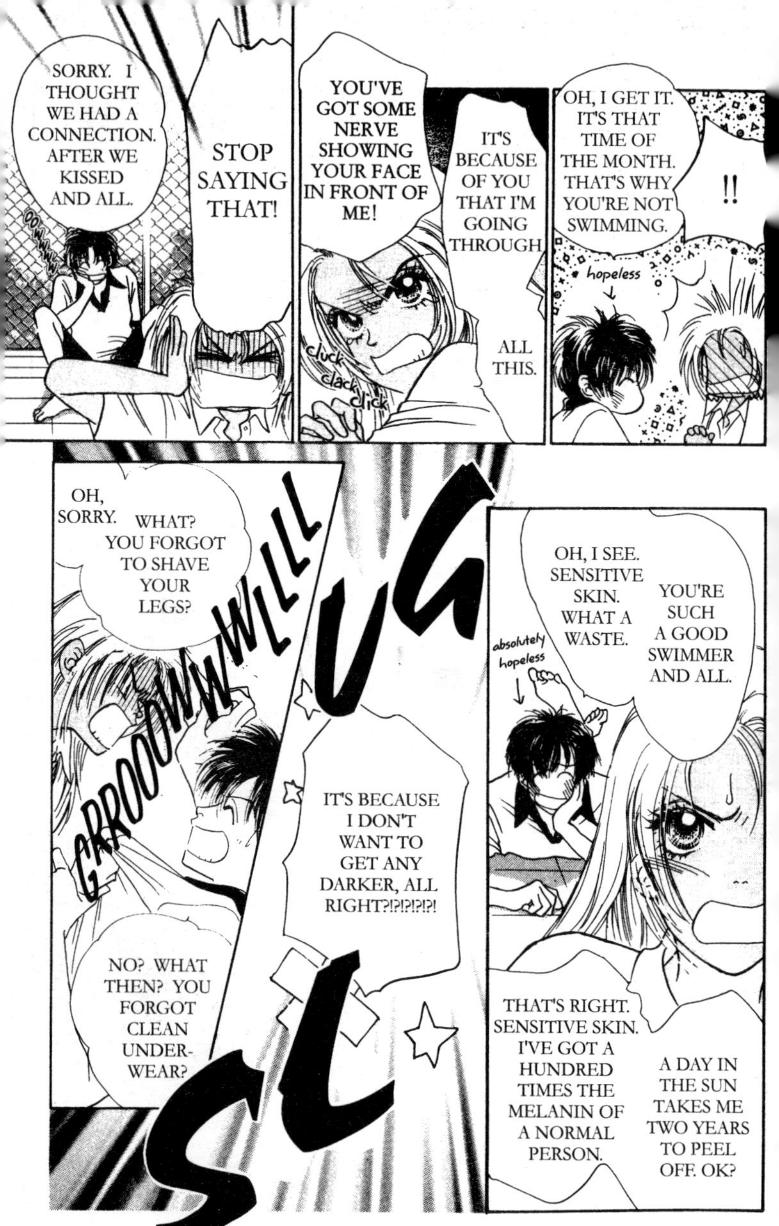
SORRY. I THOUGHT WE HAD A CONNECTION. AFTER WE KISSED AND ALL.
OOWWWW
STOP SAYING THAT!
YOU'VE GOT SOME NERVE SHOWING YOUR FACE IN FRONT OF ME!
click clack click
IT'S BECAUSE OF YOU THAT I'M GOING THROUGH
ALL THIS.
OH, I GET IT. IT'S THAT TIME OF THE MONTH. THAT'S WHY YOU'RE NOT SWIMMING.
!!
hopeless
OH, SORRY.
WHAT? YOU FORGOT TO SHAVE YOUR LEGS?
GRROOOWWWLLLL
NO? WHAT THEN? YOU FORGOT CLEAN UNDER-WEAR?
UG
IT'S BECAUSE I DON'T WANT TO GET ANY DARKER, ALL RIGHT?!?!?!?!?!
SL
OH, I SEE. SENSITIVE SKIN. WHAT A WASTE.
YOU'RE SUCH A GOOD SWIMMER AND ALL.
absolutely hopeless
THAT'S RIGHT. SENSITIVE SKIN. I'VE GOT A HUNDRED TIMES THE MELANIN OF A NORMAL PERSON.
A DAY IN THE SUN TAKES ME TWO YEARS TO PEEL OFF. OK?

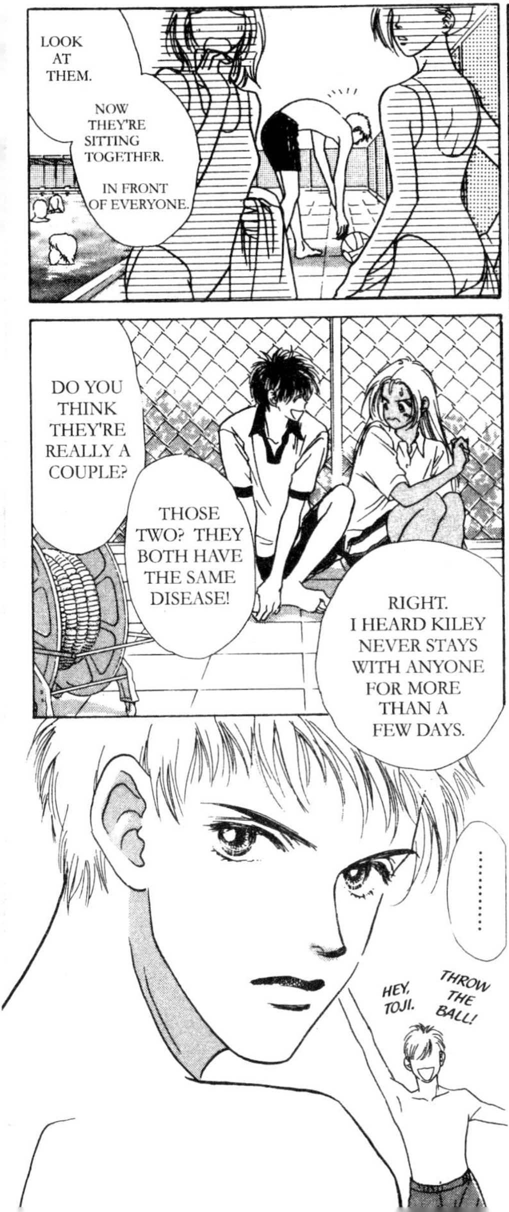
LOOK AT THEM.
NOW THEY'RE SITTING TOGETHER.
IN FRONT OF EVERYONE.
DO YOU THINK THEY'RE REALLY A COUPLE?
THOSE TWO? THEY BOTH HAVE THE SAME DISEASE!
RIGHT. I HEARD KILEY NEVER STAYS WITH ANYONE FOR MORE THAN A FEW DAYS.
....
HEY, TOJI.
THROW THE BALL!

MESSAGE FROM THE AUTHOR:

THANK YOU ALL FOR BUYING MY BOOK. JUST WANTED TO TELL YOU THAT, OF ALL THE CHARACTERS IN ALL THE COMICS I'VE EVER WRITTEN, MOMO IS THE ONE THAT'S CLOSEST IN REAL LIFE TO THE WAY I WAS. IN JR. HIGH AND HIGH SCHOOL, I WAS ALSO ON THE SWIM TEAM, BUT HAD A PROBLEM BECAUSE I TANNED SO EASILY. I USED TO WORRY ABOUT IT A LOT. OF COURSE, SINCE I BECAME A CARTOONIST, I NEVER LEAVE THE HOUSE AND I'VE GOTTEN LIGHT AGAIN. WHEN MY OLD FRIENDS FROM SCHOOL SEE ME, THEY CAN'T BELIEVE I'M THE SAME PERSON. TEE-HEE

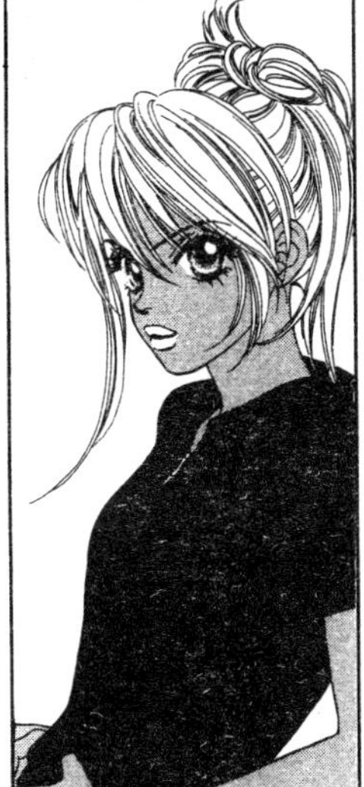

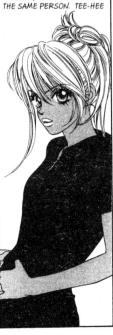

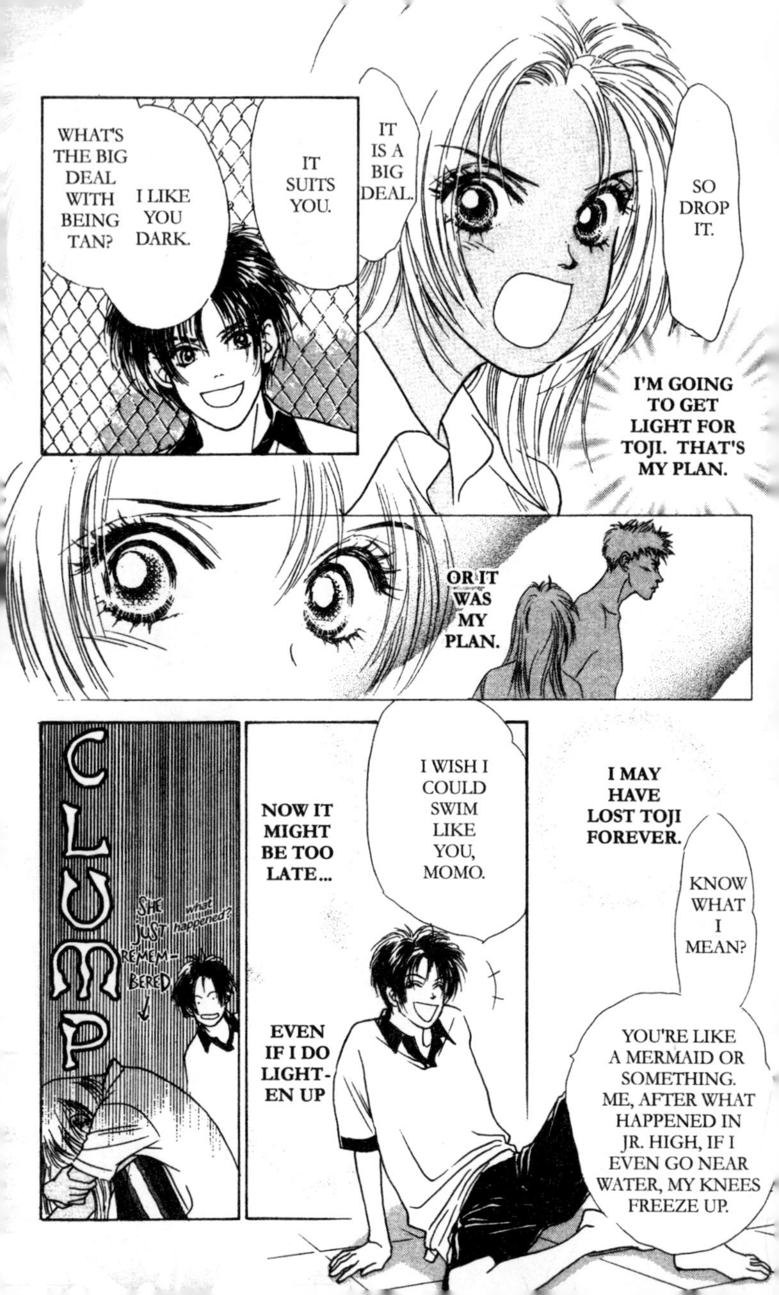
WHAT'S THE BIG DEAL WITH BEING TAN?
I LIKE YOU DARK.
IT SUITS YOU.
IT IS A BIG DEAL.
SO DROP IT.
I'M GOING TO GET LIGHT FOR TOJI. THAT'S MY PLAN.
OR IT WAS MY PLAN.
I MAY HAVE LOST TOJI FOREVER.
KNOW WHAT I MEAN?
YOU'RE LIKE A MERMAID OR SOMETHING. ME, AFTER WHAT HAPPENED IN JR. HIGH, IF I EVEN GO NEAR WATER, MY KNEES FREEZE UP.
I WISH I COULD SWIM LIKE YOU, MOMO.
NOW IT MIGHT BE TOO LATE...
EVEN IF I DO LIGHT-EN UP
what happened?
SHE JUST REMEM-BERED
CLUMP

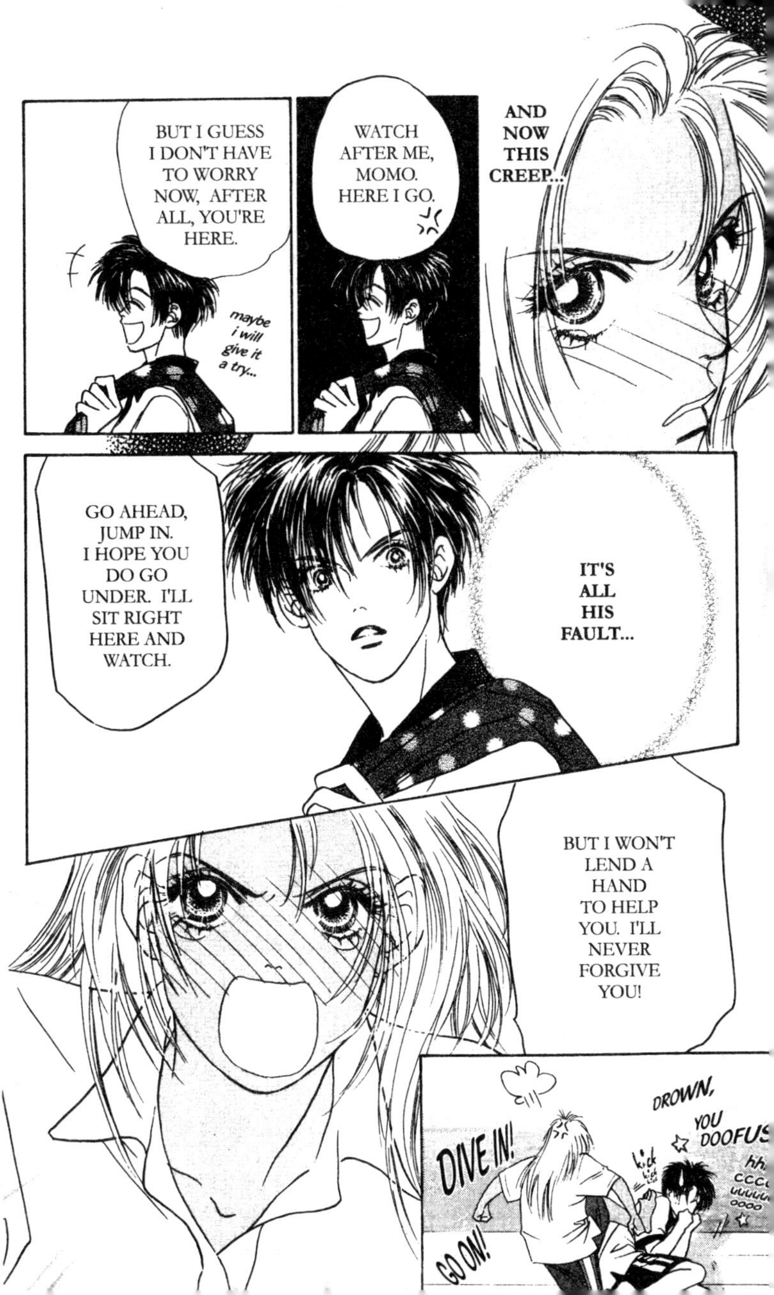
BUT I GUESS I DON'T HAVE TO WORRY NOW, AFTER ALL, YOU'RE HERE.
maybe i will give it a try...
WATCH AFTER ME, MOMO. HERE I GO.
AND NOW THIS CREEP...
GO AHEAD, JUMP IN. I HOPE YOU DO GO UNDER. I'LL SIT RIGHT HERE AND WATCH.
IT'S ALL HIS FAULT...
BUT I WON'T LEND A HAND TO HELP YOU. I'LL NEVER FORGIVE YOU!
DIVE IN!
GO ON!
DROWN, YOU DOOFUS

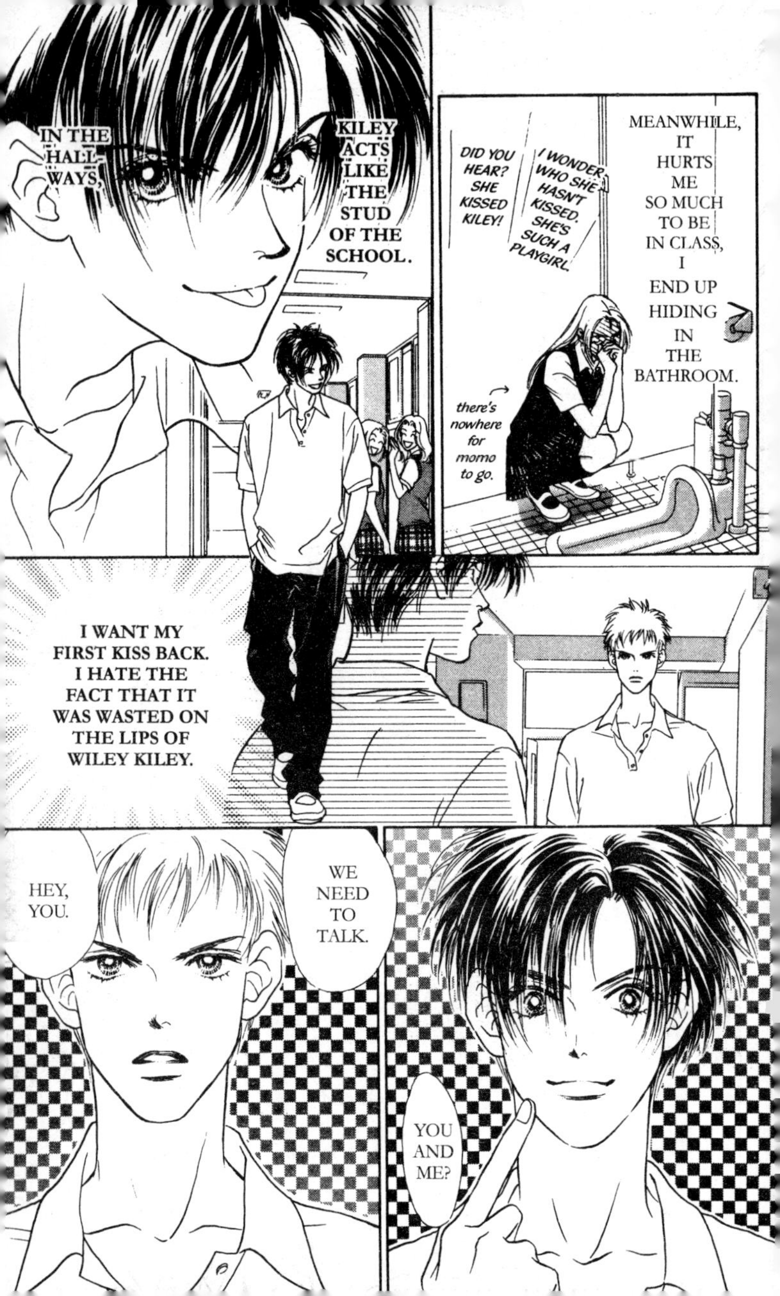
IN THE HALL-WAYS,
KILEY ACTS LIKE THE STUD OF THE SCHOOL.
DID YOU HEAR? SHE KISSED KILEY!
I WONDER WHO SHE HASN'T KISSED. SHE'S SUCH A PLAYGIRL
MEANWHILE, IT HURTS ME SO MUCH TO BE IN CLASS, I END UP HIDING IN THE BATHROOM.
there's nowhere for momo to go.
I WANT MY FIRST KISS BACK. I HATE THE FACT THAT IT WAS WASTED ON THE LIPS OF WILEY KILEY.
HEY, YOU.
WE NEED TO TALK.
YOU AND ME?

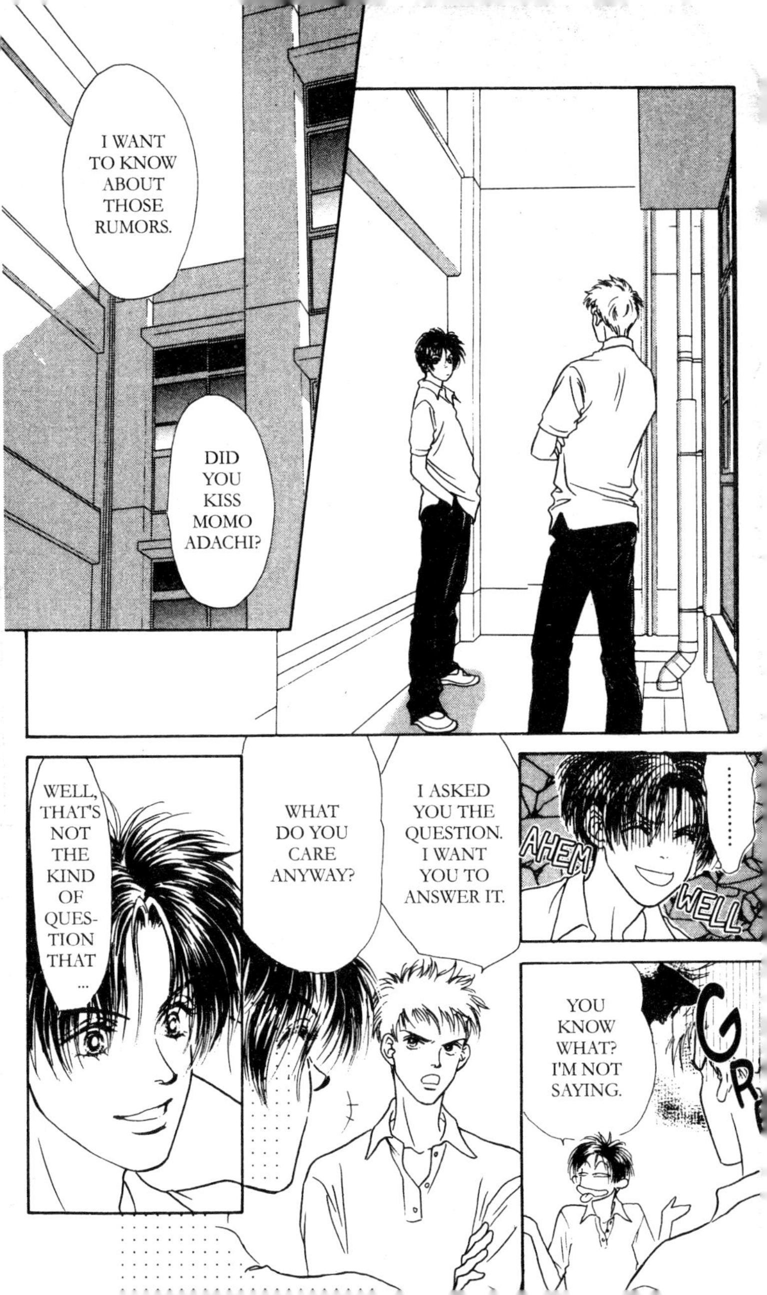
I WANT TO KNOW ABOUT THOSE RUMORS.
DID YOU KISS MOMO ADACHI?
WELL, THAT'S NOT THE KIND OF QUES-TION THAT ...
WHAT DO YOU CARE ANYWAY?
I ASKED YOU THE QUESTION. I WANT YOU TO ANSWER IT.
AHEM
......
WELL
YOU KNOW WHAT? I'M NOT SAYING.

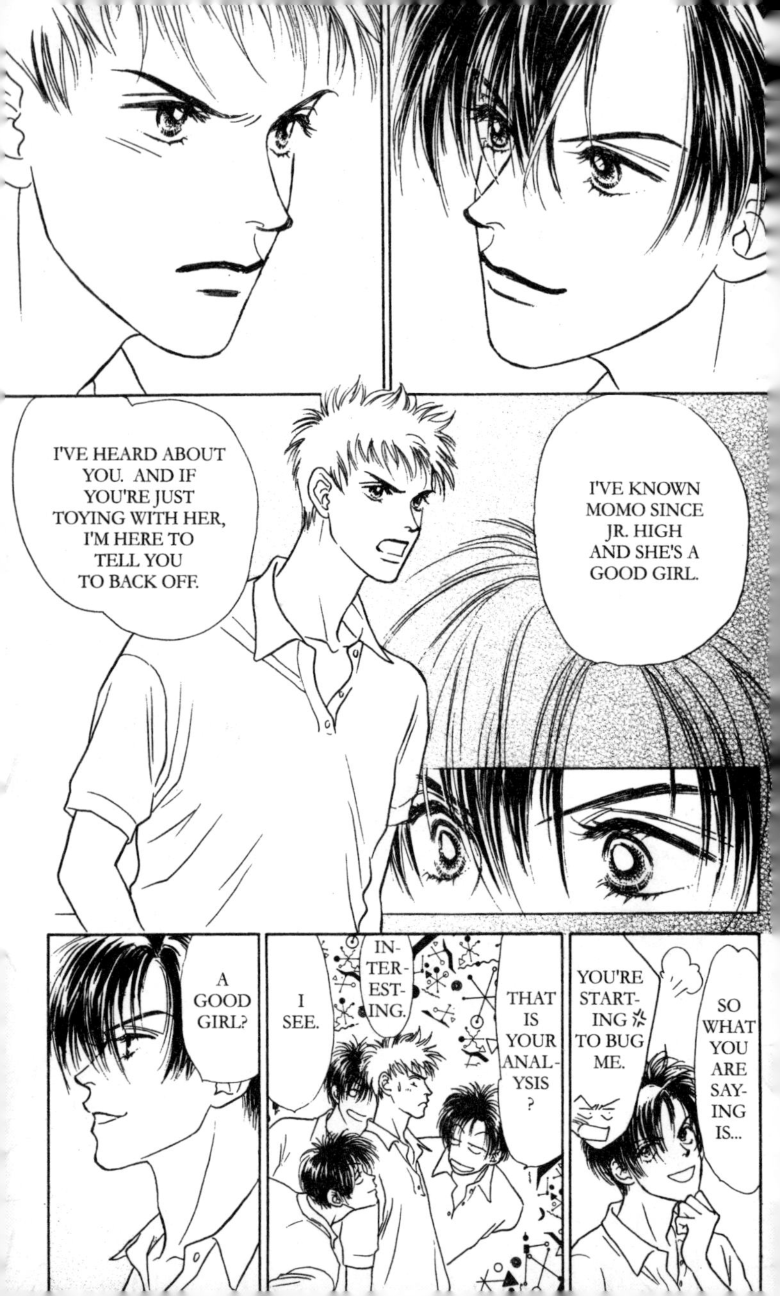
I'VE HEARD ABOUT YOU. AND IF YOU'RE JUST TOYING WITH HER, I'M HERE TO TELL YOU TO BACK OFF.
I'VE KNOWN MOMO SINCE JR. HIGH AND SHE'S A GOOD GIRL.
A GOOD GIRL?
I SEE.
IN-TER-EST-ING.
THAT IS YOUR ANAL-YSIS?
YOU'RE START-ING TO BUG ME.
SO WHAT YOU ARE SAY-ING IS...

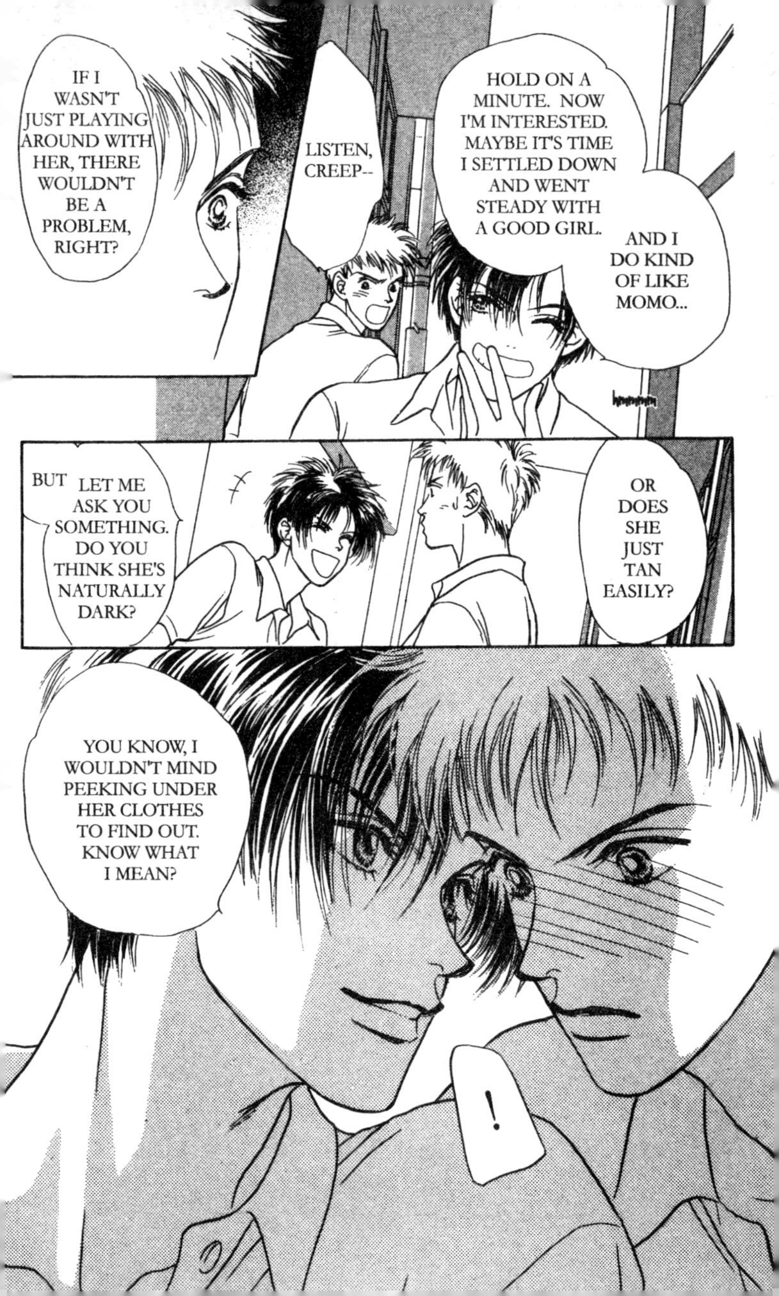
IF I WASN'T JUST PLAYING AROUND WITH HER, THERE WOULDN'T BE A PROBLEM, RIGHT?
LISTEN, CREEP--
HOLD ON A MINUTE. NOW I'M INTERESTED. MAYBE IT'S TIME I SETTLED DOWN AND WENT STEADY WITH A GOOD GIRL.
AND I DO KIND OF LIKE MOMO...
BUT LET ME ASK YOU SOMETHING. DO YOU THINK SHE'S NATURALLY DARK?
OR DOES SHE JUST TAN EASILY?
YOU KNOW, I WOULDN'T MIND PEEKING UNDER HER CLOTHES TO FIND OUT. KNOW WHAT I MEAN?
!

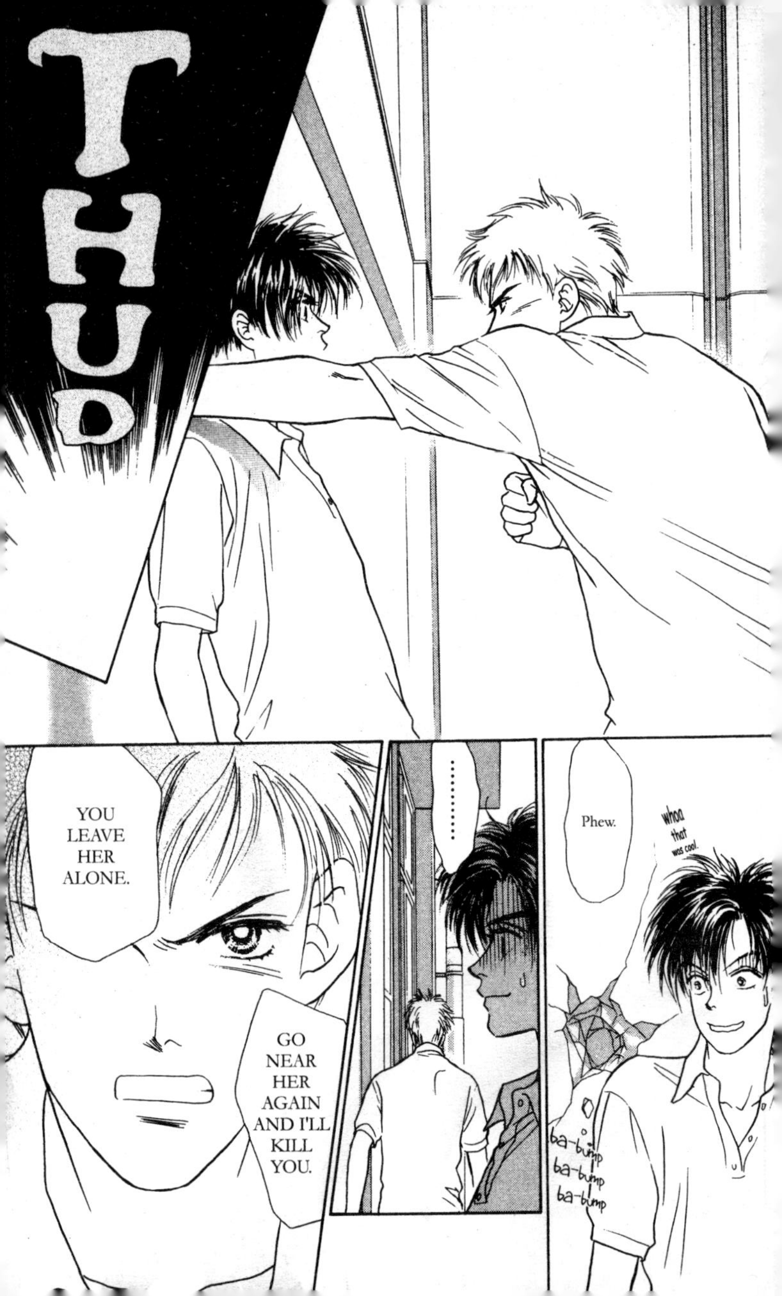
THUD
YOU LEAVE HER ALONE.
GO NEAR HER AGAIN AND I'LL KILL YOU.
....
Phew.
whoa that was cool.
ba-bump
ba-bump
ba-bump

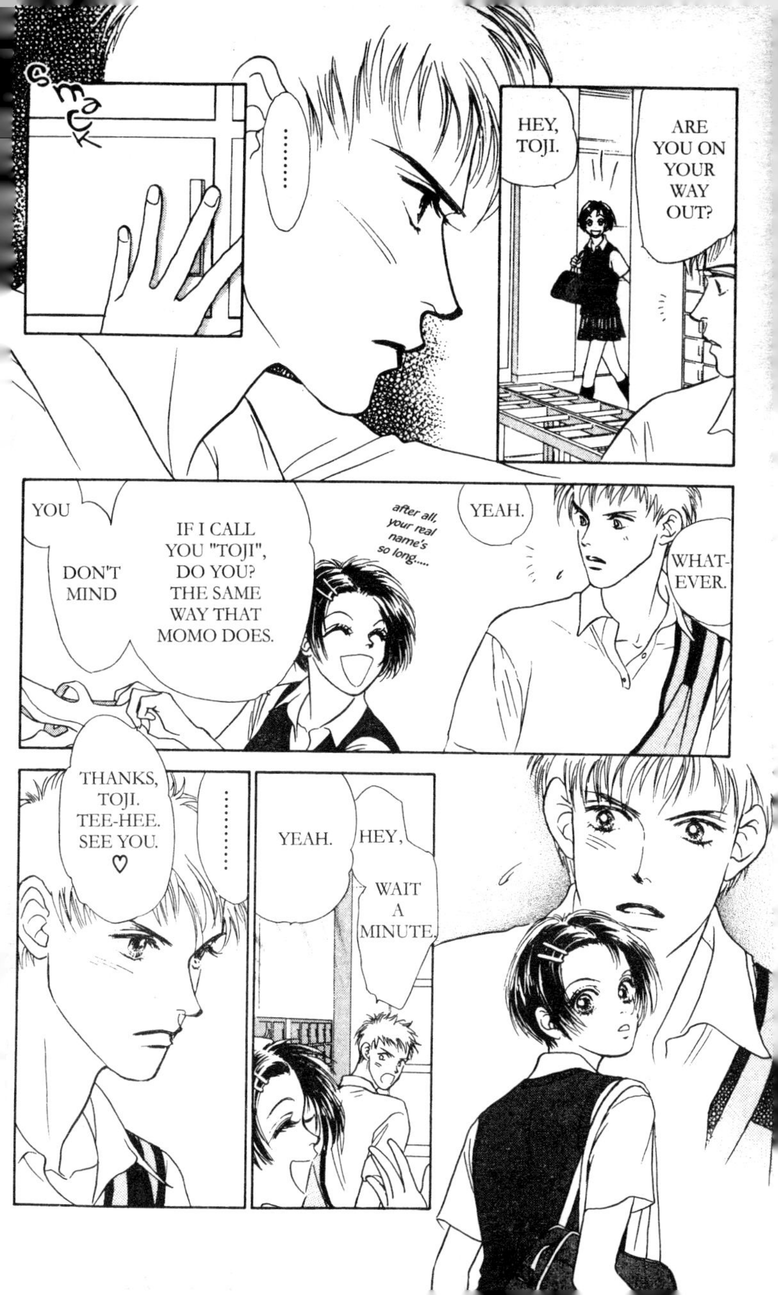
smack
......
HEY, TOJI.
ARE YOU ON YOUR WAY OUT?
YOU DON'T MIND IF I CALL YOU "TOJI", DO YOU? THE SAME WAY THAT MOMO DOES.
after all, your real name's so long....
YEAH.
WHAT-EVER.
THANKS, TOJI. TEE-HEE. SEE YOU. ♡
......
YEAH.
HEY, WAIT A MINUTE.

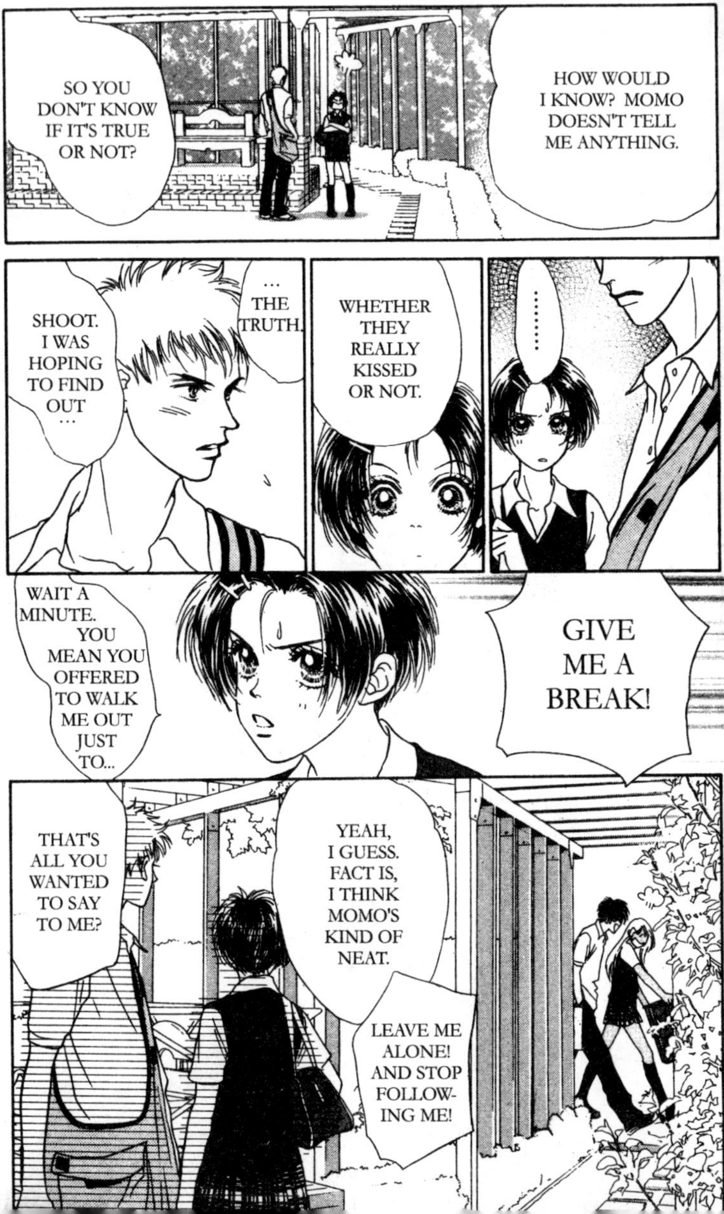
SO YOU DON'T KNOW IF IT'S TRUE OR NOT?
HOW WOULD I KNOW? MOMO DOESN'T TELL ME ANYTHING.
SHOOT. I WAS HOPING TO FIND OUT ...
... THE TRUTH.
WHETHER THEY REALLY KISSED OR NOT.
....
WAIT A MINUTE. YOU MEAN YOU OFFERED TO WALK ME OUT JUST TO...
GIVE ME A BREAK!
THAT'S ALL YOU WANTED TO SAY TO ME?
YEAH, I GUESS. FACT IS, I THINK MOMO'S KIND OF NEAT.
LEAVE ME ALONE! AND STOP FOLLOW-ING ME!

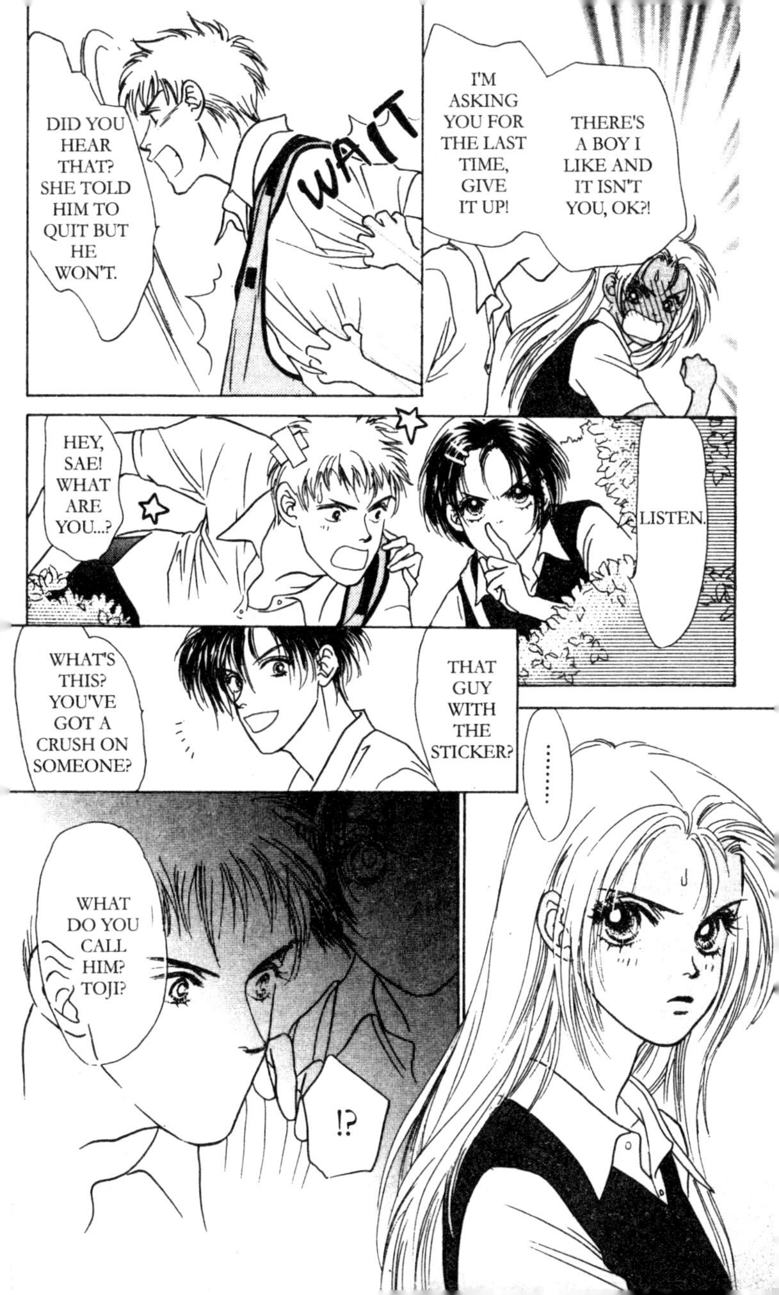
DID YOU HEAR THAT? SHE TOLD HIM TO QUIT BUT HE WON'T.
WAIT
I'M ASKING YOU FOR THE LAST TIME, GIVE IT UP!
THERE'S A BOY I LIKE AND IT ISN'T YOU, OK?!
HEY, SAE! WHAT ARE YOU...?
LISTEN.
WHAT'S THIS? YOU'VE GOT A CRUSH ON SOMEONE?
THAT GUY WITH THE STICKER?
WHAT DO YOU CALL HIM? TOJI?
!?
....

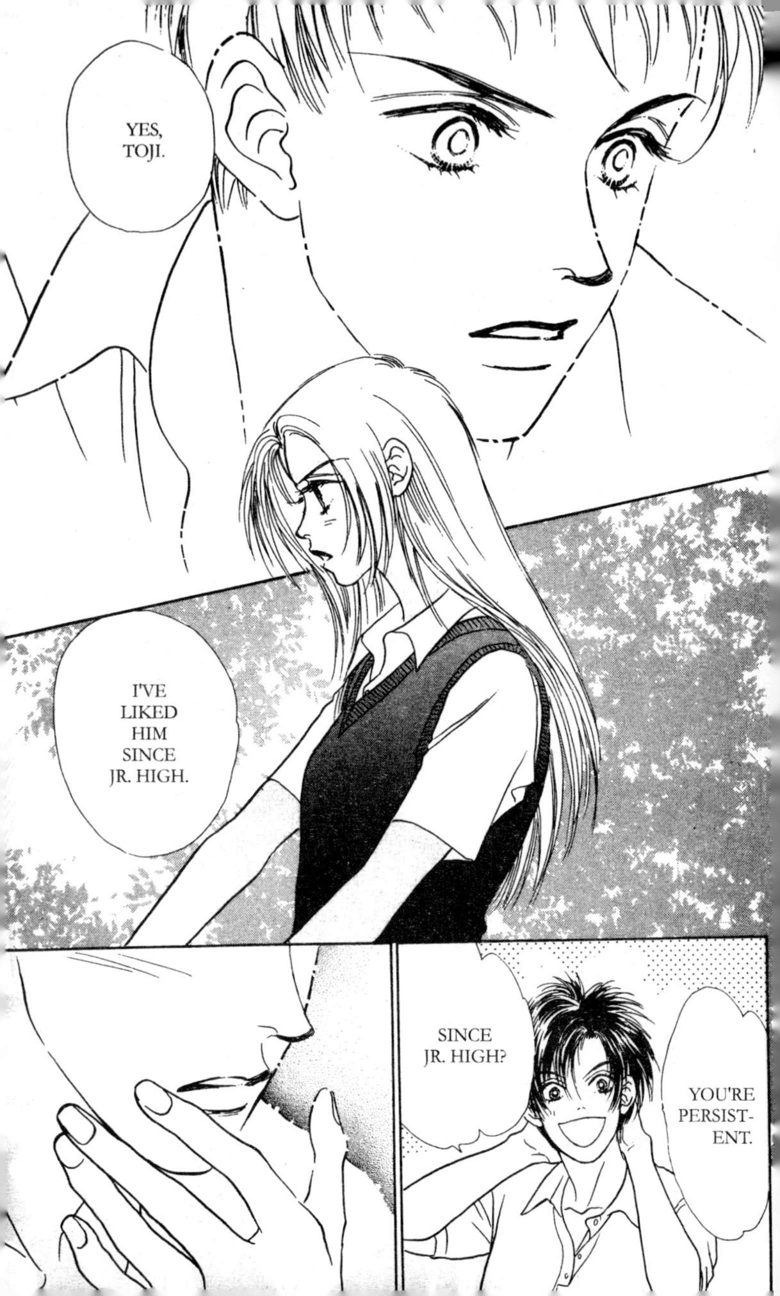
YES, TOJI.
I'VE LIKED HIM SINCE JR. HIGH.
SINCE JR. HIGH?
YOU'RE PERSIST-ENT.

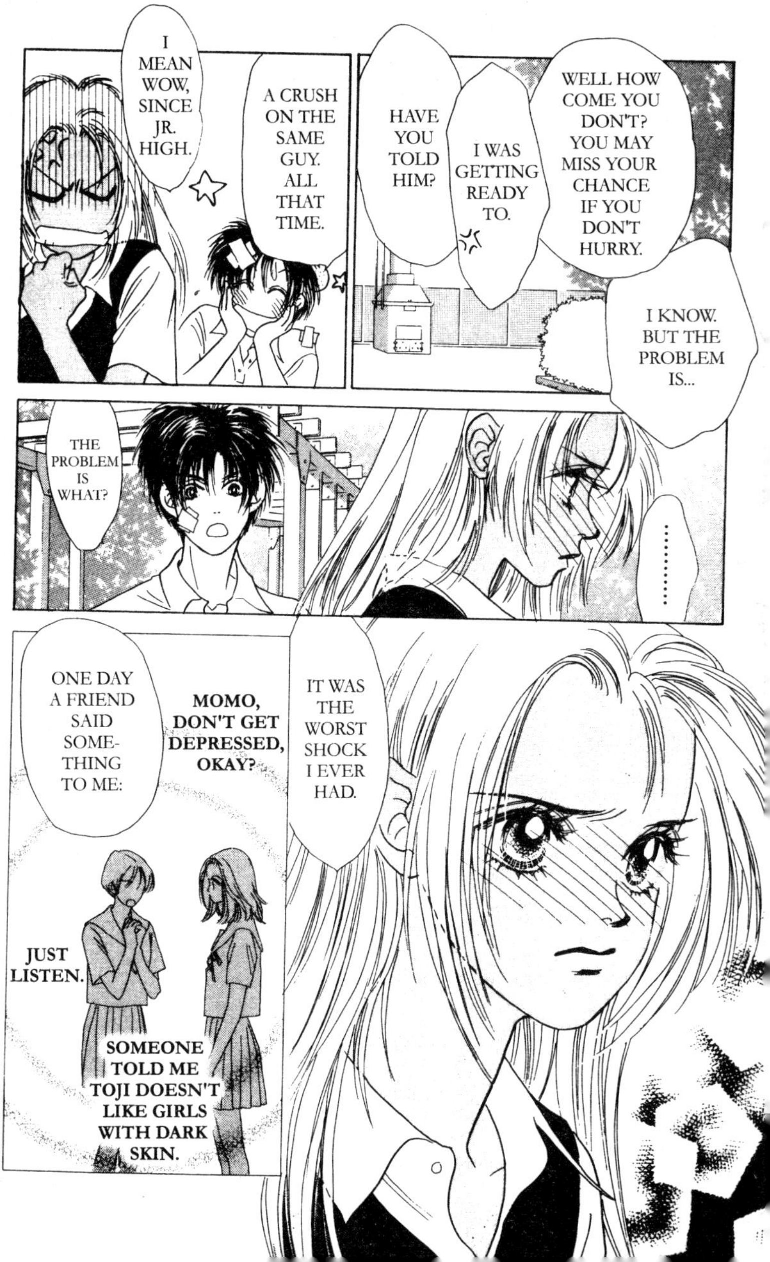
I MEAN WOW, SINCE JR. HIGH.
A CRUSH ON THE SAME GUY. ALL THAT TIME.
HAVE YOU TOLD HIM?
I WAS GETTING READY TO.
WELL HOW COME YOU DON'T? YOU MAY MISS YOUR CHANCE IF YOU DON'T HURRY.
I KNOW. BUT THE PROBLEM IS...
THE PROBLEM IS WHAT?
....
ONE DAY A FRIEND SAID SOME-THING TO ME:
MOMO, DON'T GET DEPRESSED, OKAY?
JUST LISTEN.
SOMEONE TOLD ME TOJI DOESN'T LIKE GIRLS WITH DARK SKIN.
IT WAS THE WORST SHOCK I EVER HAD.

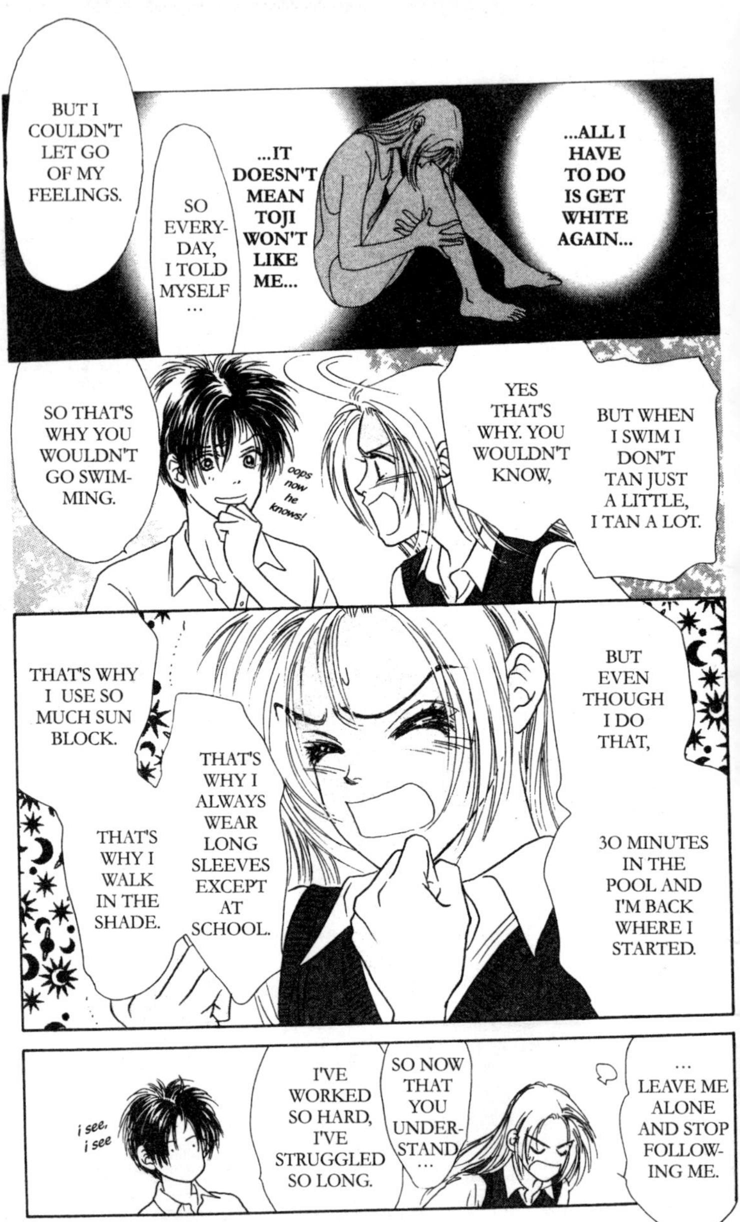
BUT I COULDN'T LET GO OF MY FEELINGS.
SO EVERY-DAY, I TOLD MYSELF …
...IT DOESN'T MEAN TOJI WON'T LIKE ME...
...ALL I HAVE TO DO IS GET WHITE AGAIN...
SO THAT'S WHY YOU WOULDN'T GO SWIM-MING.
oops now he knows!
YES THAT'S WHY. YOU WOULDN'T KNOW,
BUT WHEN I SWIM I DON'T TAN JUST A LITTLE, I TAN A LOT.
THAT'S WHY I USE SO MUCH SUN BLOCK.
THAT'S WHY I ALWAYS WEAR LONG SLEEVES EXCEPT AT SCHOOL.
THAT'S WHY I WALK IN THE SHADE.
BUT EVEN THOUGH I DO THAT,
30 MINUTES IN THE POOL AND I'M BACK WHERE I STARTED.
i see, i see
I'VE WORKED SO HARD, I'VE STRUGGLED SO LONG.
SO NOW THAT YOU UNDER-STAND …
… LEAVE ME ALONE AND STOP FOLLOW-ING ME.

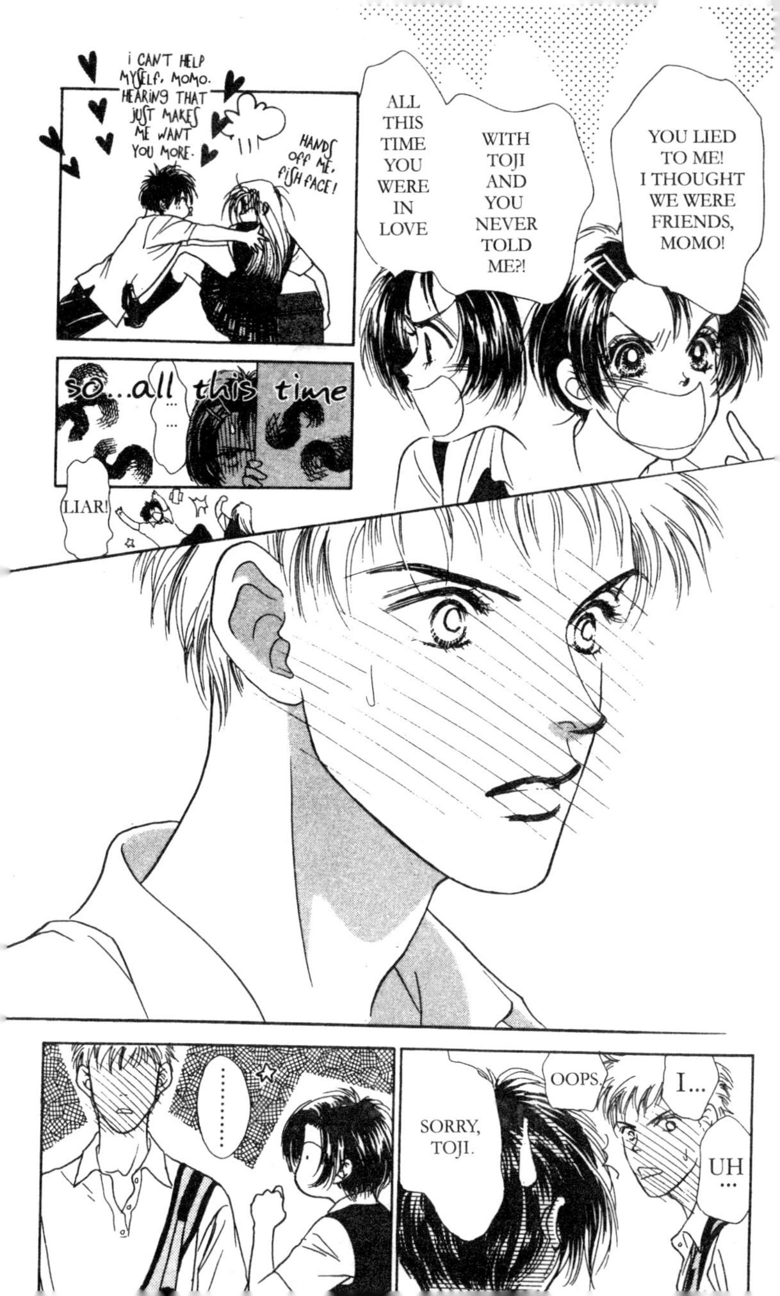
I CAN'T HELP MYSELF, MOMO. HEARING THAT JUST MAKES ME WANT YOU MORE.
HANDS OFF ME, FISH FACE!
so...all this time
...
...
LIAR!
ALL THIS TIME YOU WERE IN LOVE
WITH TOJI AND YOU NEVER TOLD ME?!
YOU LIED TO ME! I THOUGHT WE WERE FRIENDS, MOMO!
....
SORRY, TOJI.
OOPS.
I...
UH...

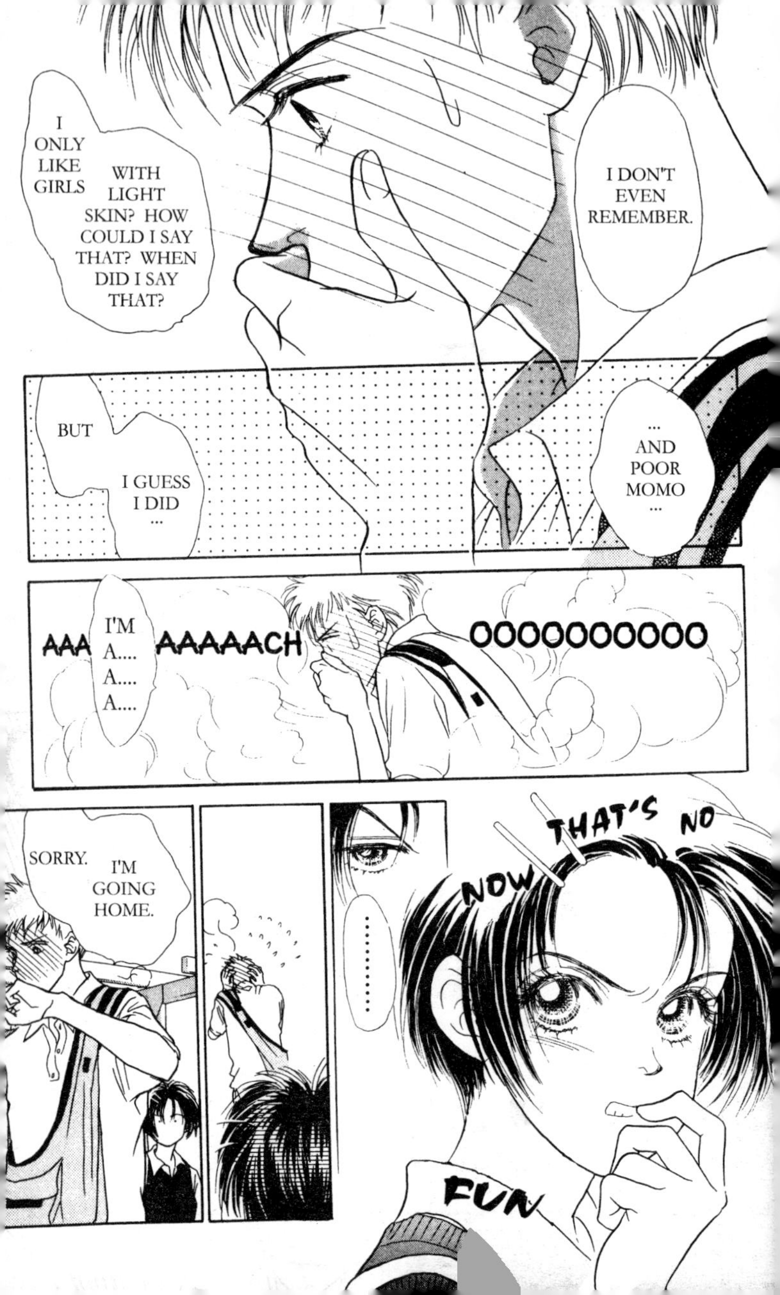
I ONLY LIKE GIRLS WITH LIGHT SKIN? HOW COULD I SAY THAT? WHEN DID I SAY THAT?
I DON'T EVEN REMEMBER.
BUT
I GUESS I DID ...
... AND POOR MOMO ...
AAA
I'M A.... A.... A....
AAAAACH
OOOOOOOOOO
SORRY.
I'M GOING HOME.
....
NOW THAT'S NO FUN

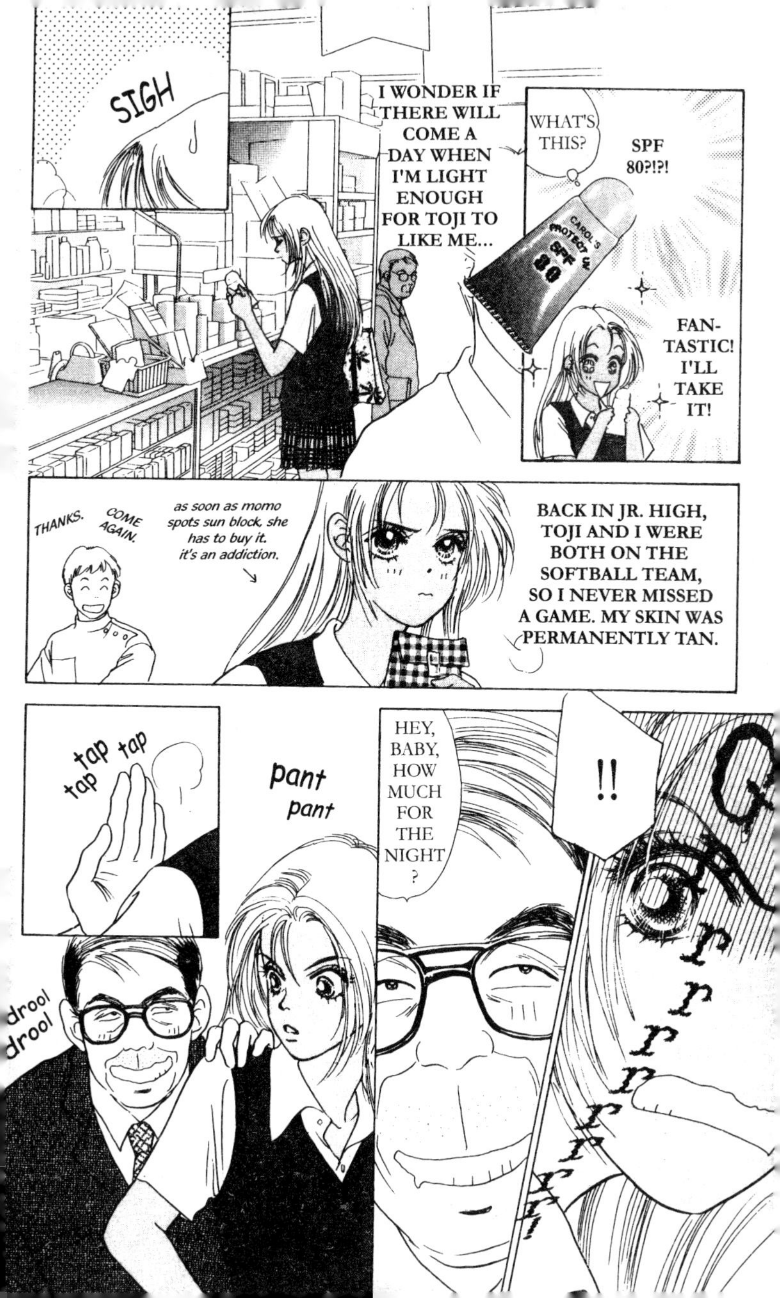
SIGH
I WONDER IF THERE WILL COME A DAY WHEN I'M LIGHT ENOUGH FOR TOJI TO LIKE ME...
WHAT'S THIS?
SPF 80?!?!
CAROL'S PROTECT U SPF 80
FAN-TASTIC! I'LL TAKE IT!
THANKS.
COME AGAIN.
as soon as momo spots sun block, she has to buy it. it's an addiction.
BACK IN JR. HIGH, TOJI AND I WERE BOTH ON THE SOFTBALL TEAM, SO I NEVER MISSED A GAME. MY SKIN WAS PERMANENTLY TAN.
tap tap tap
pant pant
drool drool
HEY, BABY, HOW MUCH FOR THE NIGHT?
!!
Grrrrrrrr

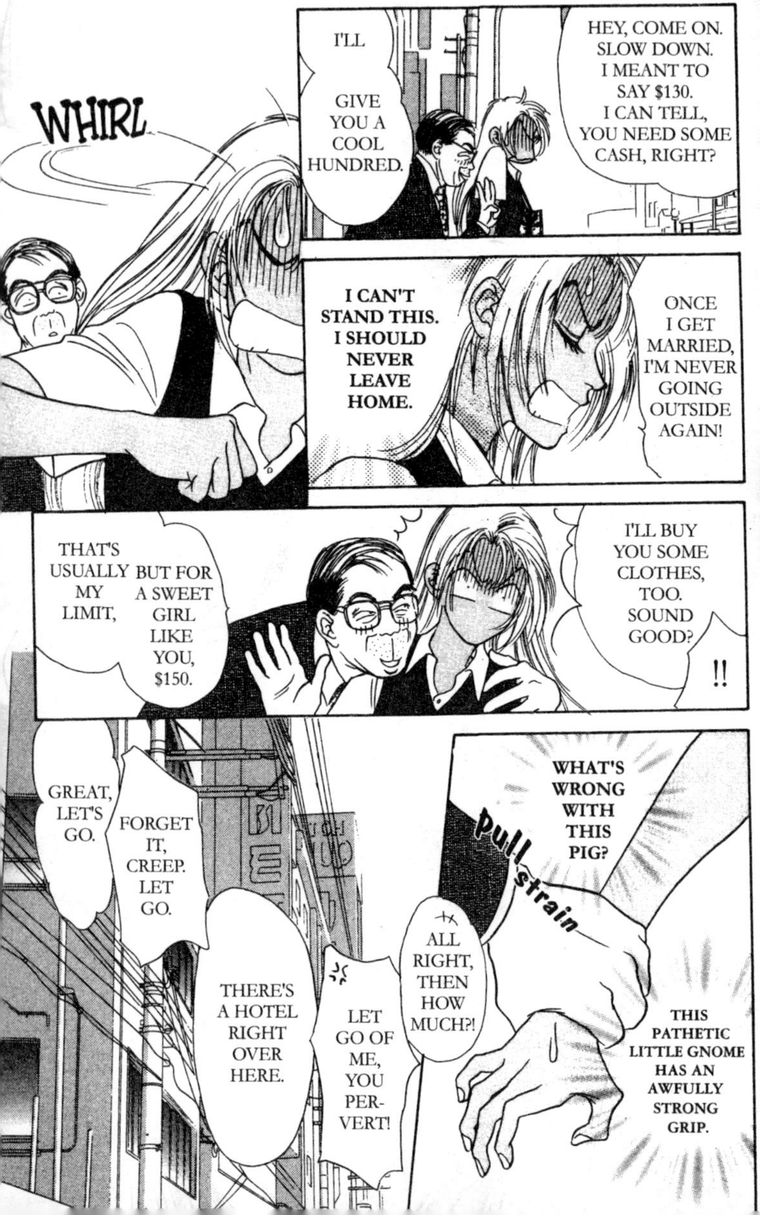
WHIRL
I'LL
GIVE YOU A COOL HUNDRED.
HEY, COME ON. SLOW DOWN. I MEANT TO SAY $130. I CAN TELL, YOU NEED SOME CASH, RIGHT?
I CAN'T STAND THIS. I SHOULD NEVER LEAVE HOME.
ONCE I GET MARRIED, I'M NEVER GOING OUTSIDE AGAIN!
THAT'S USUALLY MY LIMIT,
BUT FOR A SWEET GIRL LIKE YOU, $150.
I'LL BUY YOU SOME CLOTHES, TOO. SOUND GOOD?
!!
GREAT, LET'S GO.
FORGET IT, CREEP. LET GO.
THERE'S A HOTEL RIGHT OVER HERE.
LET GO OF ME, YOU PER-VERT!
ALL RIGHT, THEN HOW MUCH?!
WHAT'S WRONG WITH THIS PIG?
Pull strain
THIS PATHETIC LITTLE GNOME HAS AN AWFULLY STRONG GRIP.

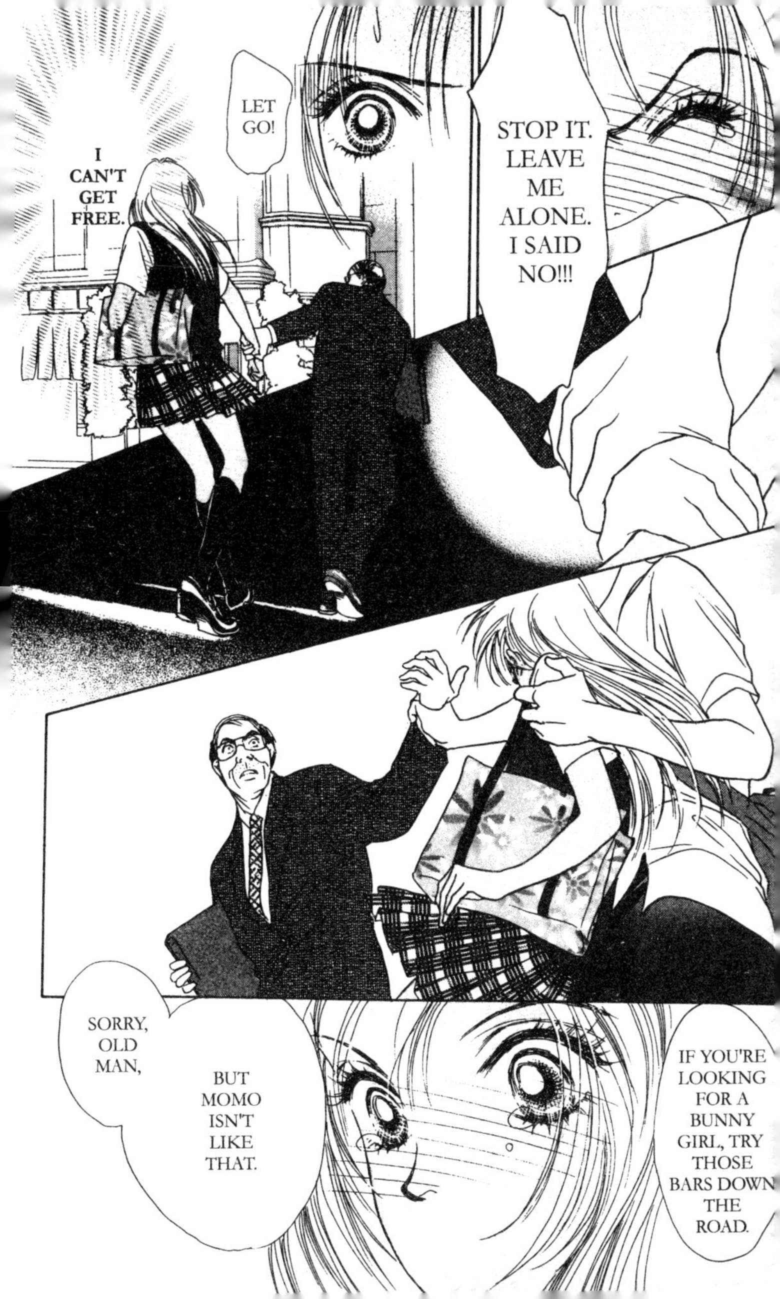
I CAN'T GET FREE.
LET GO!
STOP IT. LEAVE ME ALONE. I SAID NO!!!
SORRY, OLD MAN,
BUT MOMO ISN'T LIKE THAT.
IF YOU'RE LOOKING FOR A BUNNY GIRL, TRY THOSE BARS DOWN THE ROAD.

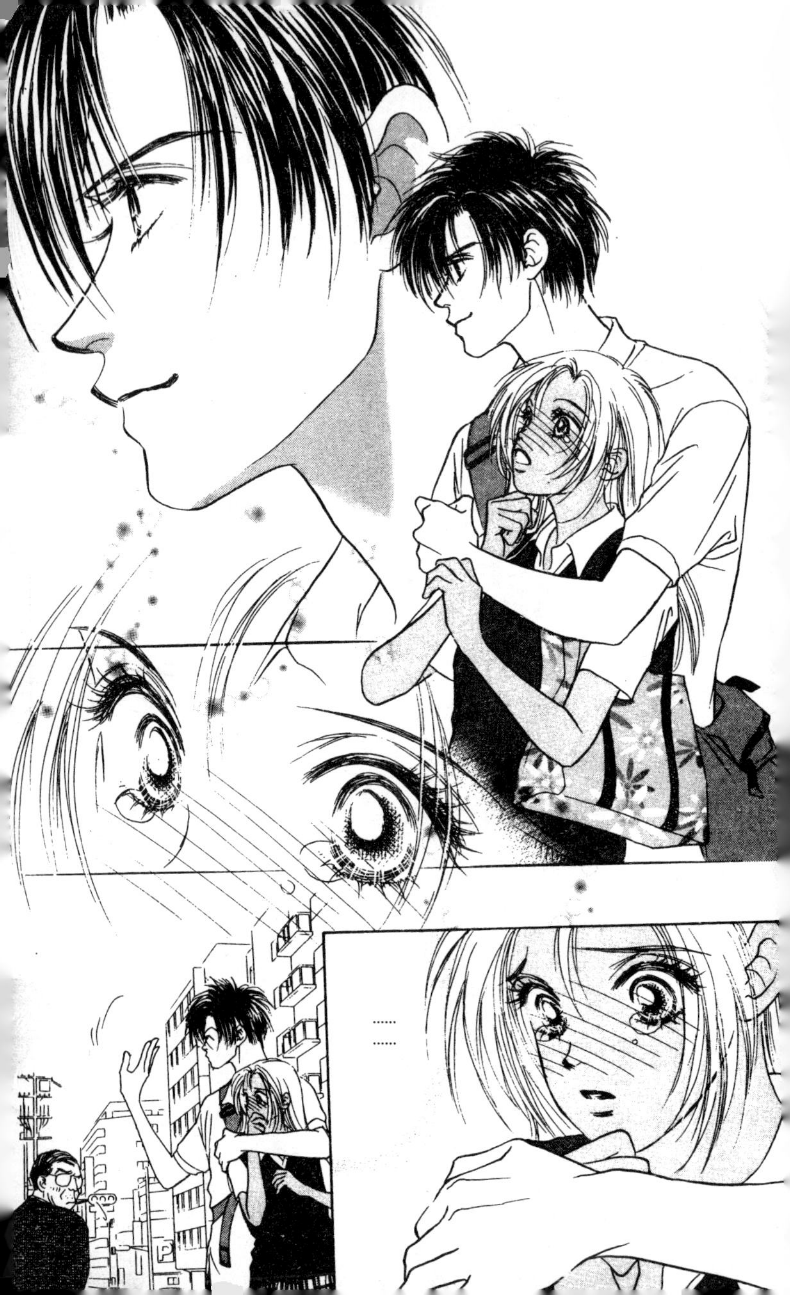
......
......

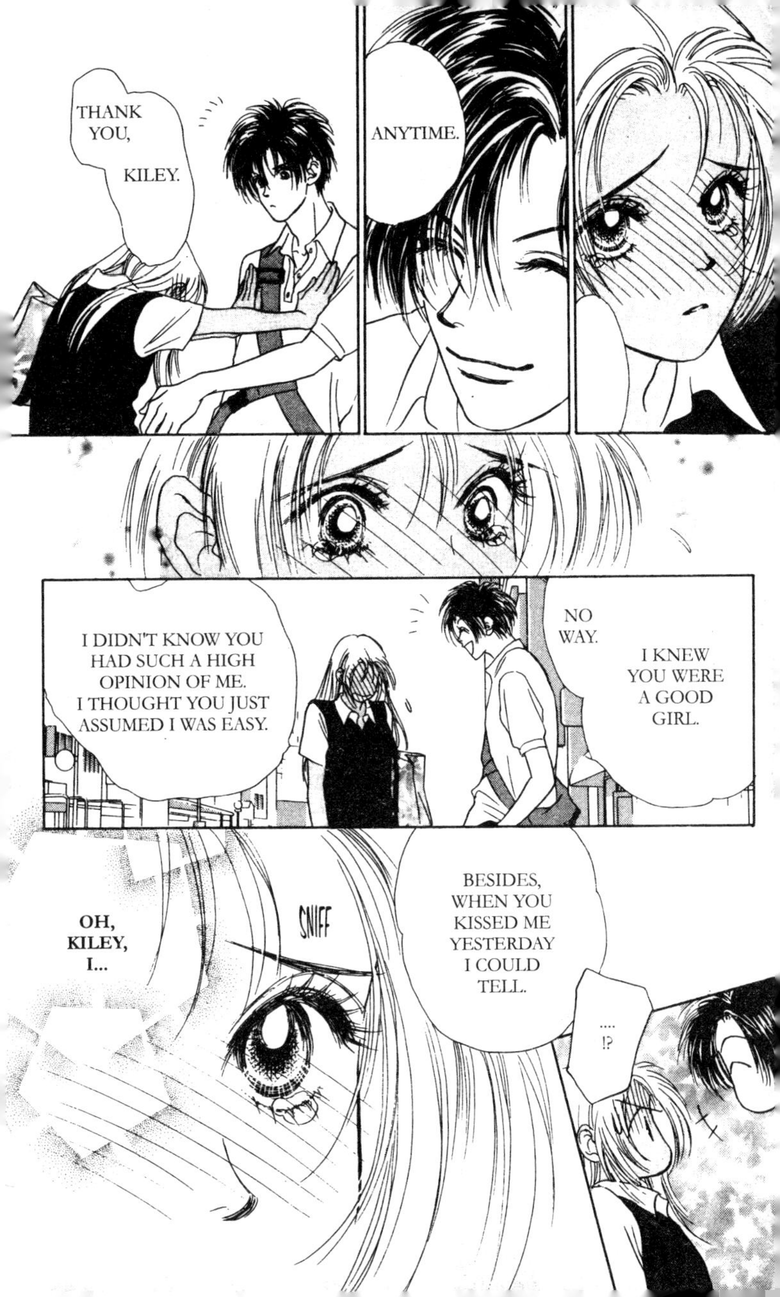

THANK YOU, KILEY.
ANYTIME.
I DIDN'T KNOW YOU HAD SUCH A HIGH OPINION OF ME. I THOUGHT YOU JUST ASSUMED I WAS EASY.
NO WAY.
I KNEW YOU WERE A GOOD GIRL.
OH, KILEY, I...
SNIFF
BESIDES, WHEN YOU KISSED ME YESTERDAY I COULD TELL.
....!?

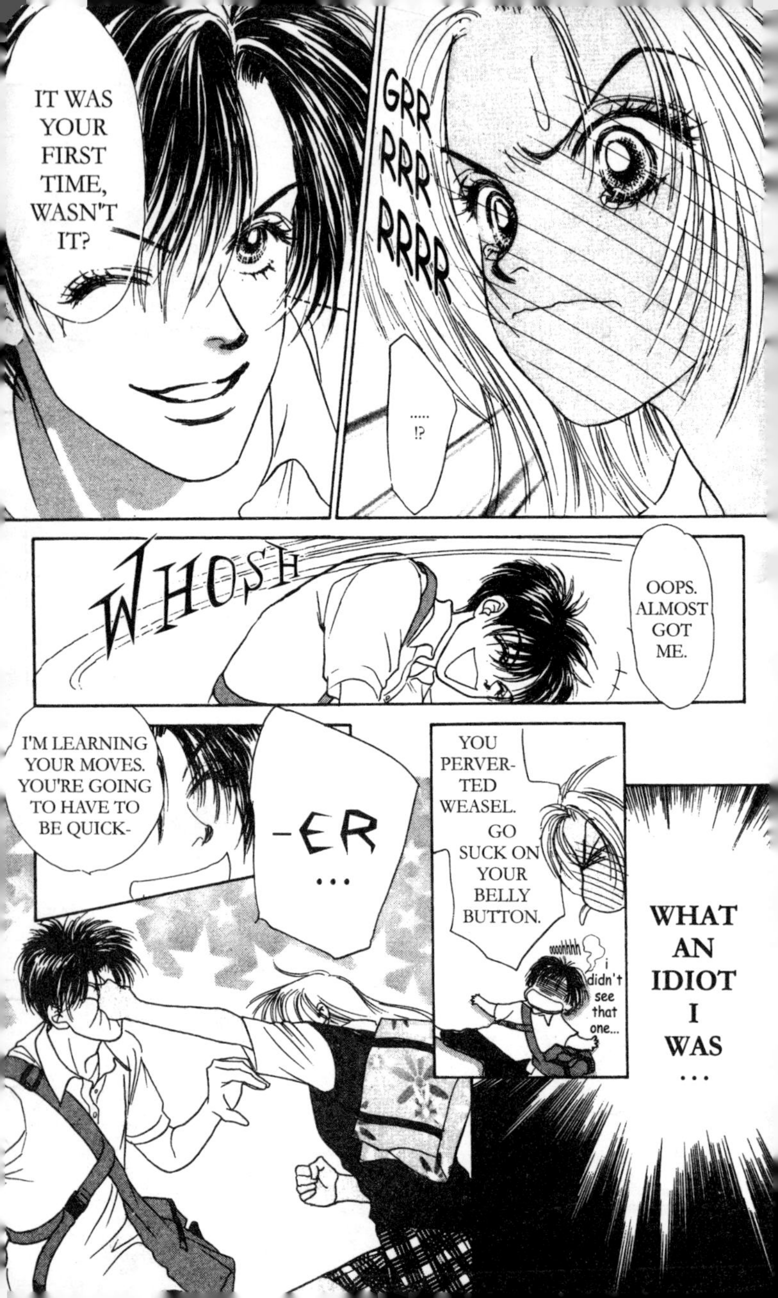
IT WAS YOUR FIRST TIME, WASN'T IT?
GRRRRRRRRRR
.....!?
WHOSH
OOPS. ALMOST GOT ME.
I'M LEARNING YOUR MOVES. YOU'RE GOING TO HAVE TO BE QUICK-
-ER ...
YOU PERVER-TED WEASEL. GO SUCK ON YOUR BELLY BUTTON.
ooohhhh
i didn't see that one...
WHAT AN IDIOT I WAS ...

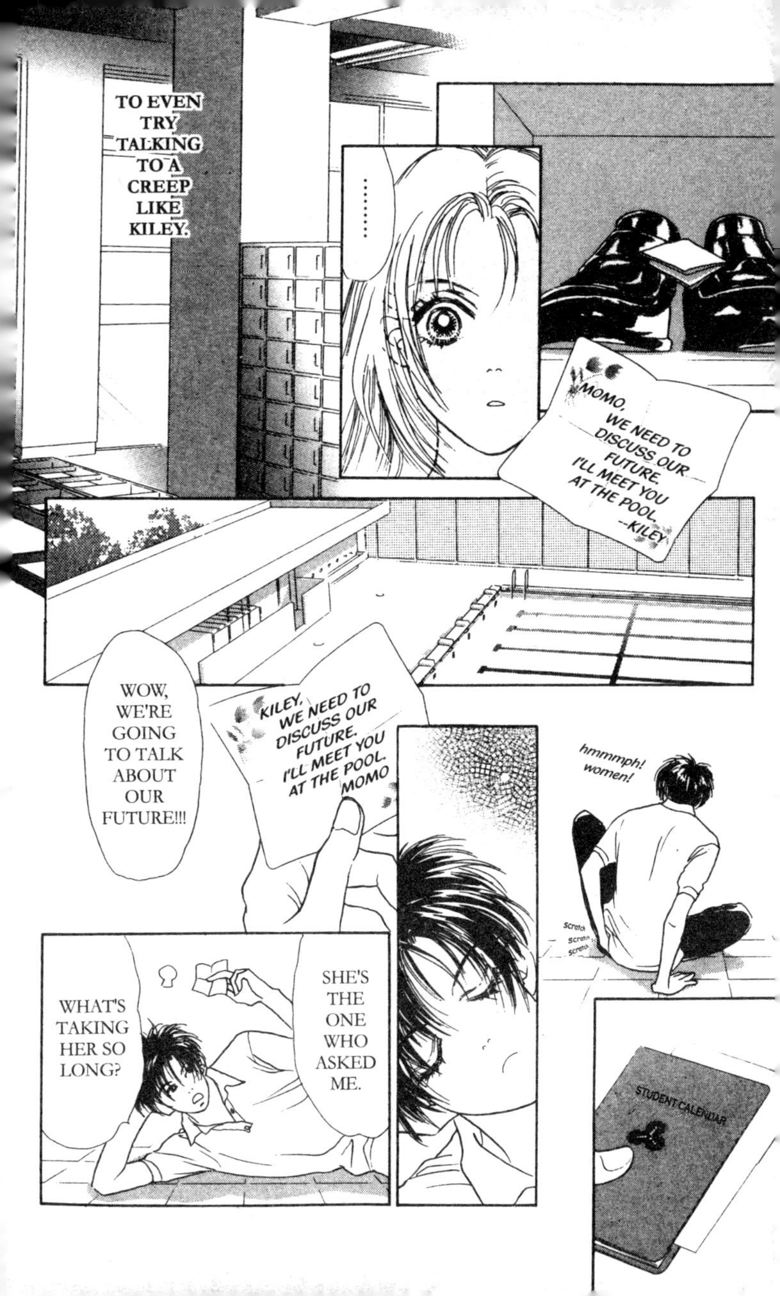
TO EVEN TRY TALKING TO A CREEP LIKE KILEY.
......
MOMO, WE NEED TO DISCUSS OUR FUTURE. I'LL MEET YOU AT THE POOL. --KILEY
WOW, WE'RE GOING TO TALK ABOUT OUR FUTURE!!!
KILEY, WE NEED TO DISCUSS OUR FUTURE. I'LL MEET YOU AT THE POOL. MOMO
hmmmph! women!
Scratch
Scratch
Scratch
WHAT'S TAKING HER SO LONG?
SHE'S THE ONE WHO ASKED ME.
STUDENT CALENDAR

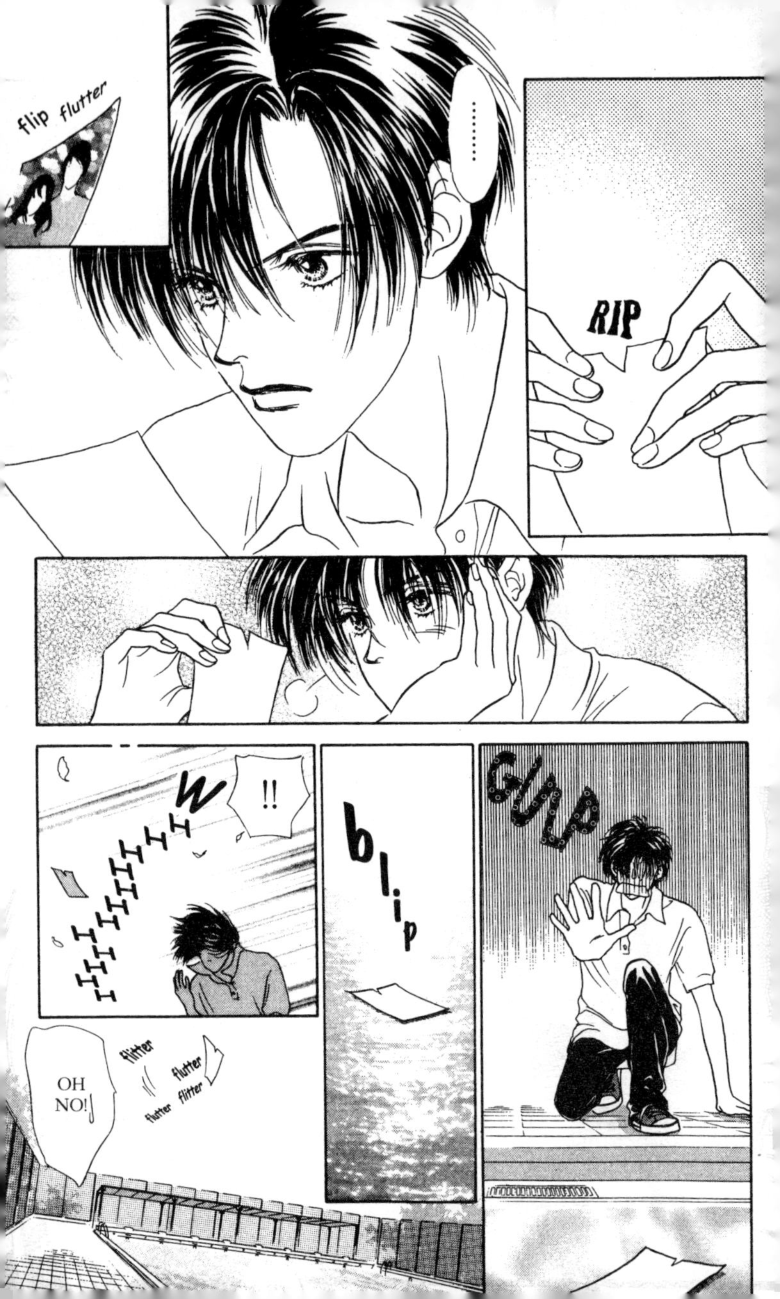
flip flutter
......
RIP
WHHHHHHHHHHHHHHH
!!
blip
GULP
OH NO!
flitter
flutter
flutter flitter

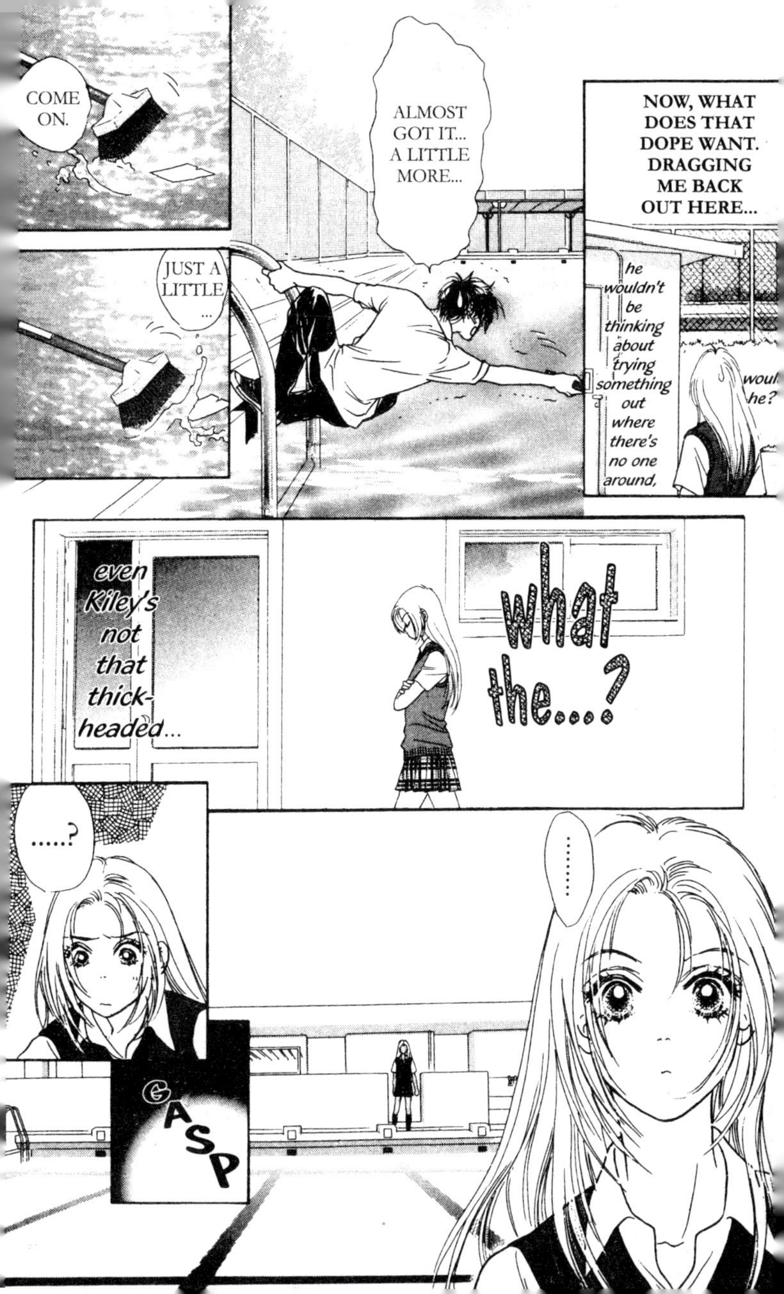
COME ON.
JUST A LITTLE ...
ALMOST GOT IT... A LITTLE MORE...
NOW, WHAT DOES THAT DOPE WANT. DRAGGING ME BACK OUT HERE...
he wouldn't be thinking about trying something out where there's no one around,
woul he?
even Kiley's not that thick-headed...
what the...?
.....?
GASP
....

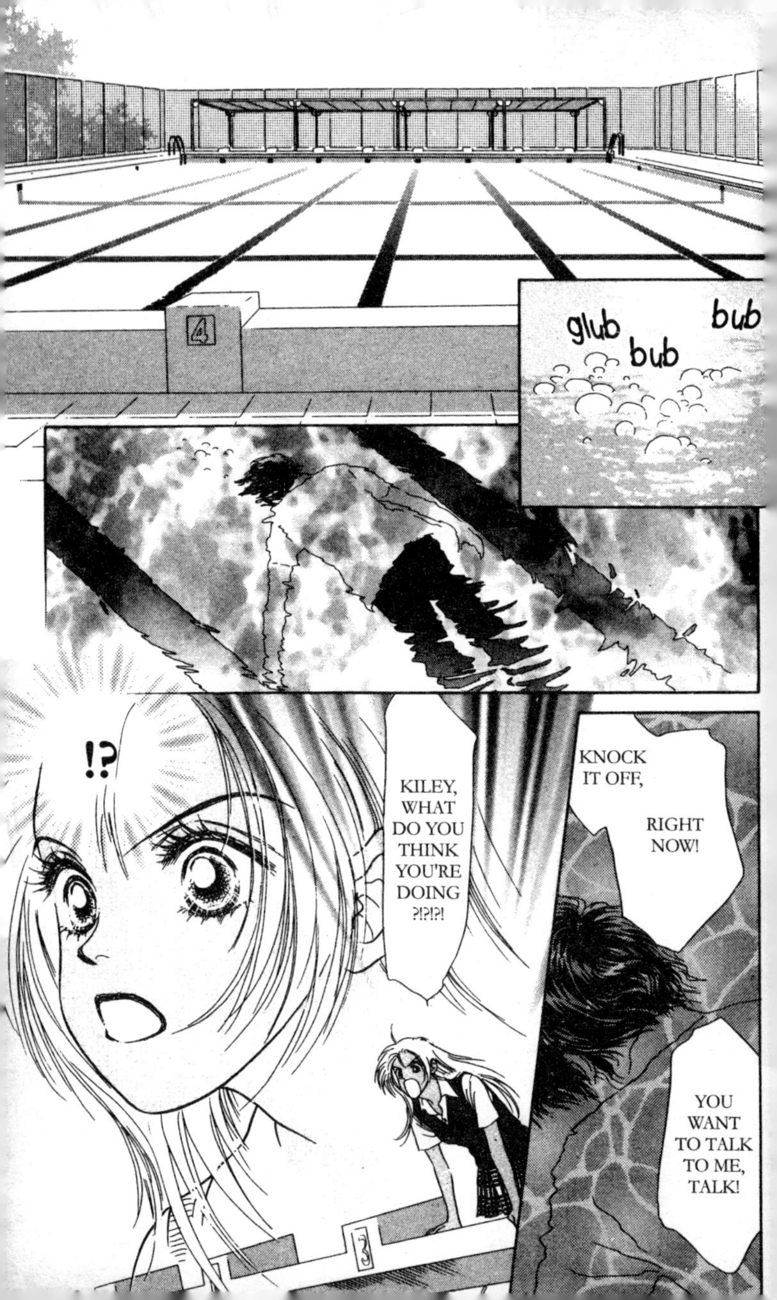
glub
bub
bub
!?
KILEY, WHAT DO YOU THINK YOU'RE DOING ?!?!?!
KNOCK IT OFF,
RIGHT NOW!
YOU WANT TO TALK TO ME, TALK!

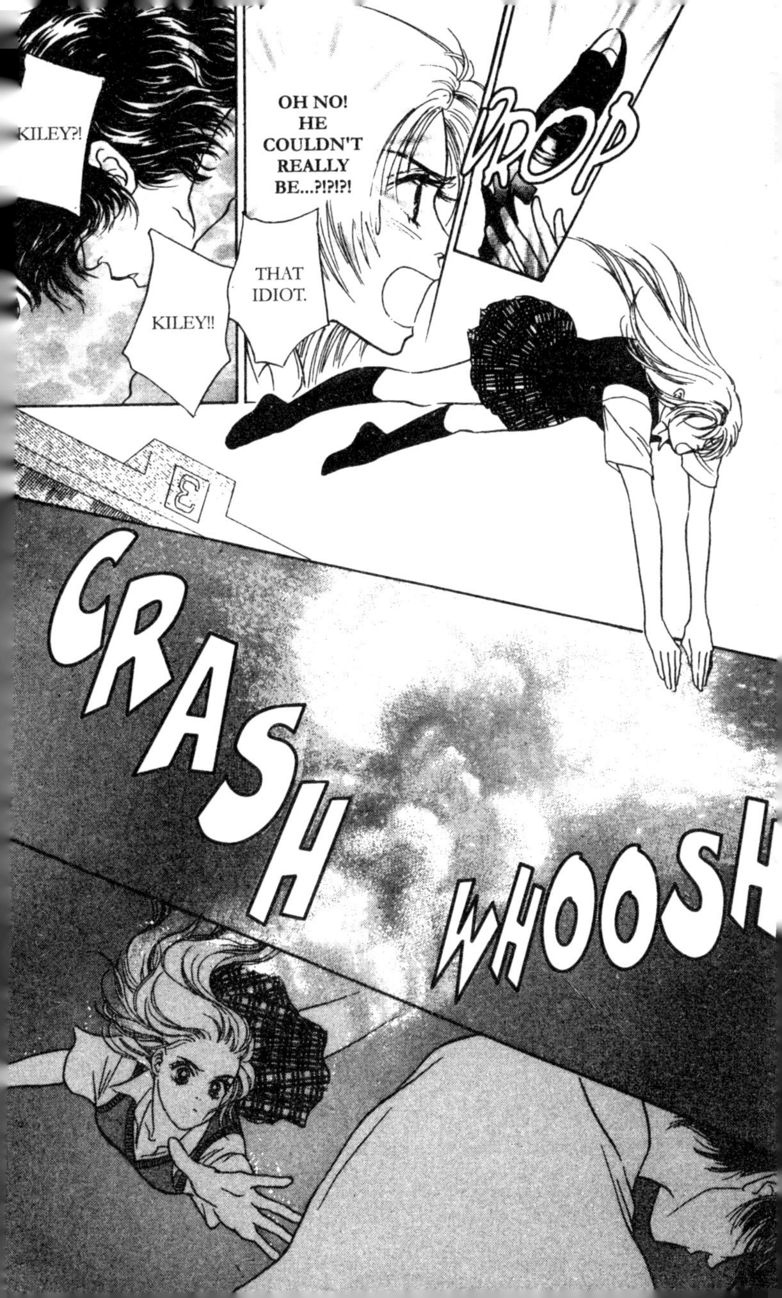
KILEY?!
KILEY!!
OH NO! HE COULDN'T REALLY BE...?!?!?!
THAT IDIOT.
DROP
3
CRASH
WHOOSH

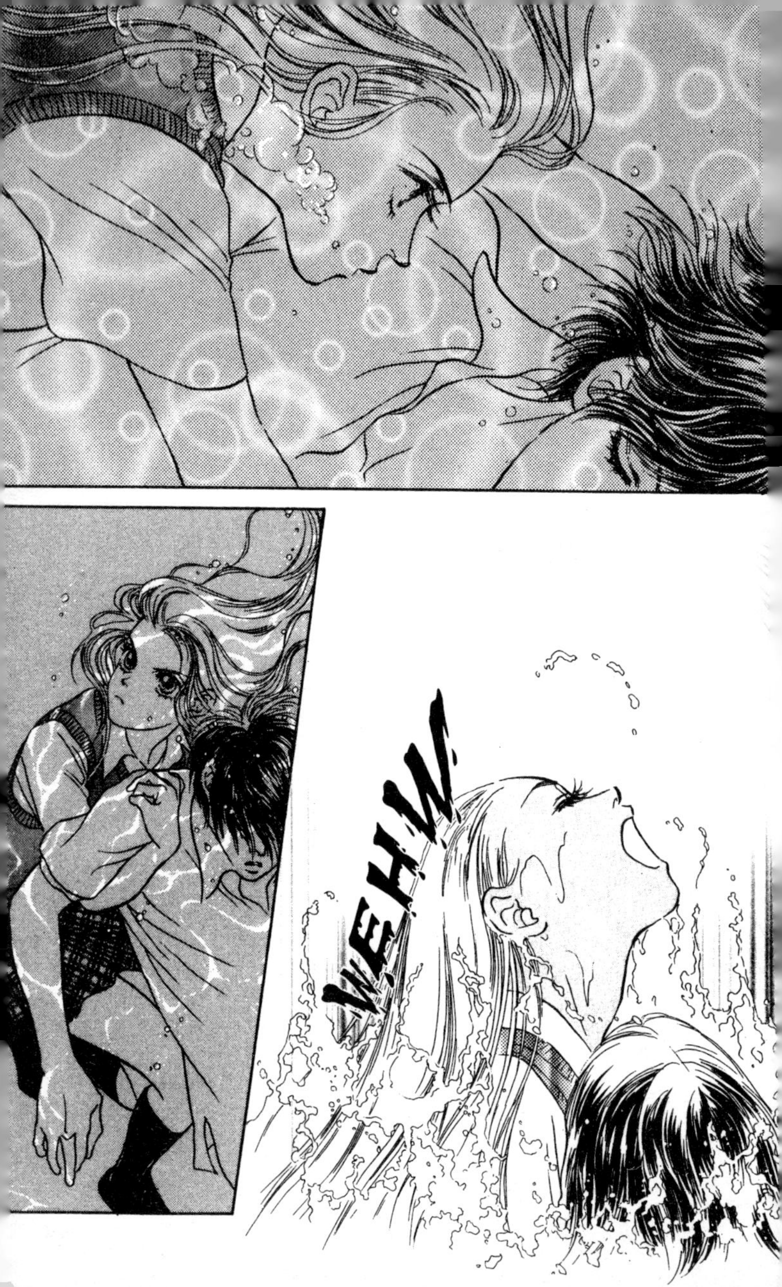
WEHW!

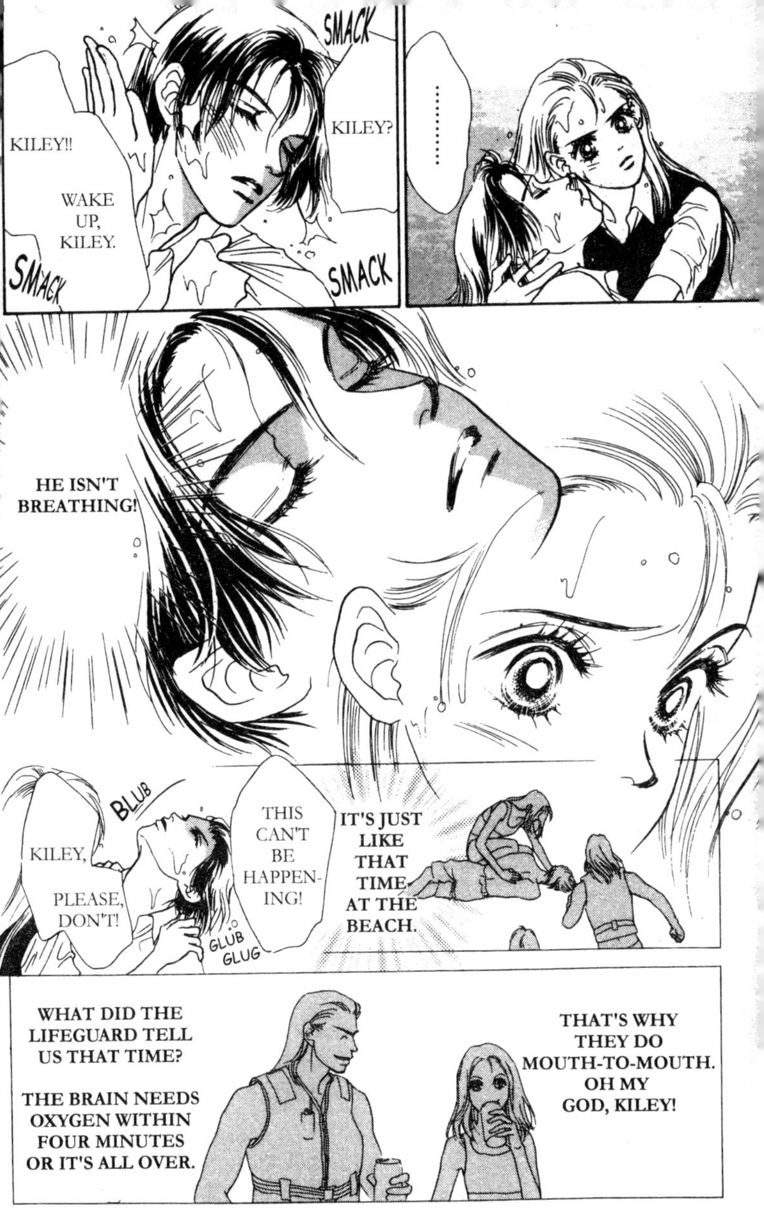

SMACK
KILEY!!
WAKE UP, KILEY.
SMACK
KILEY?
SMACK
......
HE ISN'T BREATHING!
BLUB
KILEY,
PLEASE, DON'T!
GLUB GLUG
THIS CAN'T BE HAPPEN-ING!
IT'S JUST LIKE THAT TIME AT THE BEACH.
WHAT DID THE LIFEGUARD TELL US THAT TIME?
THE BRAIN NEEDS OXYGEN WITHIN FOUR MINUTES OR IT'S ALL OVER.
THAT'S WHY THEY DO MOUTH-TO-MOUTH. OH MY GOD, KILEY!

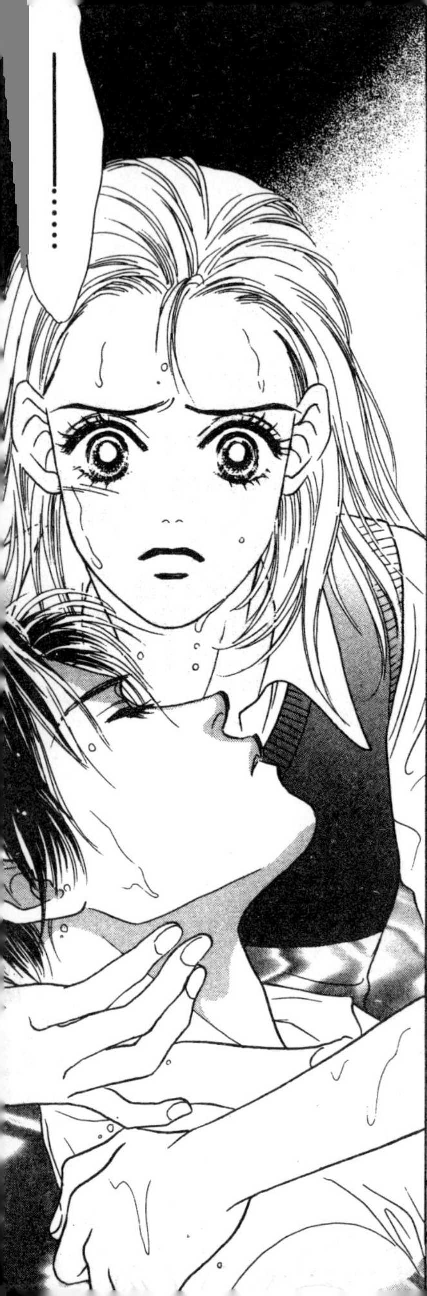
......

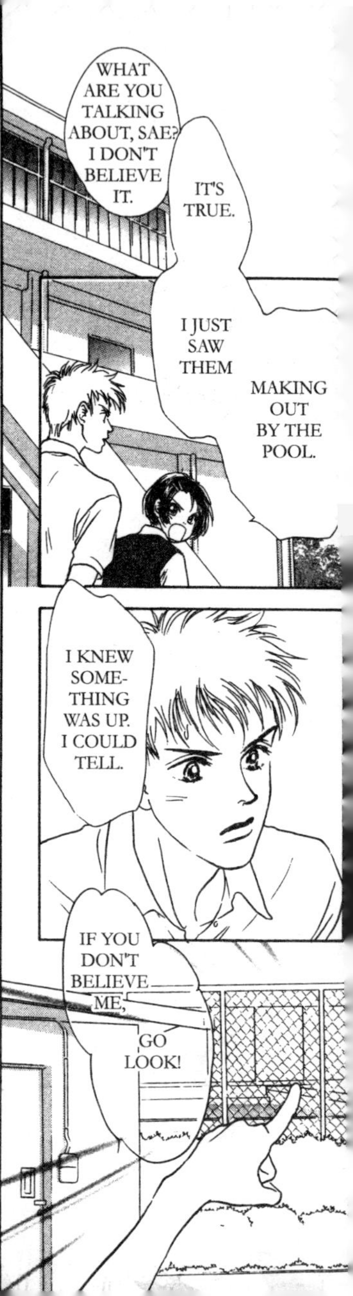
WHAT ARE YOU TALKING ABOUT, SAE? I DON'T BELIEVE IT.
IT'S TRUE.
I JUST SAW THEM
MAKING OUT BY THE POOL.
I KNEW SOME-THING WAS UP. I COULD TELL.
IF YOU DON'T BELIEVE ME,
GO LOOK!

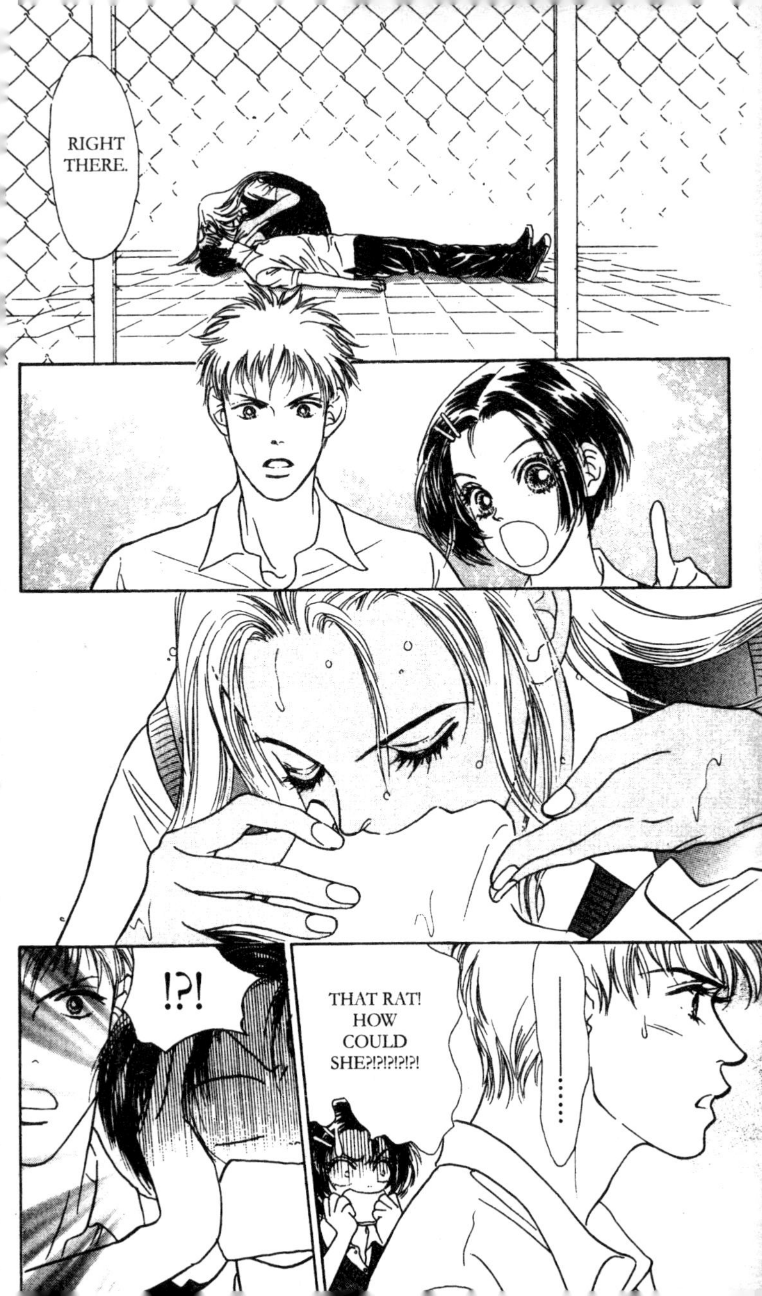
RIGHT THERE.
!?!
THAT RAT! HOW COULD SHE?!?!?!?!?!
......

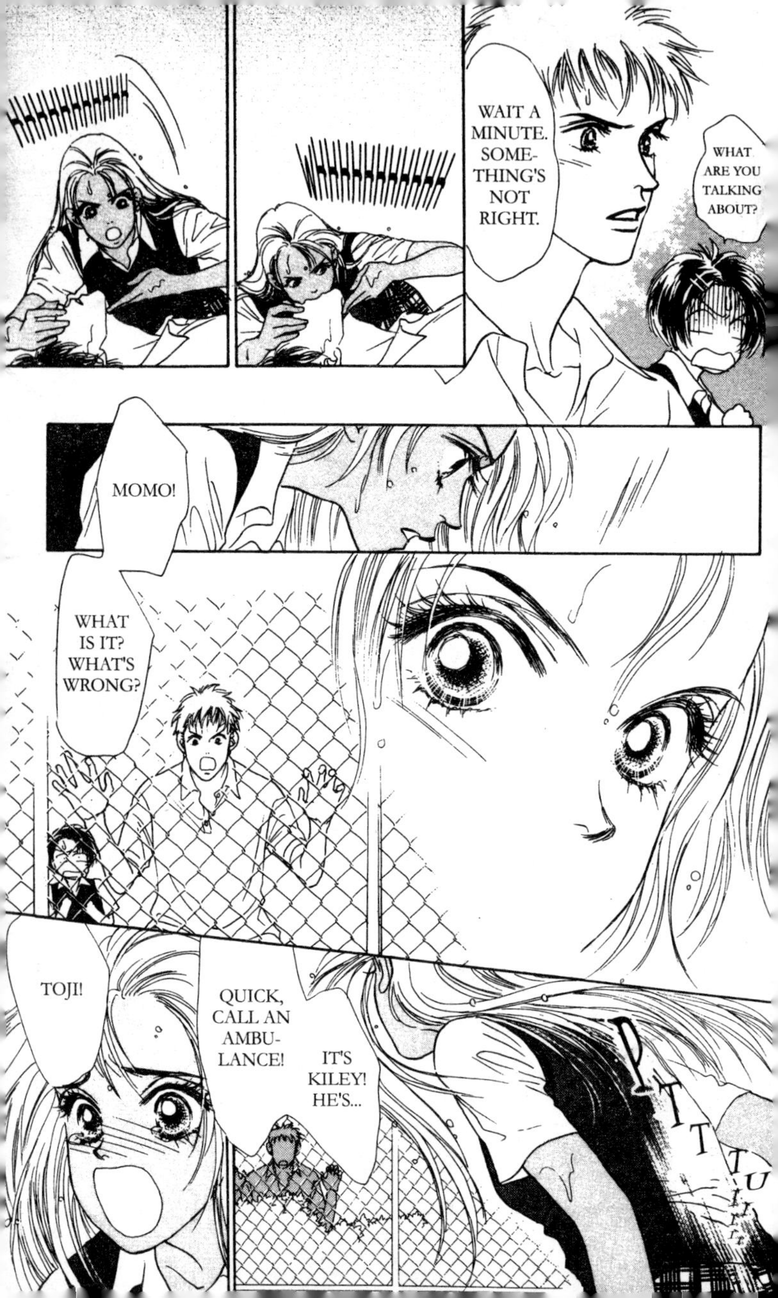
WAIT A MINUTE. SOME-THING'S NOT RIGHT.
WHAT ARE YOU TALKING ABOUT?
MOMO!
WHAT IS IT? WHAT'S WRONG?
TOJI!
QUICK, CALL AN AMBU-LANCE!
IT'S KILEY! HE'S...

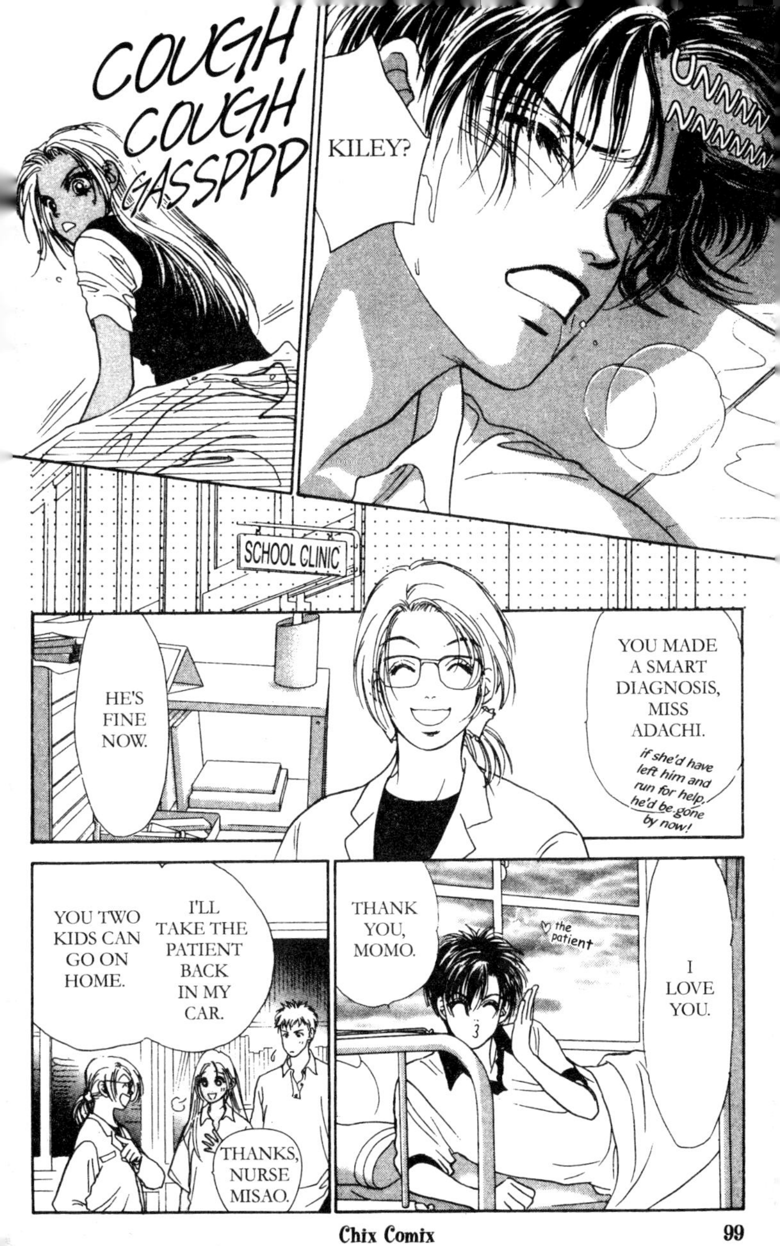
COUGH COUGH GASSPPP
KILEY?
UNNNNNNNNNNN
SCHOOL CLINIC
HE'S FINE NOW.
YOU MADE A SMART DIAGNOSIS, MISS ADACHI.
if she'd have left him and run for help, he'd be gone by now!
YOU TWO KIDS CAN GO ON HOME.
I'LL TAKE THE PATIENT BACK IN MY CAR.
THANKS, NURSE MISAO.
THANK YOU, MOMO.
♡ the patient
I LOVE YOU.

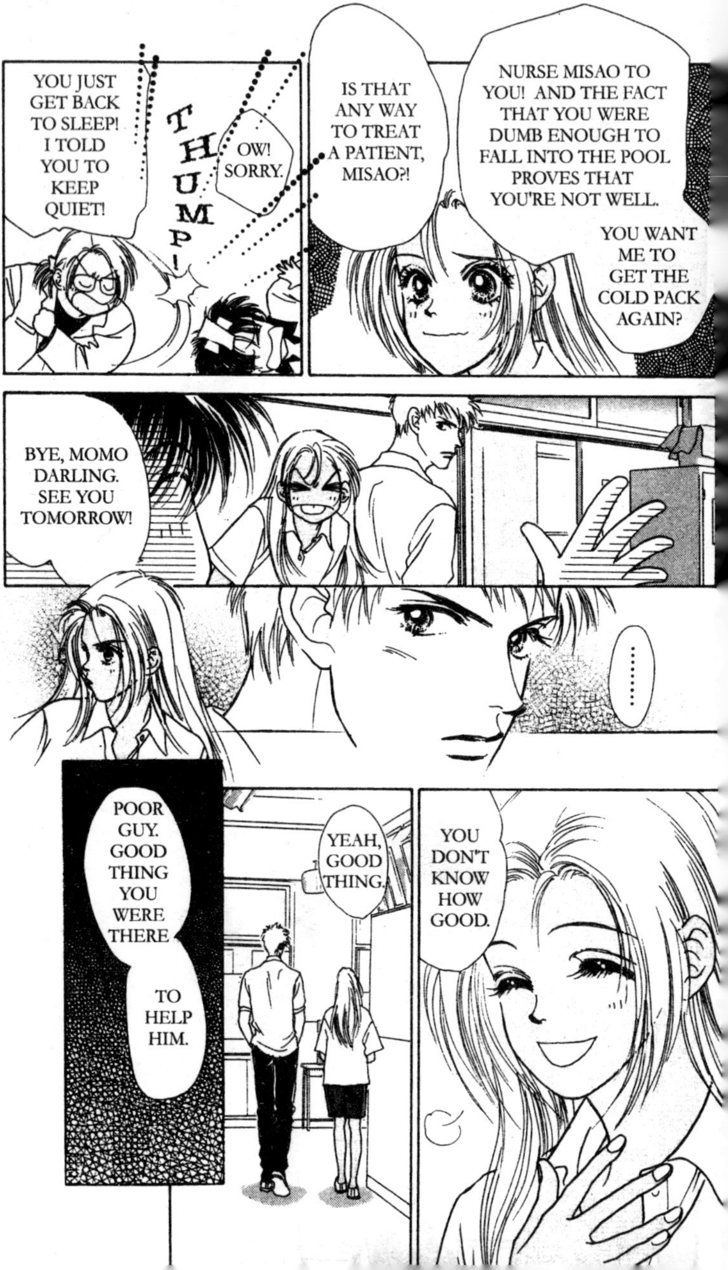
YOU JUST GET BACK TO SLEEP! I TOLD YOU TO KEEP QUIET!
THUMP!
OW! SORRY.
IS THAT ANY WAY TO TREAT A PATIENT, MISAO?!
NURSE MISAO TO YOU! AND THE FACT THAT YOU WERE DUMB ENOUGH TO FALL INTO THE POOL PROVES THAT YOU'RE NOT WELL.
YOU WANT ME TO GET THE COLD PACK AGAIN?
BYE, MOMO DARLING. SEE YOU TOMORROW!
......
POOR GUY. GOOD THING YOU WERE THERE
TO HELP HIM.
YEAH, GOOD THING.
YOU DON'T KNOW HOW GOOD.

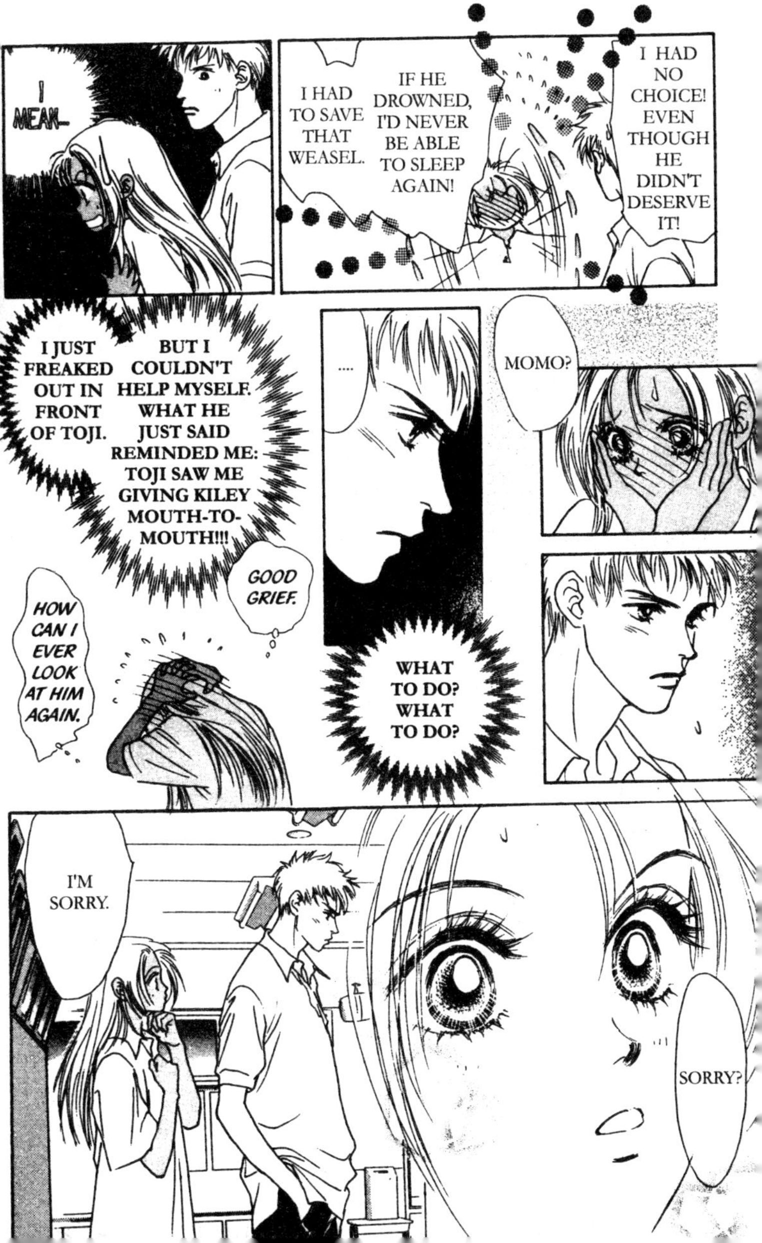
I MEAN...
I HAD TO SAVE THAT WEASEL.
IF HE DROWNED, I'D NEVER BE ABLE TO SLEEP AGAIN!
I HAD NO CHOICE! EVEN THOUGH HE DIDN'T DESERVE IT!
I JUST FREAKED OUT IN FRONT OF TOJI.
BUT I COULDN'T HELP MYSELF. WHAT HE JUST SAID REMINDED ME: TOJI SAW ME GIVING KILEY MOUTH-TO-MOUTH!!!
HOW CAN I EVER LOOK AT HIM AGAIN.
GOOD GRIEF.
....
WHAT TO DO? WHAT TO DO?
MOMO?
I'M SORRY.
SORRY?

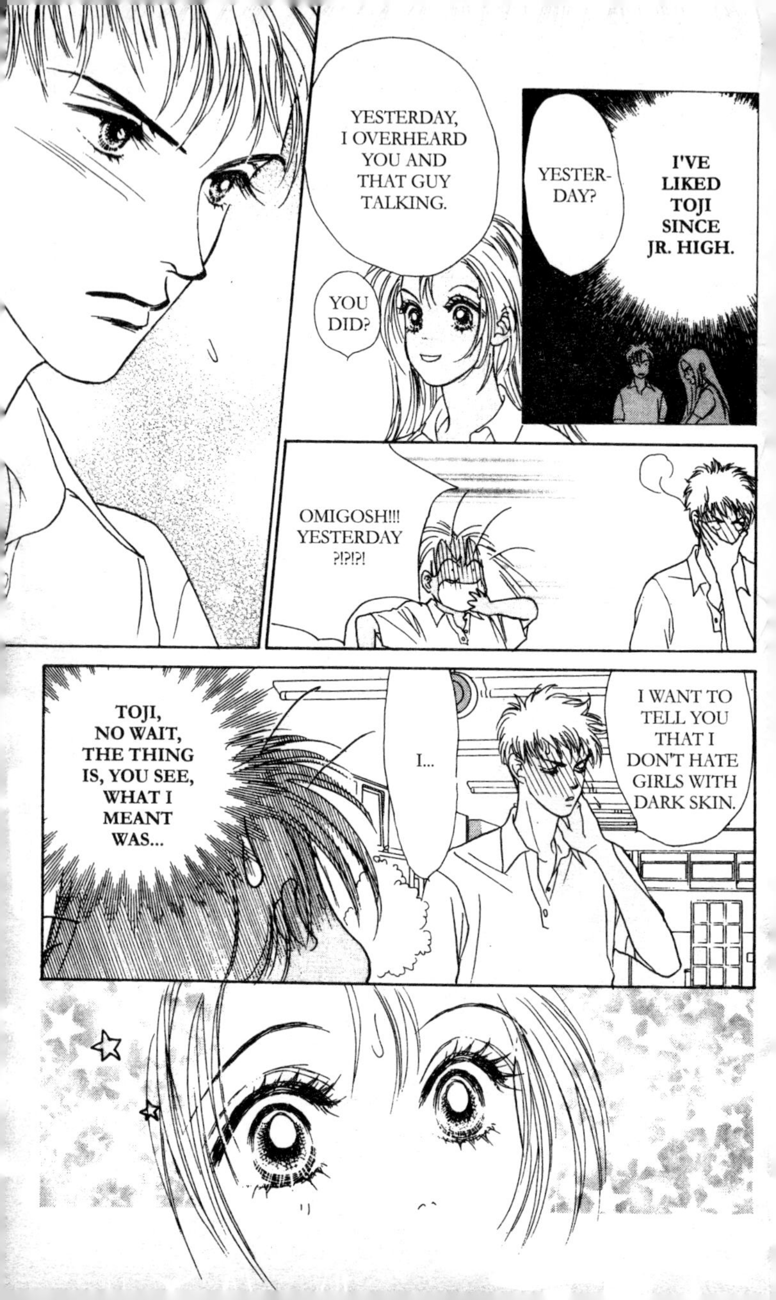

YESTERDAY, I OVERHEARD YOU AND THAT GUY TALKING.
YOU DID?
YESTER-DAY?
I'VE LIKED TOJI SINCE JR. HIGH.
OMIGOSH!!! YESTERDAY ?!?!?!
TOJI, NO WAIT, THE THING IS, YOU SEE, WHAT I MEANT WAS...
I...
I WANT TO TELL YOU THAT I DON'T HATE GIRLS WITH DARK SKIN.

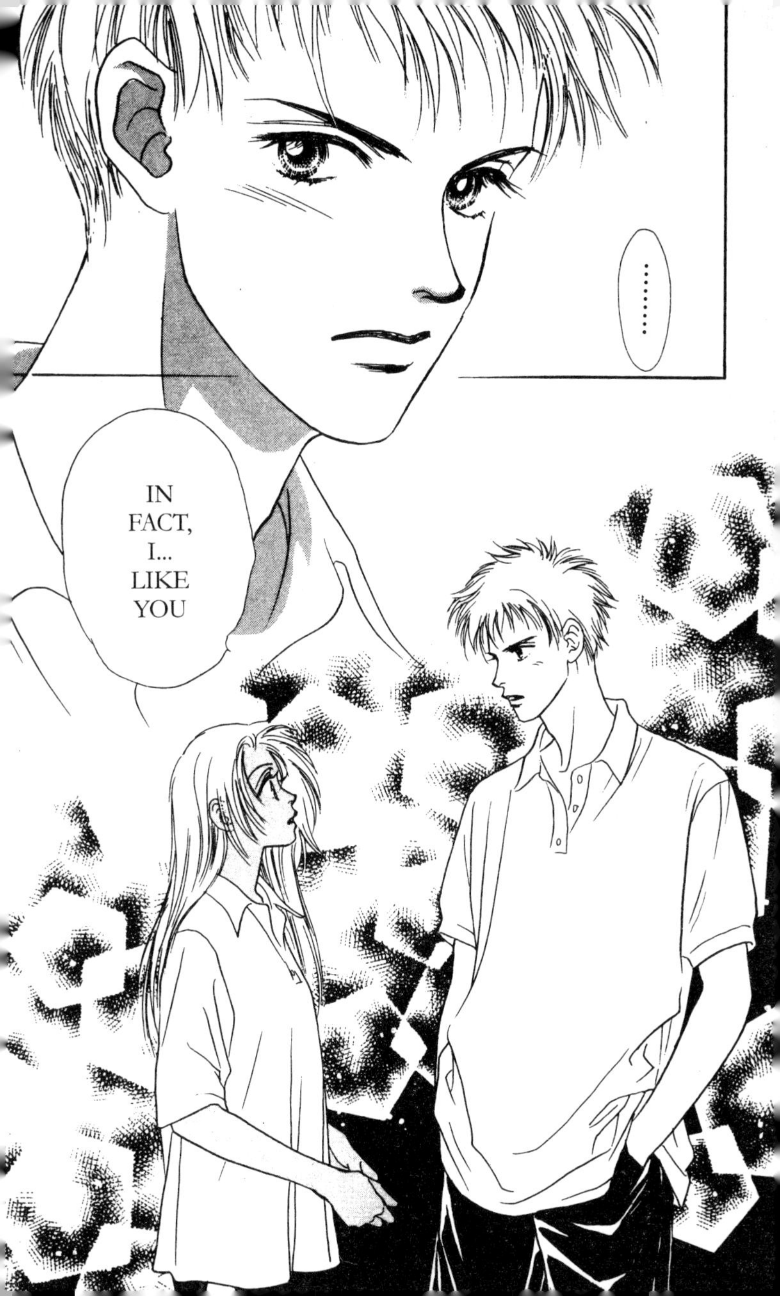

....
IN FACT, I... LIKE YOU

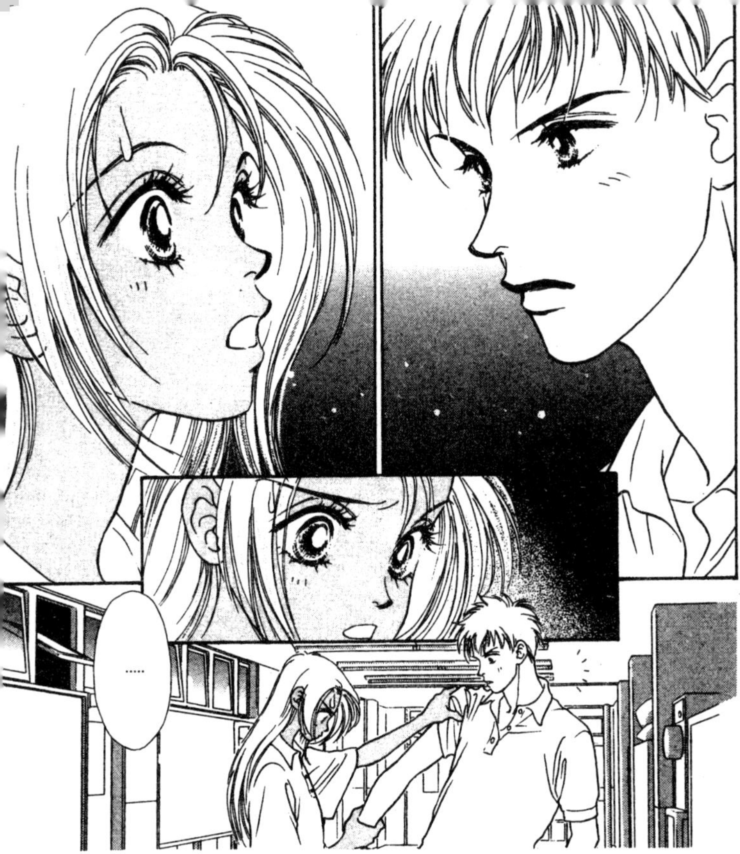
.....

PEACH CLUB CORNER

QUESTION: WHATEVER HAPPENED TO THAT BAG THAT SAE BOUGHT?
ANSWER: GOOD QUESTION. WHAT DID HAPPEN TO IT. WE CAN BE SURE THAT MOMO WOULD NOT HAVE TAKEN IT. SO SAE PROBABLY PICKED IT UP LATER, DRAGGED IT HOME, AND THREW IT INTO THE BACK OF HER CLOSET AND THAT'S WHERE IT SITS TODAY. IN ANY EVENT, BAGS LIKE THESE ARE A POPULAR ITEM IN THE FORMER JAPANESE CAPITAL OF KYOTO. SO IF YOU WANT TO GET ONE LIKE IT, BOOK A TRIP NEXT CHANCE YOU GET AND HAPPY HUNTING!!!

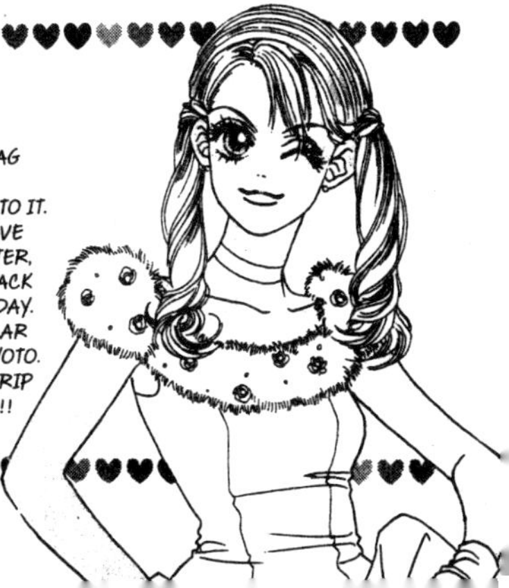

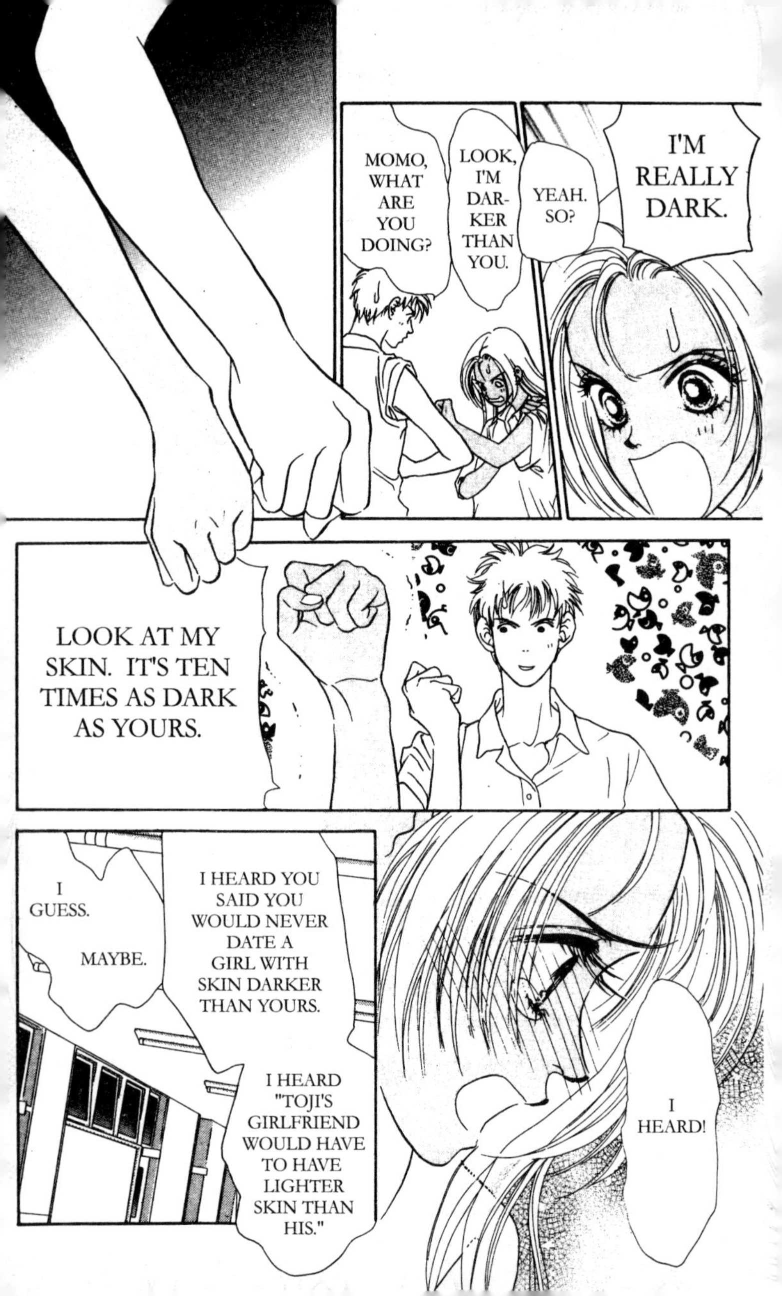
MOMO, WHAT ARE YOU DOING?
LOOK, I'M DAR-KER THAN YOU.
YEAH. SO?
I'M REALLY DARK.
LOOK AT MY SKIN. IT'S TEN TIMES AS DARK AS YOURS.
I GUESS.
MAYBE.
I HEARD YOU SAID YOU WOULD NEVER DATE A GIRL WITH SKIN DARKER THAN YOURS.
I HEARD "TOJI'S GIRLFRIEND WOULD HAVE TO HAVE LIGHTER SKIN THAN HIS."
I HEARD!

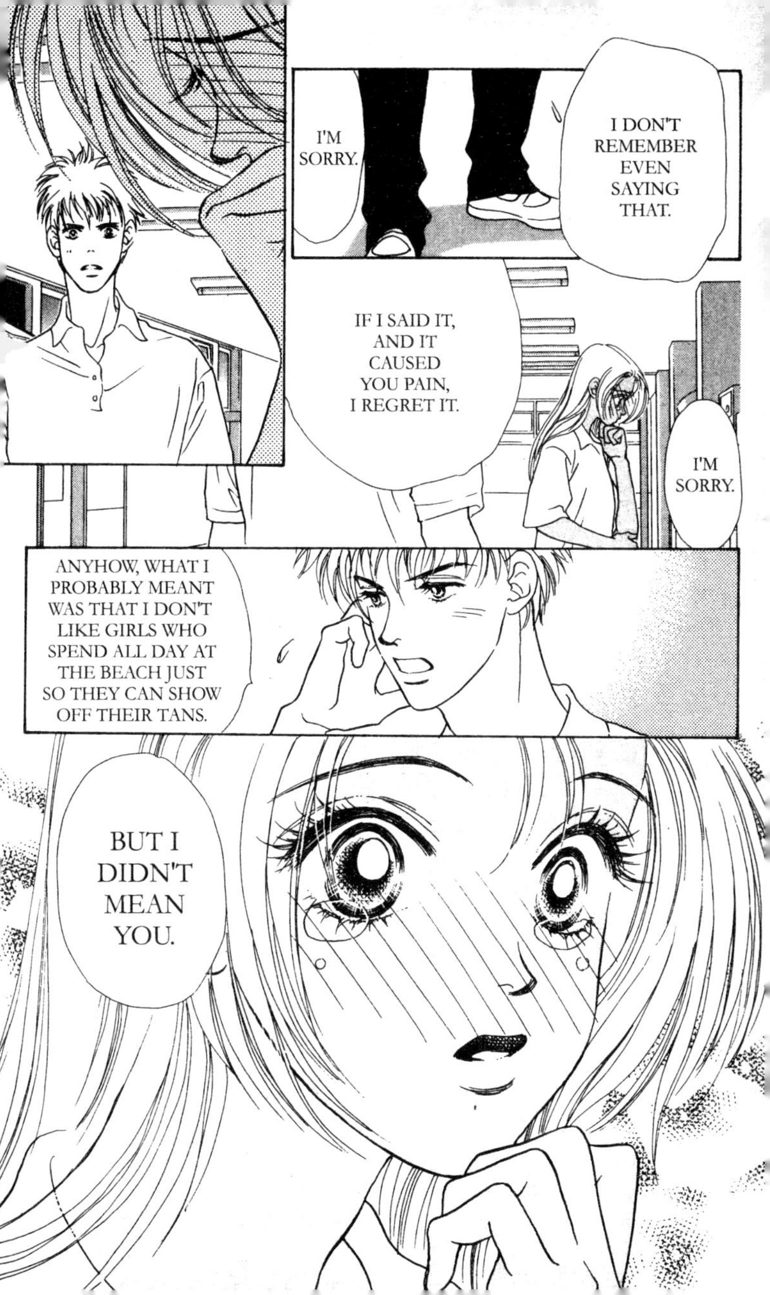
I'M SORRY.
I DON'T REMEMBER EVEN SAYING THAT.
IF I SAID IT, AND IT CAUSED YOU PAIN, I REGRET IT.
I'M SORRY.
ANYHOW, WHAT I PROBABLY MEANT WAS THAT I DON'T LIKE GIRLS WHO SPEND ALL DAY AT THE BEACH JUST SO THEY CAN SHOW OFF THEIR TANS.
BUT I DIDN'T MEAN YOU.

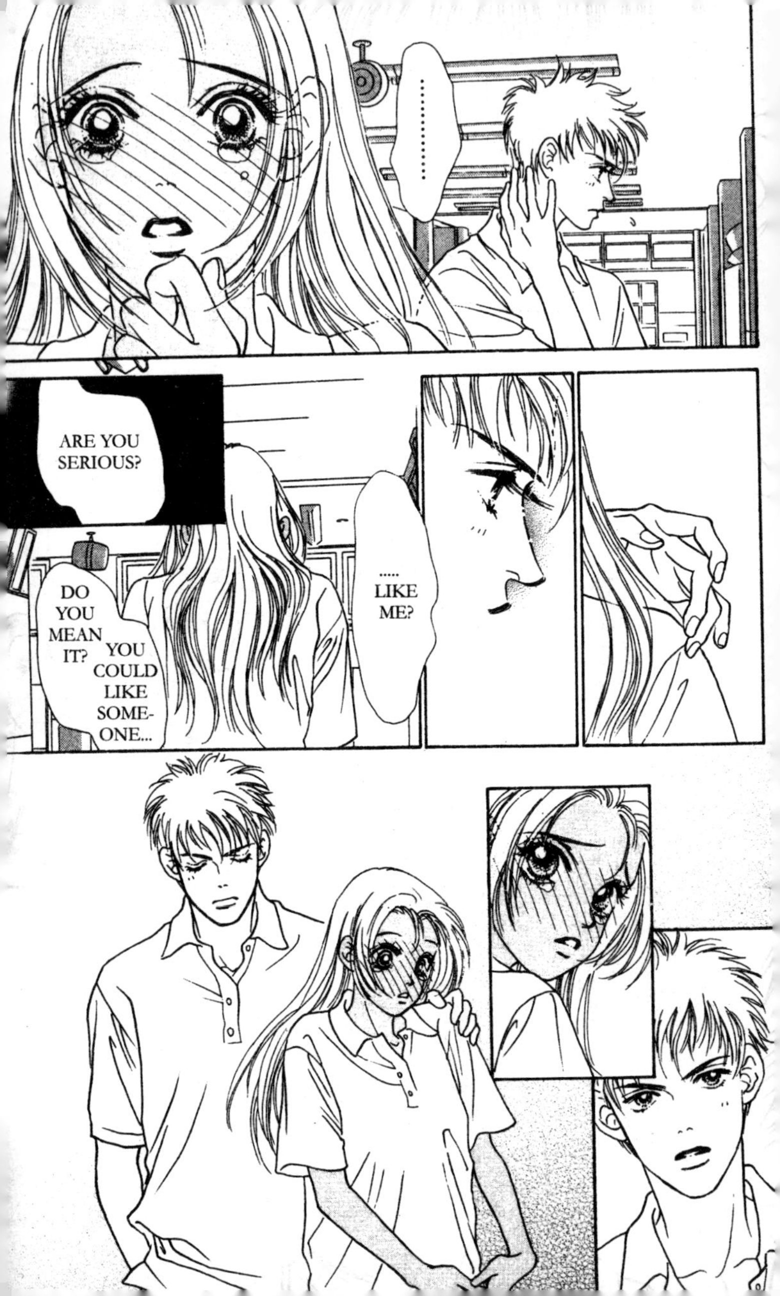
......
ARE YOU SERIOUS?
DO YOU MEAN IT?
YOU COULD LIKE SOME-ONE...
..... LIKE ME?

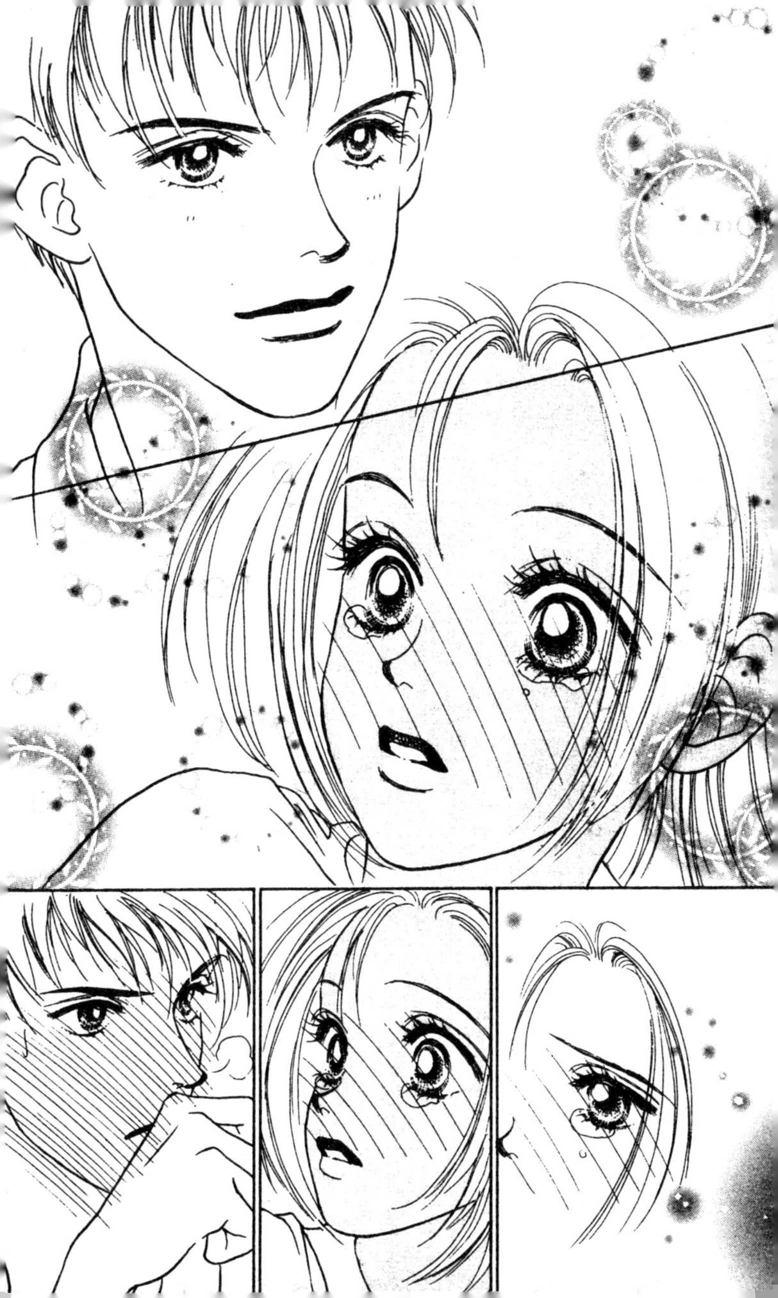

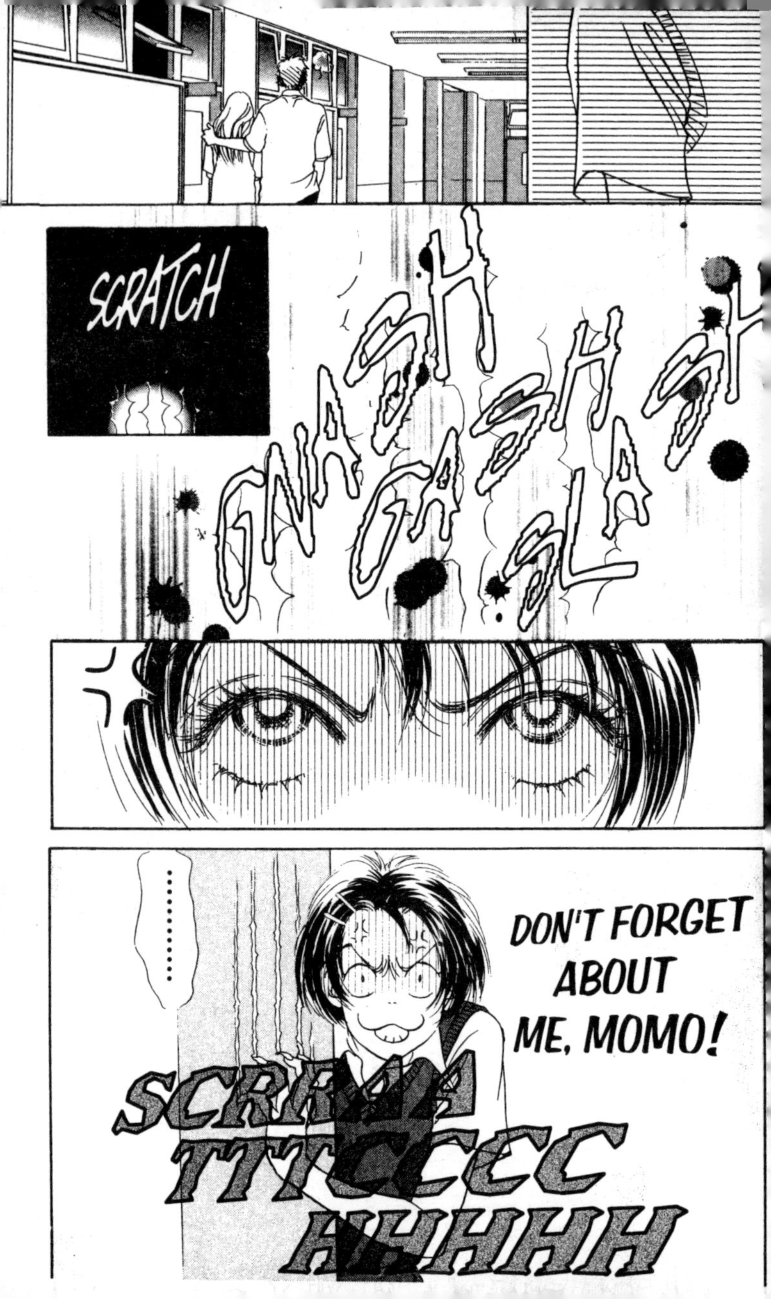
SCRATCH
GNASH GNASH GNASH
GASH GASH
SLASH SLASH
......
DON'T FORGET ABOUT ME, MOMO!
SCRRAA TTTCCCC HHHHH

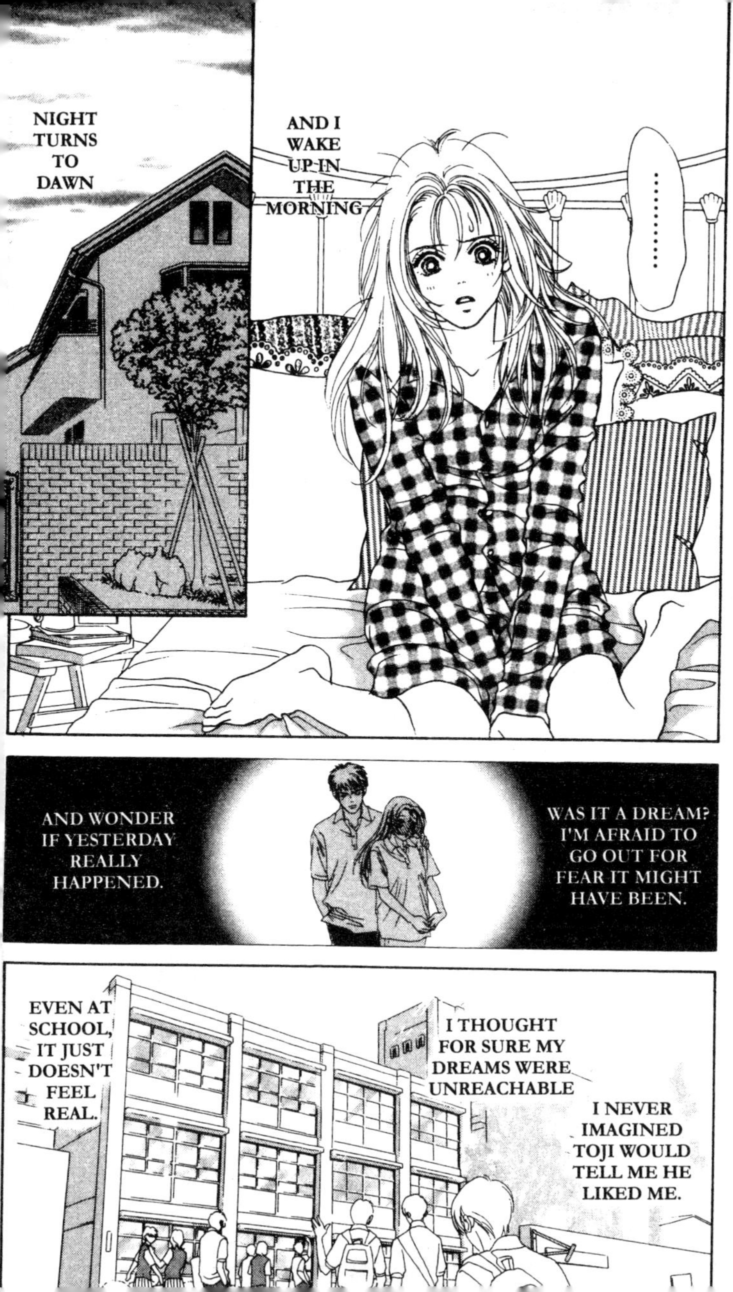
NIGHT TURNS TO DAWN
AND I WAKE UP IN THE MORNING
....
AND WONDER IF YESTERDAY REALLY HAPPENED.
WAS IT A DREAM? I'M AFRAID TO GO OUT FOR FEAR IT MIGHT HAVE BEEN.
EVEN AT SCHOOL, IT JUST DOESN'T FEEL REAL.
I THOUGHT FOR SURE MY DREAMS WERE UNREACHABLE
I NEVER IMAGINED TOJI WOULD TELL ME HE LIKED ME.

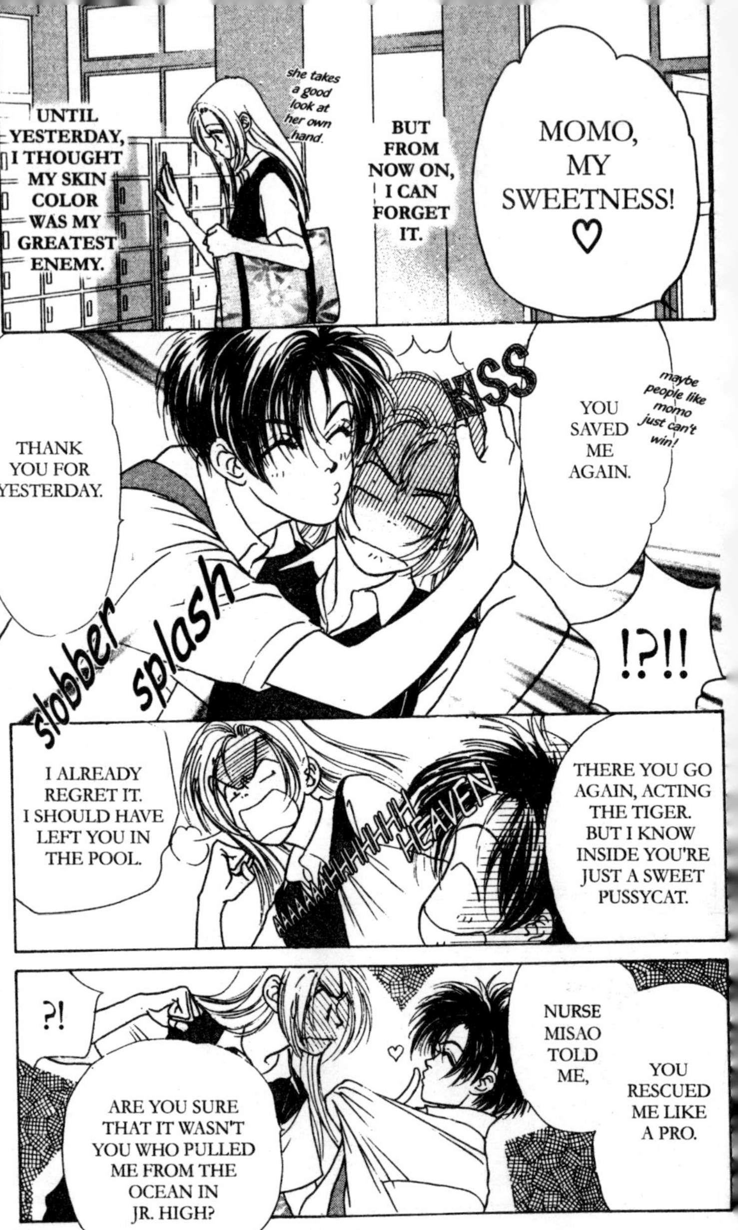
UNTIL YESTERDAY, I THOUGHT MY SKIN COLOR WAS MY GREATEST ENEMY.
she takes a good look at her own hand.
BUT FROM NOW ON, I CAN FORGET IT.
MOMO, MY SWEETNESS! ♡
THANK YOU FOR YESTERDAY.
slobber
splash
KISS
YOU SAVED ME AGAIN.
maybe people like momo just can't win!
!?!!
I ALREADY REGRET IT. I SHOULD HAVE LEFT YOU IN THE POOL.
AAAAAHHHHHH HEAVEN
THERE YOU GO AGAIN, ACTING THE TIGER. BUT I KNOW INSIDE YOU'RE JUST A SWEET PUSSYCAT.
?!
NURSE MISAO TOLD ME,
YOU RESCUED ME LIKE A PRO.
ARE YOU SURE THAT IT WASN'T YOU WHO PULLED ME FROM THE OCEAN IN JR. HIGH?

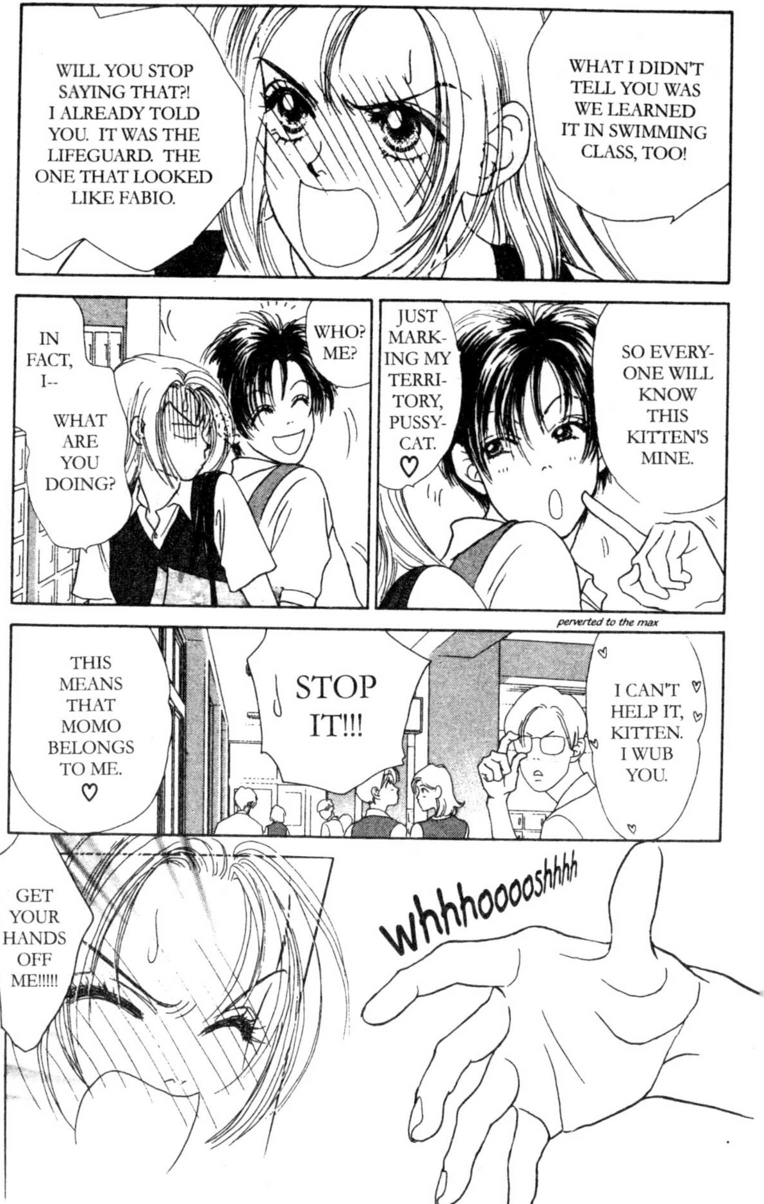
WILL YOU STOP SAYING THAT?! I ALREADY TOLD YOU. IT WAS THE LIFEGUARD. THE ONE THAT LOOKED LIKE FABIO.
WHAT I DIDN'T TELL YOU WAS WE LEARNED IT IN SWIMMING CLASS, TOO!
IN FACT, I--
WHAT ARE YOU DOING?
WHO? ME?
JUST MARKING MY TERRITORY, PUSSYCAT. ♡
SO EVERYONE WILL KNOW THIS KITTEN'S MINE.
perverted to the max
THIS MEANS THAT MOMO BELONGS TO ME. ♡
STOP IT!!!
I CAN'T HELP IT, KITTEN. I WUB YOU.
GET YOUR HANDS OFF ME!!!!!
whhhoooshhhh

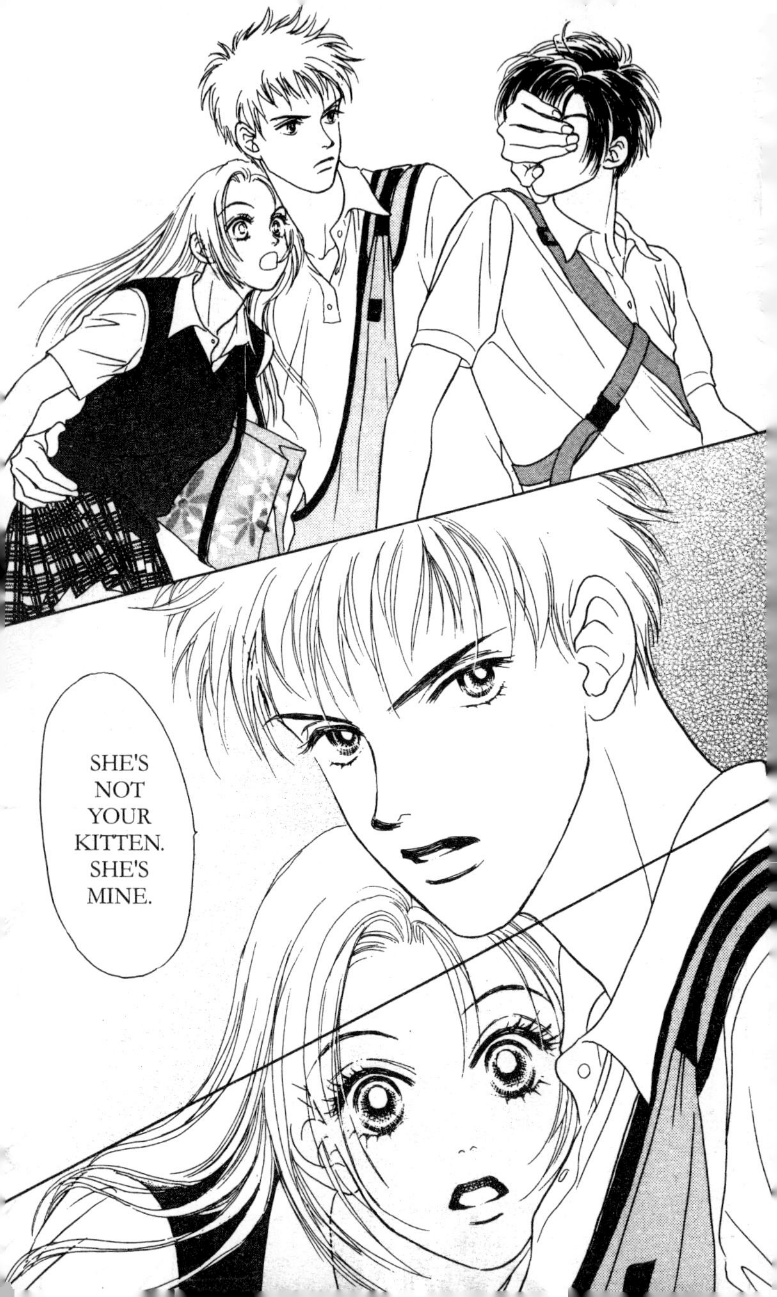
SHE'S NOT YOUR KITTEN. SHE'S MINE.

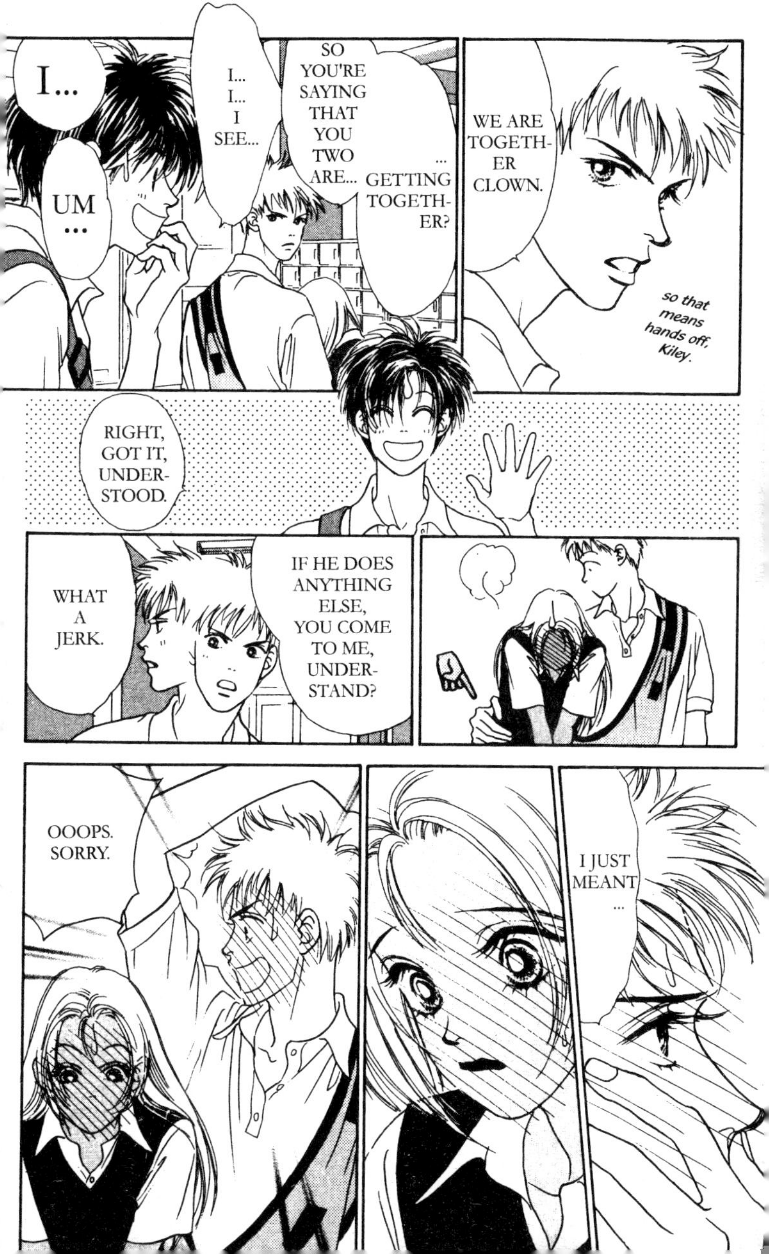
I...
UM ...
I... I... I SEE...
SO YOU'RE SAYING THAT YOU TWO ARE...
... GETTING TOGETHER?
WE ARE TOGETHER CLOWN.
so that means hands off, Kiley.
RIGHT, GOT IT, UNDERSTOOD.
WHAT A JERK.
IF HE DOES ANYTHING ELSE, YOU COME TO ME, UNDERSTAND?
OOOPS. SORRY.
I JUST MEANT ...

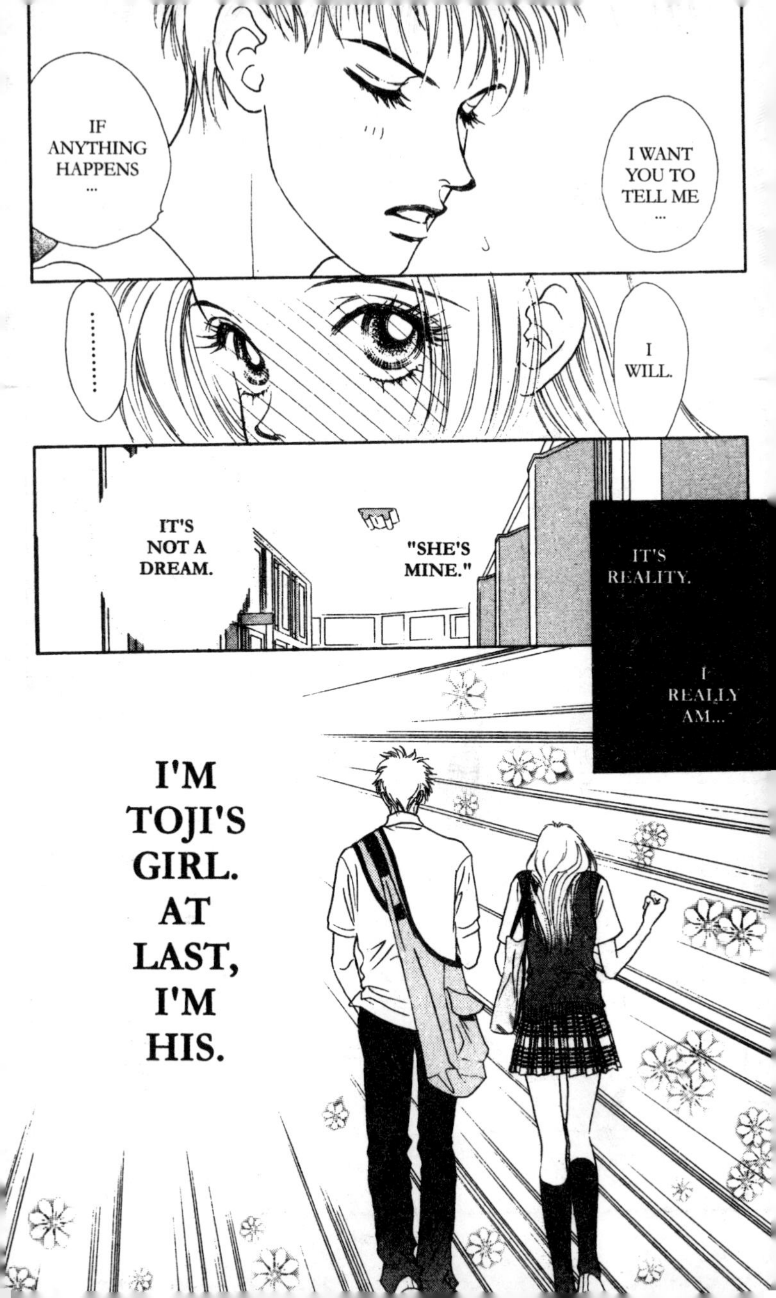
IF ANYTHING HAPPENS ...
I WANT YOU TO TELL ME ...
....
I WILL.
IT'S NOT A DREAM.
"SHE'S MINE."
IT'S REALITY.
I REALLY AM...
I'M TOJI'S GIRL. AT LAST, I'M HIS.

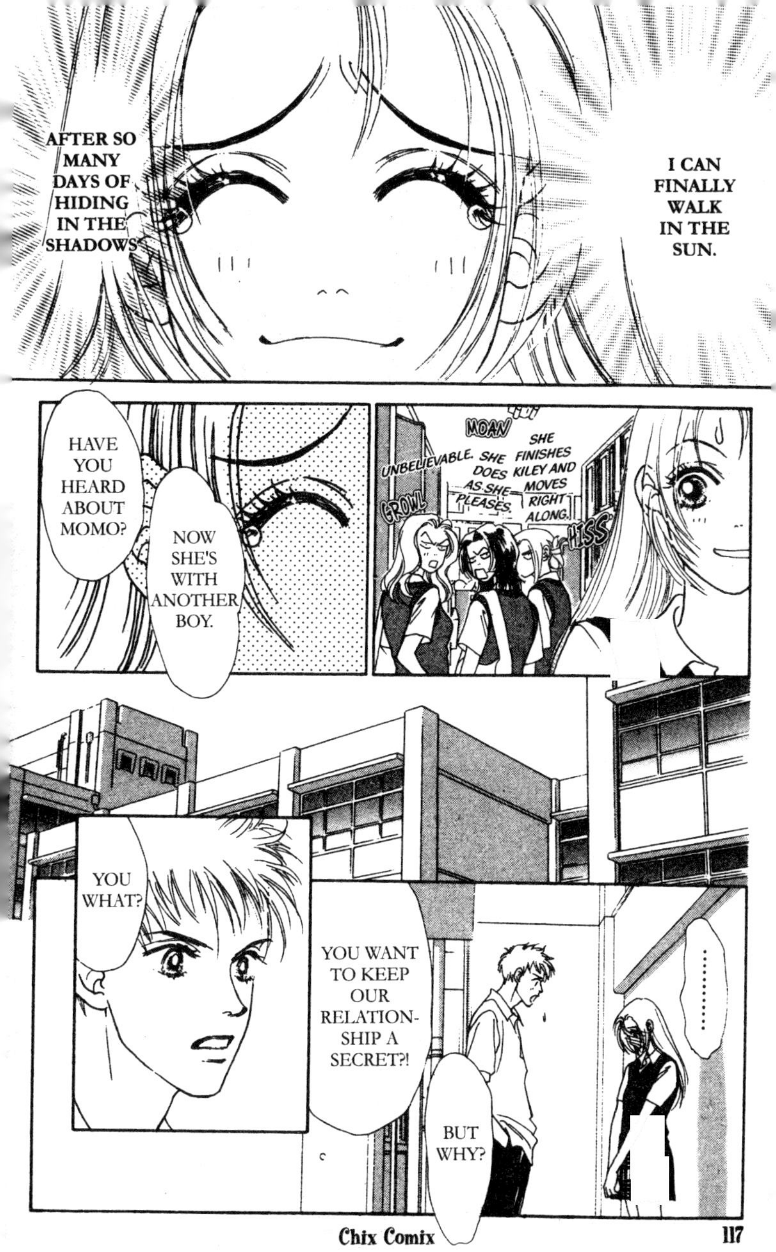
AFTER SO MANY DAYS OF HIDING IN THE SHADOWS
I CAN FINALLY WALK IN THE SUN.
HAVE YOU HEARD ABOUT MOMO?
NOW SHE'S WITH ANOTHER BOY.
MOAN
UNBELIEVABLE. SHE DOES AS SHE PLEASES.
SHE FINISHES KILEY AND MOVES RIGHT ALONG.
GROWL
HISS
YOU WHAT?
YOU WANT TO KEEP OUR RELATIONSHIP A SECRET?!
BUT WHY?
....

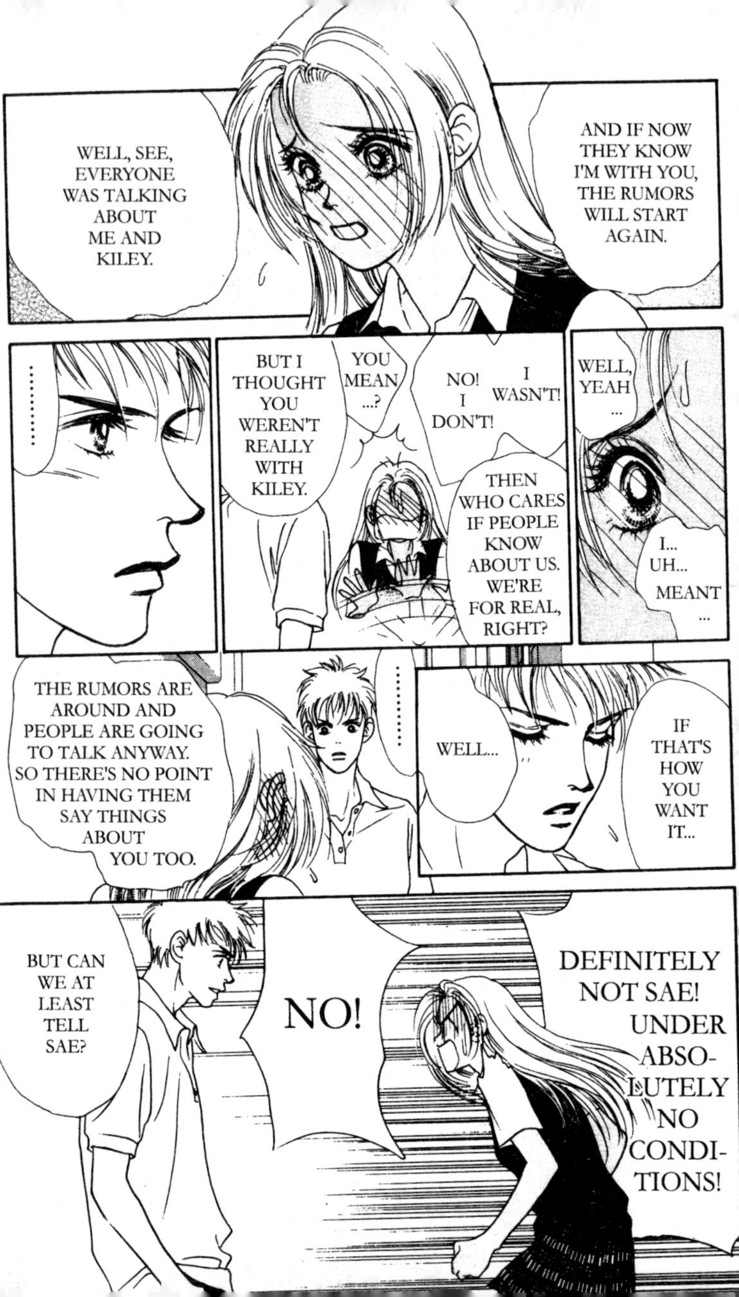
WELL, SEE, EVERYONE WAS TALKING ABOUT ME AND KILEY.
AND IF NOW THEY KNOW I'M WITH YOU, THE RUMORS WILL START AGAIN.
....
BUT I THOUGHT YOU WEREN'T REALLY WITH KILEY.
YOU MEAN ...?
NO! I DON'T!
I WASN'T!
THEN WHO CARES IF PEOPLE KNOW ABOUT US. WE'RE FOR REAL, RIGHT?
WELL, YEAH ...
I... UH... MEANT ...
THE RUMORS ARE AROUND AND PEOPLE ARE GOING TO TALK ANYWAY. SO THERE'S NO POINT IN HAVING THEM SAY THINGS ABOUT YOU TOO.
....
WELL...
IF THAT'S HOW YOU WANT IT...
BUT CAN WE AT LEAST TELL SAE?
NO!
DEFINITELY NOT SAE! UNDER ABSO-LUTELY NO CONDI-TIONS!

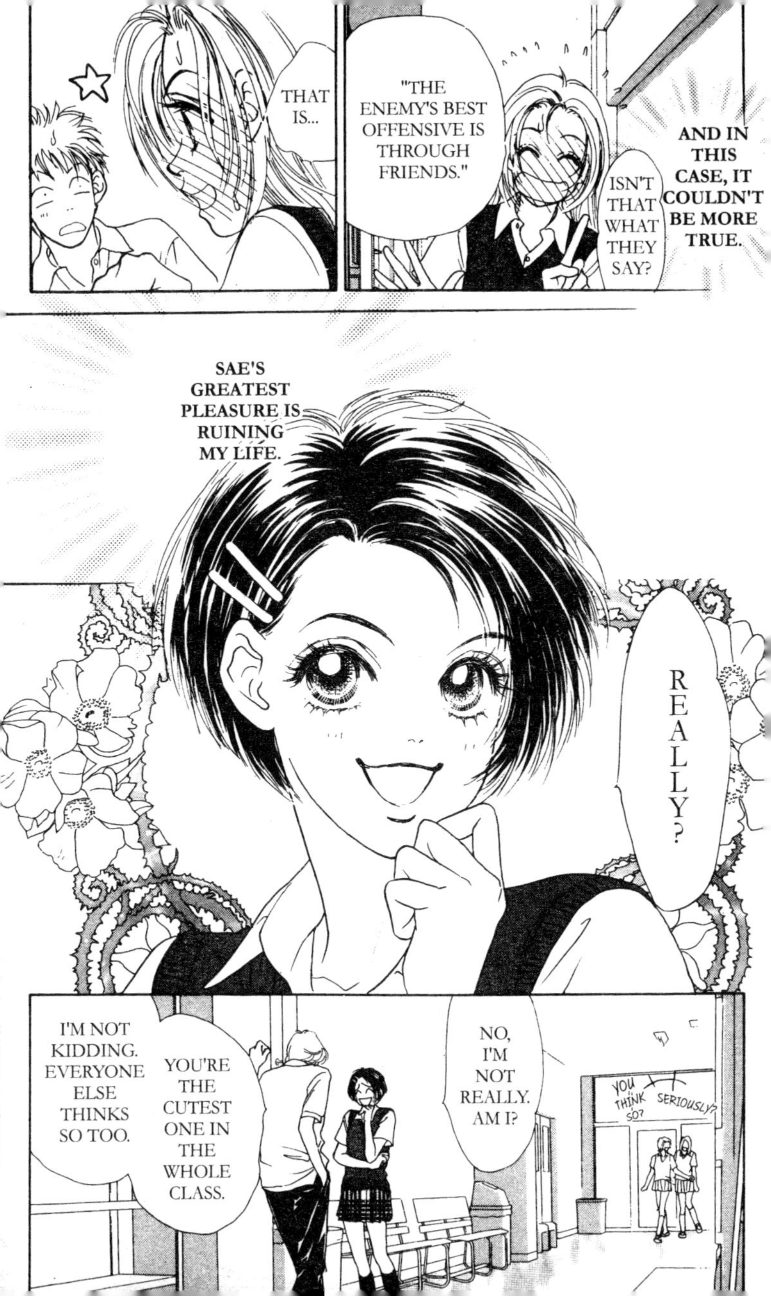
THAT IS...
"THE ENEMY'S BEST OFFENSIVE IS THROUGH FRIENDS."
ISN'T THAT WHAT THEY SAY?
AND IN THIS CASE, IT COULDN'T BE MORE TRUE.
SAE'S GREATEST PLEASURE IS RUINING MY LIFE.
REALLY?
I'M NOT KIDDING. EVERYONE ELSE THINKS SO TOO.
YOU'RE THE CUTEST ONE IN THE WHOLE CLASS.
NO, I'M NOT REALLY. AM I?
YOU THINK SO?
SERIOUSLY?

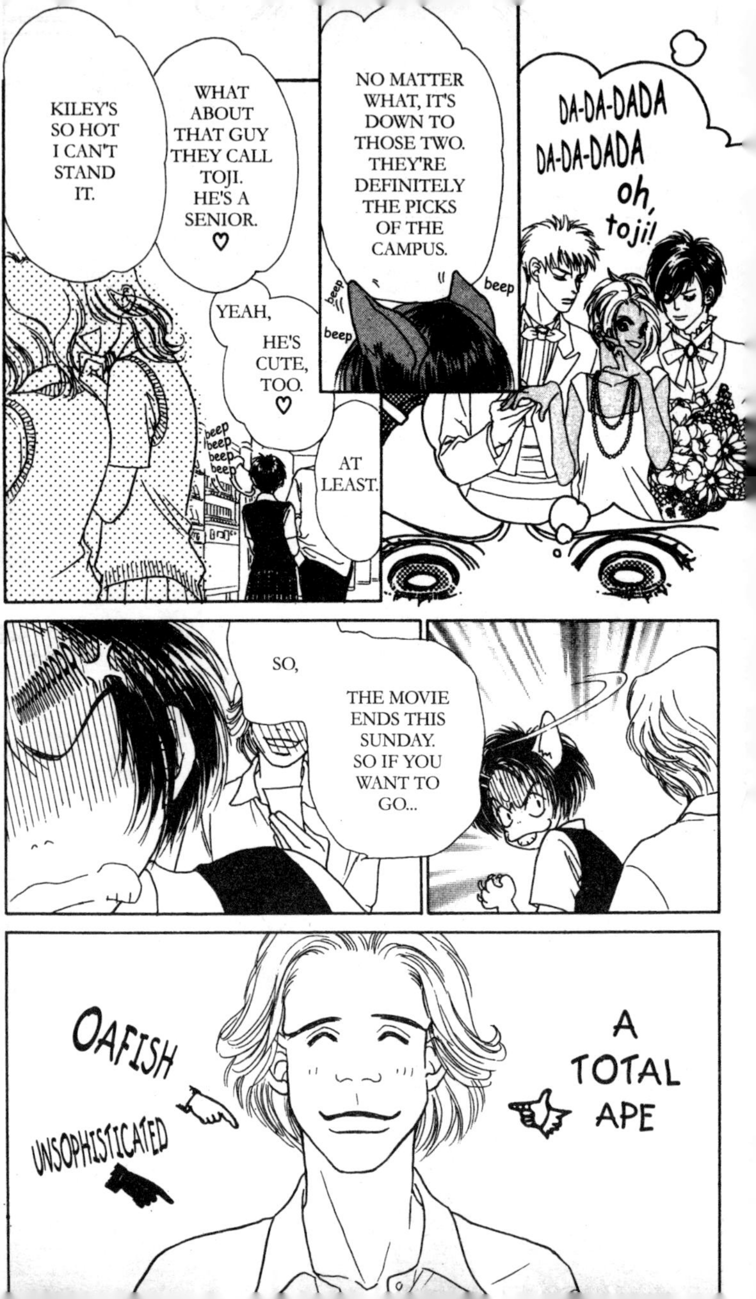
KILEY'S SO HOT I CAN'T STAND IT.
WHAT ABOUT THAT GUY THEY CALL TOJI. HE'S A SENIOR. ♡
YEAH,
HE'S CUTE, TOO. ♡
beep beep beep beep
AT LEAST.
NO MATTER WHAT, IT'S DOWN TO THOSE TWO. THEY'RE DEFINITELY THE PICKS OF THE CAMPUS.
beep
beep
beep
DA-DA-DADA DA-DA-DADA
oh, toji!
SO,
THE MOVIE ENDS THIS SUNDAY. SO IF YOU WANT TO GO...
OAFISH
UNSOPHISTICATED
A TOTAL APE

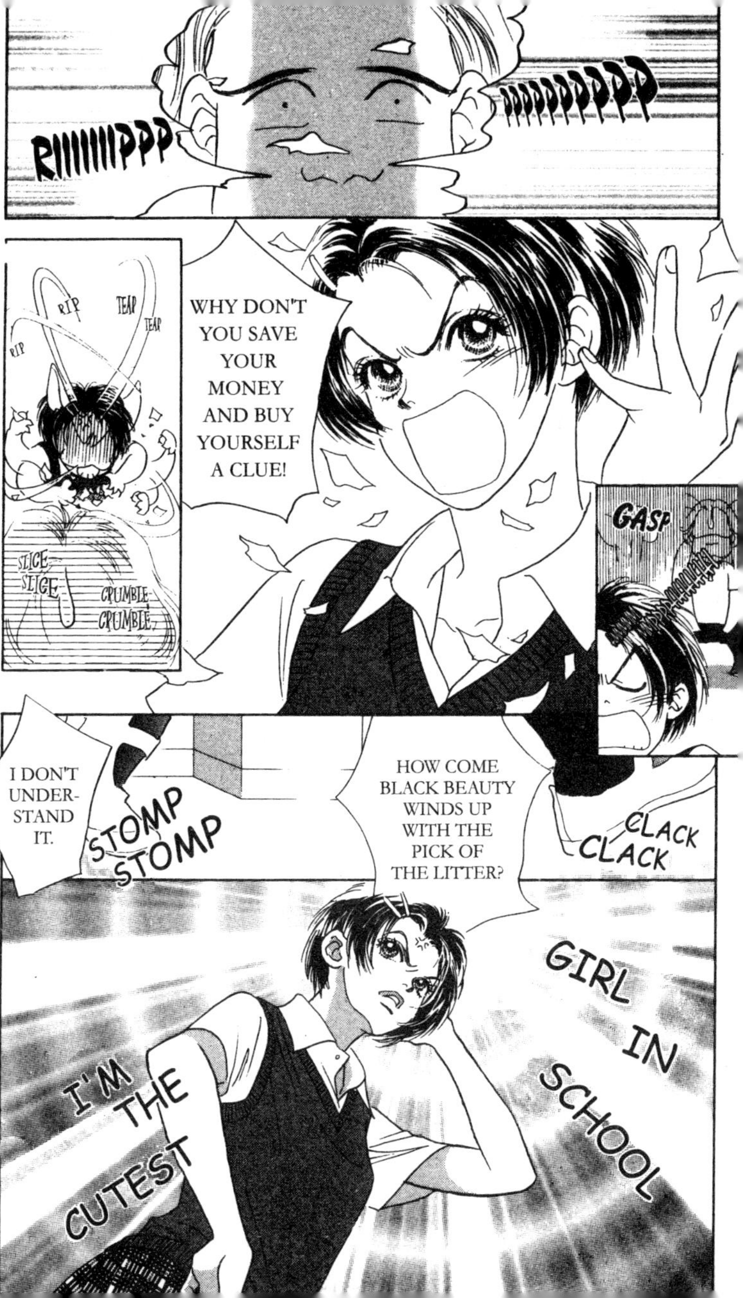

RIIIIIIPPP
PPPPPPPPPPP
RIP
TEAR
TEAR
RIP
SLICE
SLICE
CRUMBLE
CRUMBLE
WHY DON'T YOU SAVE YOUR MONEY AND BUY YOURSELF A CLUE!
GASP
I DON'T UNDER-STAND IT.
STOMP STOMP
HOW COME BLACK BEAUTY WINDS UP WITH THE PICK OF THE LITTER?
CLACK CLACK
I'M THE CUTEST GIRL IN SCHOOL

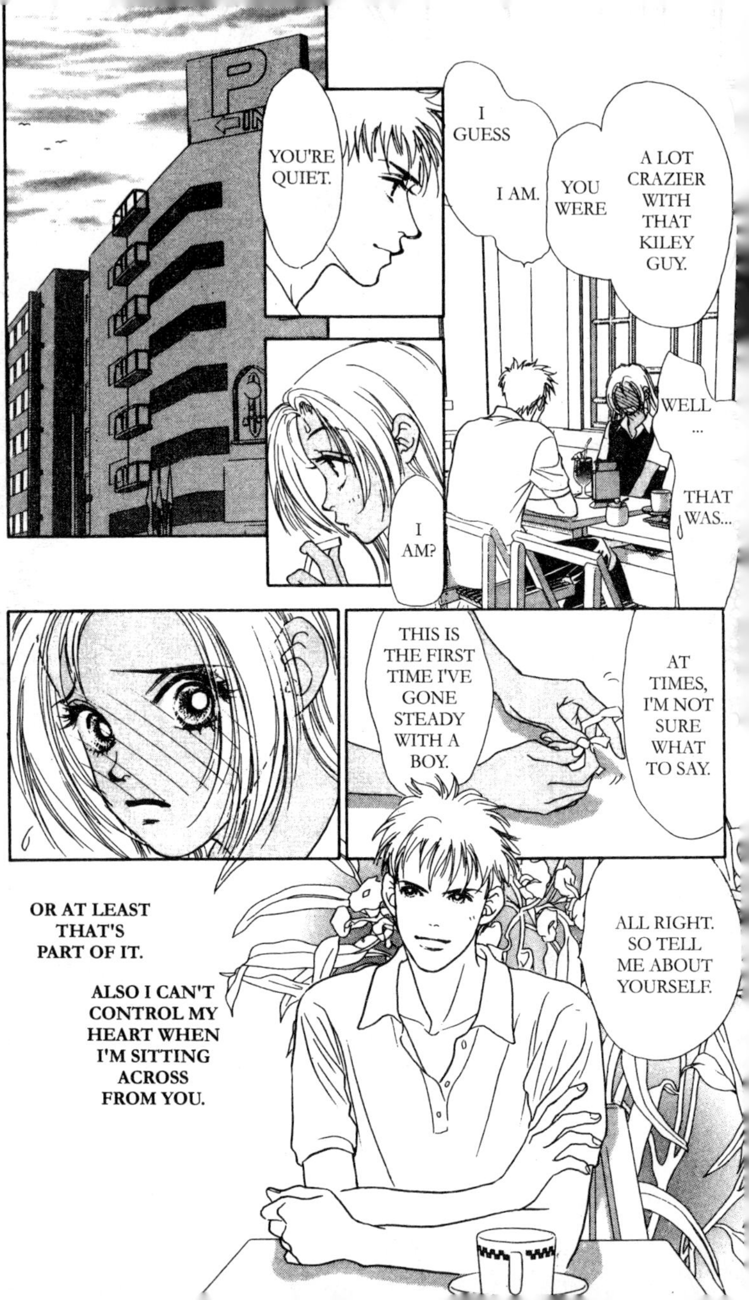
YOU'RE QUIET.
I GUESS
I AM.
YOU WERE
A LOT CRAZIER WITH THAT KILEY GUY.
I AM?
WELL ...
THAT WAS...
THIS IS THE FIRST TIME I'VE GONE STEADY WITH A BOY.
AT TIMES, I'M NOT SURE WHAT TO SAY.
OR AT LEAST THAT'S PART OF IT.
ALSO I CAN'T CONTROL MY HEART WHEN I'M SITTING ACROSS FROM YOU.
ALL RIGHT. SO TELL ME ABOUT YOURSELF.

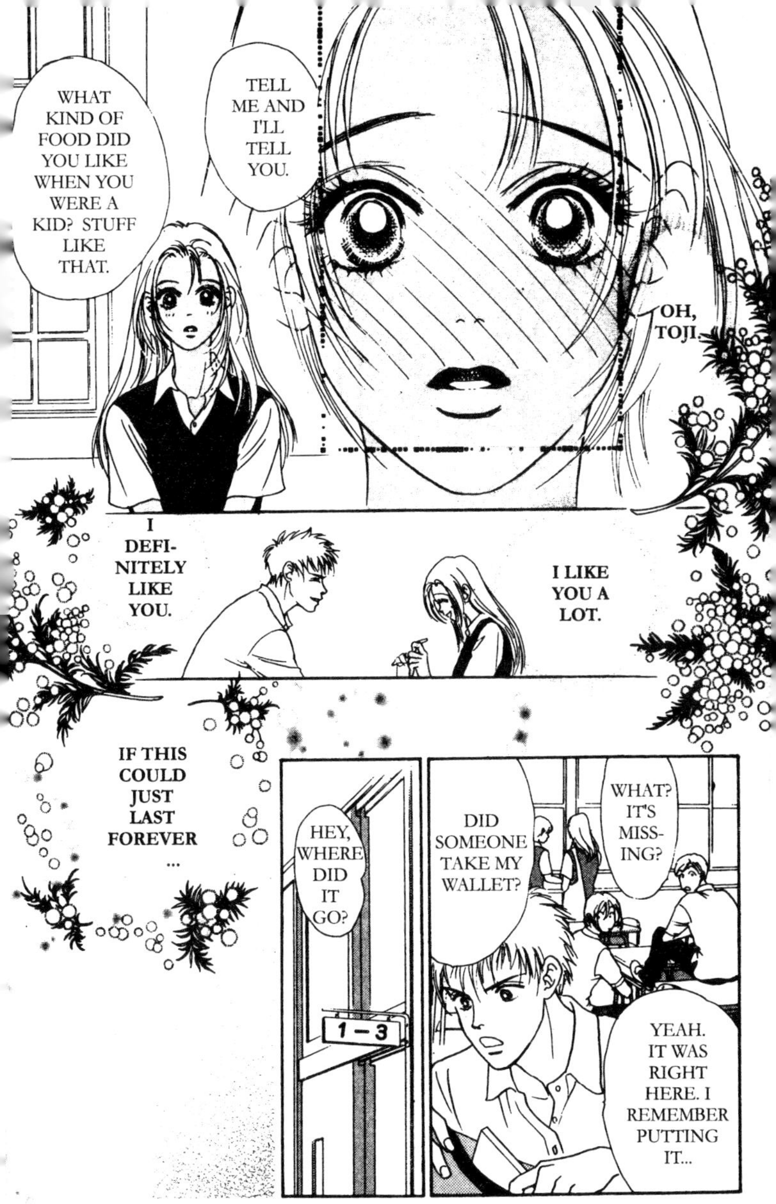
WHAT KIND OF FOOD DID YOU LIKE WHEN YOU WERE A KID? STUFF LIKE THAT.
TELL ME AND I'LL TELL YOU.
OH, TOJI.
I DEFINITELY LIKE YOU.
I LIKE YOU A LOT.
IF THIS COULD JUST LAST FOREVER ...
HEY, WHERE DID IT GO?
1 — 3
DID SOMEONE TAKE MY WALLET?
WHAT? IT'S MISSING?
YEAH. IT WAS RIGHT HERE. I REMEMBER PUTTING IT...

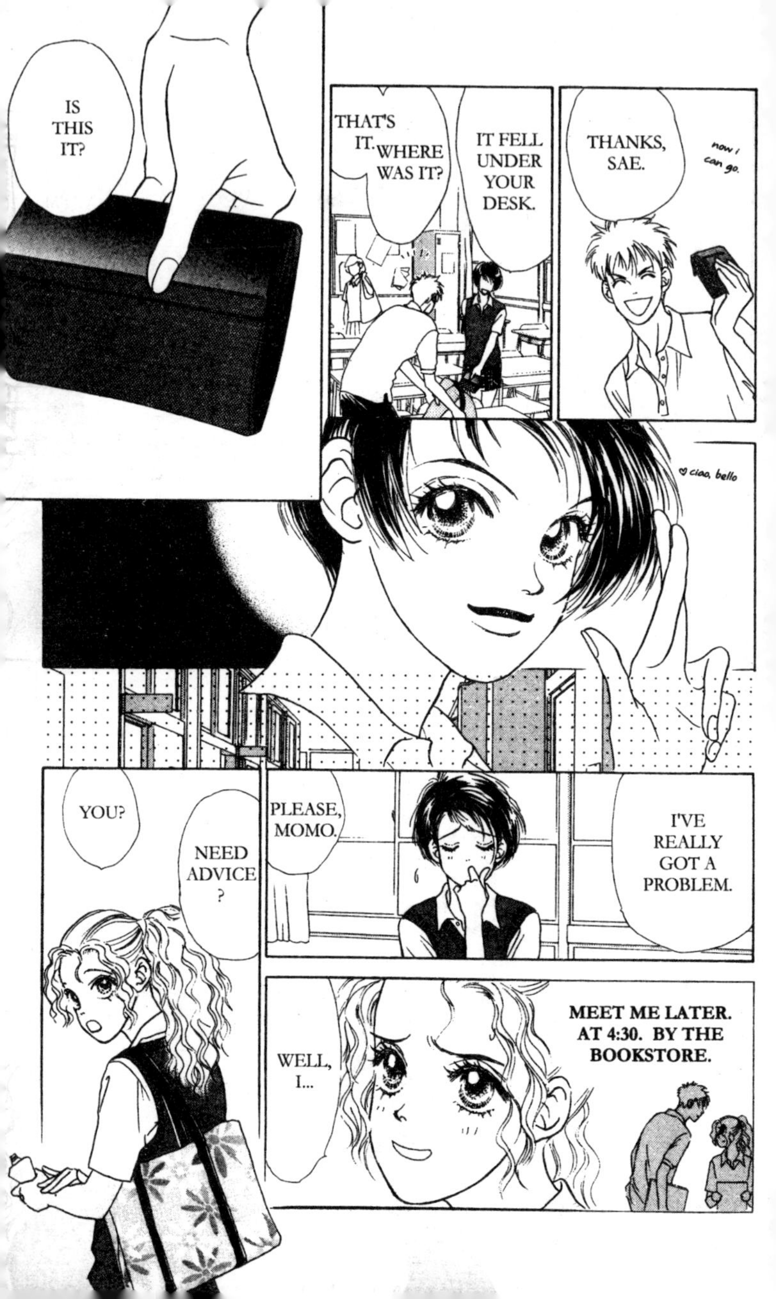

IS THIS IT?
THAT'S IT.
WHERE WAS IT?
IT FELL UNDER YOUR DESK.
THANKS, SAE.
now i can go.
♡ ciao, bello
YOU?
NEED ADVICE ?
PLEASE, MOMO.
I'VE REALLY GOT A PROBLEM.
WELL, I...
MEET ME LATER. AT 4:30. BY THE BOOKSTORE.

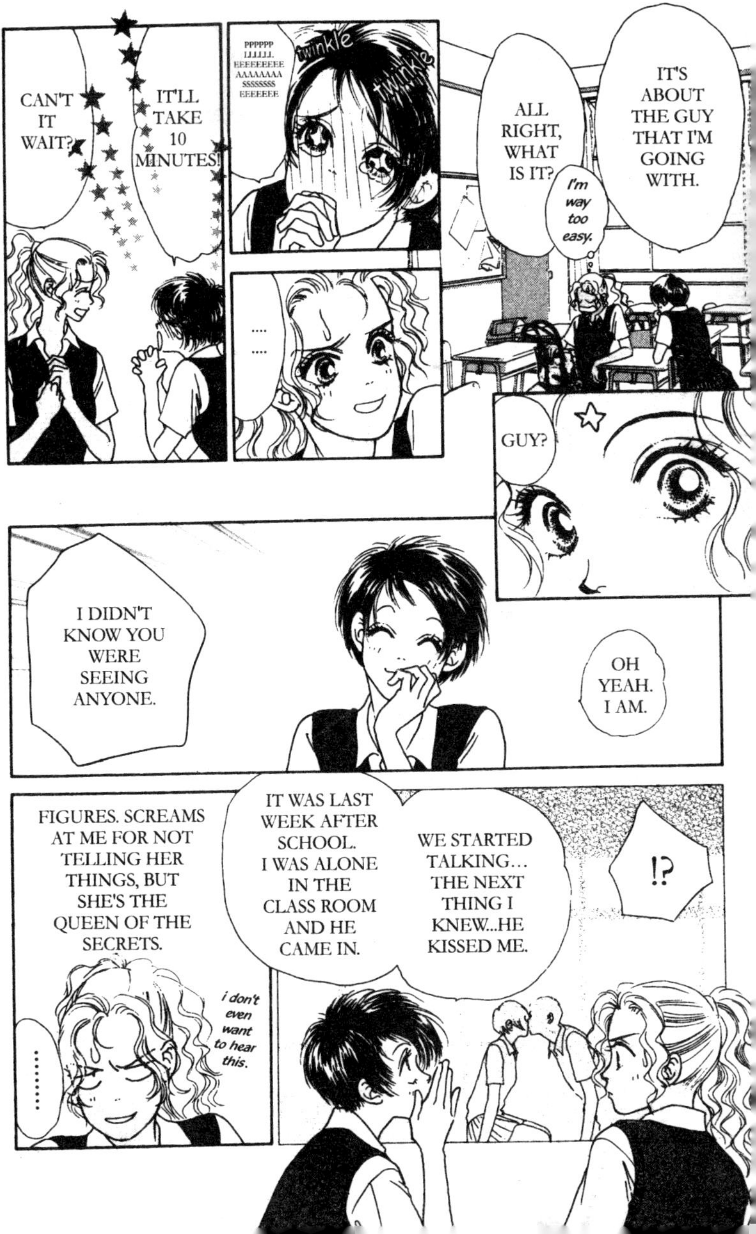

CAN'T IT WAIT?
IT'LL TAKE 10 MINUTES!
PPPPPP LLLLLL EEEEEEEEE AAAAAAAA SSSSSSSS EEEEEEE
twinkle twinkle
....
....
ALL RIGHT, WHAT IS IT?
I'm way too easy.
IT'S ABOUT THE GUY THAT I'M GOING WITH.
GUY?
I DIDN'T KNOW YOU WERE SEEING ANYONE.
OH YEAH. I AM.
FIGURES. SCREAMS AT ME FOR NOT TELLING HER THINGS, BUT SHE'S THE QUEEN OF THE SECRETS.
....
i don't even want to hear this.
IT WAS LAST WEEK AFTER SCHOOL. I WAS ALONE IN THE CLASS ROOM AND HE CAME IN.
WE STARTED TALKING... THE NEXT THING I KNEW...HE KISSED ME.
!?

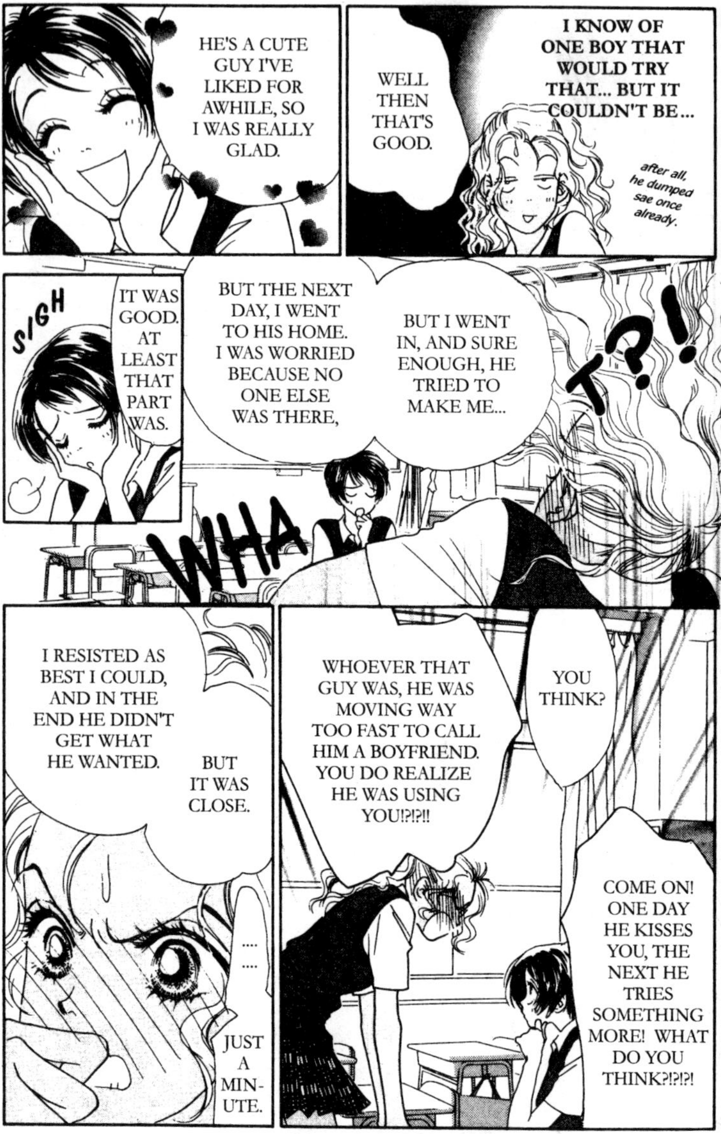
HE'S A CUTE GUY I'VE LIKED FOR AWHILE, SO I WAS REALLY GLAD.
WELL THEN THAT'S GOOD.
I KNOW OF ONE BOY THAT WOULD TRY THAT... BUT IT COULDN'T BE...
after all, he dumped sae once already.
SIGH
IT WAS GOOD. AT LEAST THAT PART WAS.
BUT THE NEXT DAY, I WENT TO HIS HOME. I WAS WORRIED BECAUSE NO ONE ELSE WAS THERE,
BUT I WENT IN, AND SURE ENOUGH, HE TRIED TO MAKE ME...
T?!
WHA
I RESISTED AS BEST I COULD, AND IN THE END HE DIDN'T GET WHAT HE WANTED.
BUT IT WAS CLOSE.
....
....
JUST A MIN-UTE.
WHOEVER THAT GUY WAS, HE WAS MOVING WAY TOO FAST TO CALL HIM A BOYFRIEND. YOU DO REALIZE HE WAS USING YOU!?!?!!
YOU THINK?
COME ON! ONE DAY HE KISSES YOU, THE NEXT HE TRIES SOMETHING MORE! WHAT DO YOU THINK?!?!?!

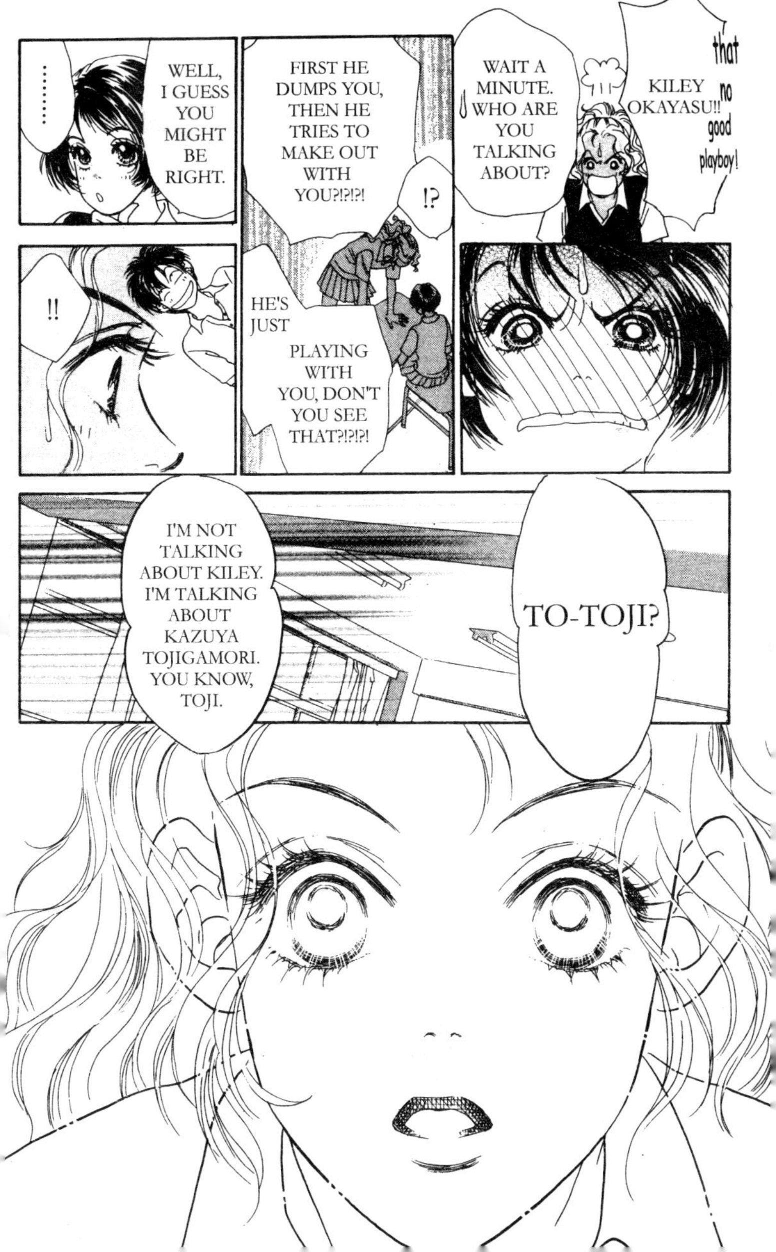

......
WELL, I GUESS YOU MIGHT BE RIGHT.
FIRST HE DUMPS YOU, THEN HE TRIES TO MAKE OUT WITH YOU?!?!?!
!?
WAIT A MINUTE. WHO ARE YOU TALKING ABOUT?
KILEY OKAYASU!!
that no good playboy!
!!
HE'S JUST PLAYING WITH YOU, DON'T YOU SEE THAT?!?!?!
I'M NOT TALKING ABOUT KILEY. I'M TALKING ABOUT KAZUYA TOJIGAMORI. YOU KNOW, TOJI.
TO-TOJI?

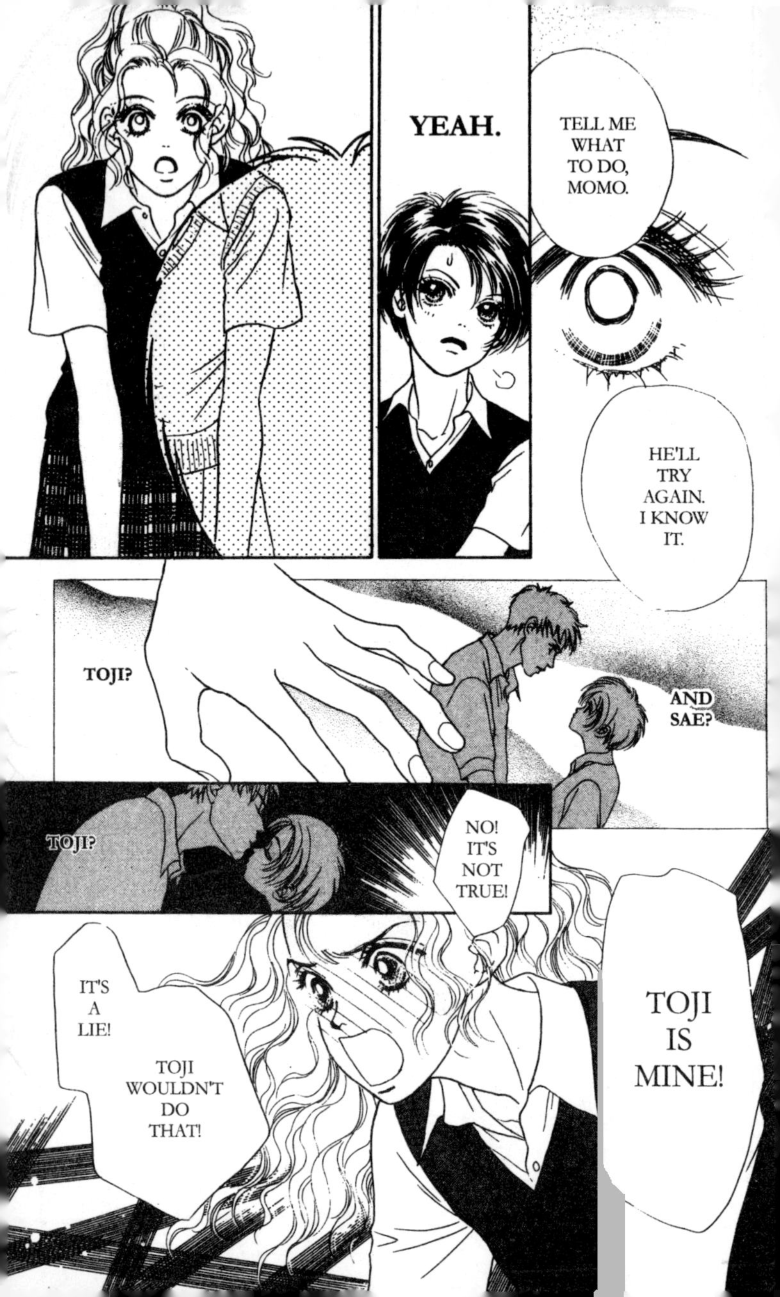
YEAH.
TELL ME WHAT TO DO, MOMO.
HE'LL TRY AGAIN. I KNOW IT.
TOJI?
AND SAE?
TOJI?
NO! IT'S NOT TRUE!
IT'S A LIE!
TOJI WOULDN'T DO THAT!
TOJI IS MINE!

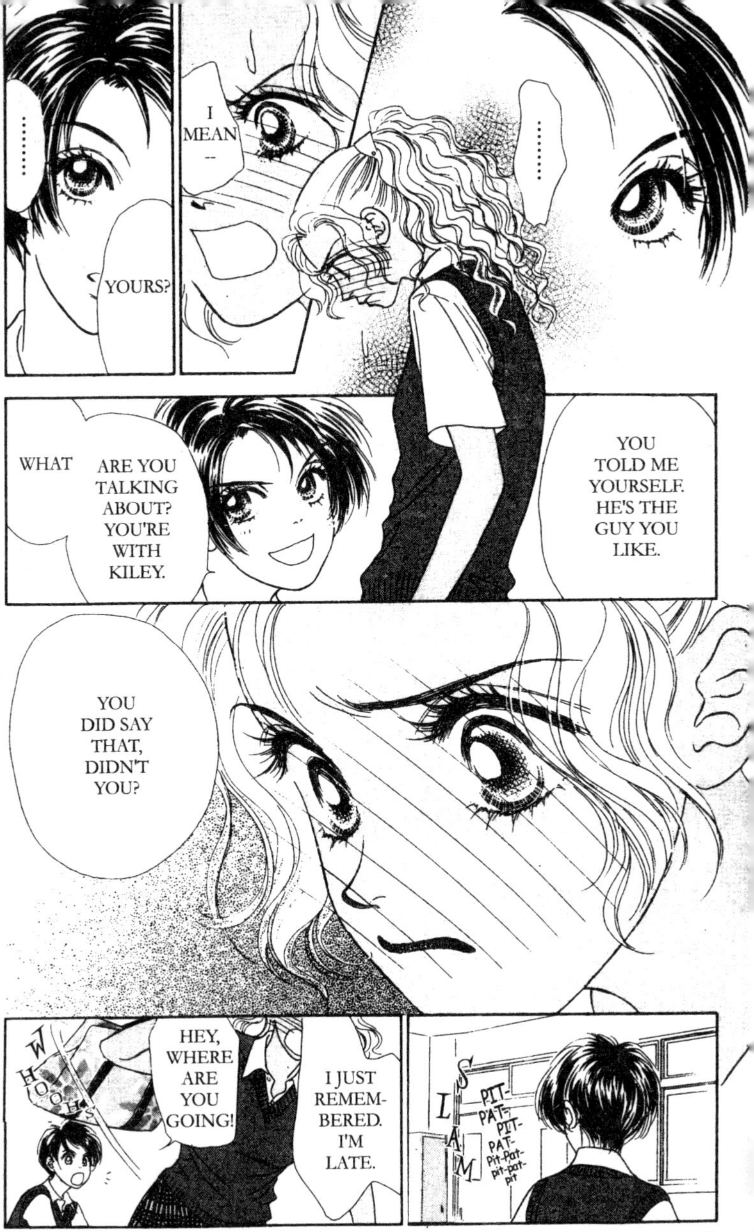

......
YOURS?
I MEAN --
......
WHAT ARE YOU TALKING ABOUT? YOU'RE WITH KILEY.
YOU TOLD ME YOURSELF. HE'S THE GUY YOU LIKE.
YOU DID SAY THAT, DIDN'T YOU?
WHOOSH
HEY, WHERE ARE YOU GOING!
I JUST REMEMBERED. I'M LATE.
SLAM
PIT-PAT-PIT-PAT-Pit-Pat-pit-pat-pit

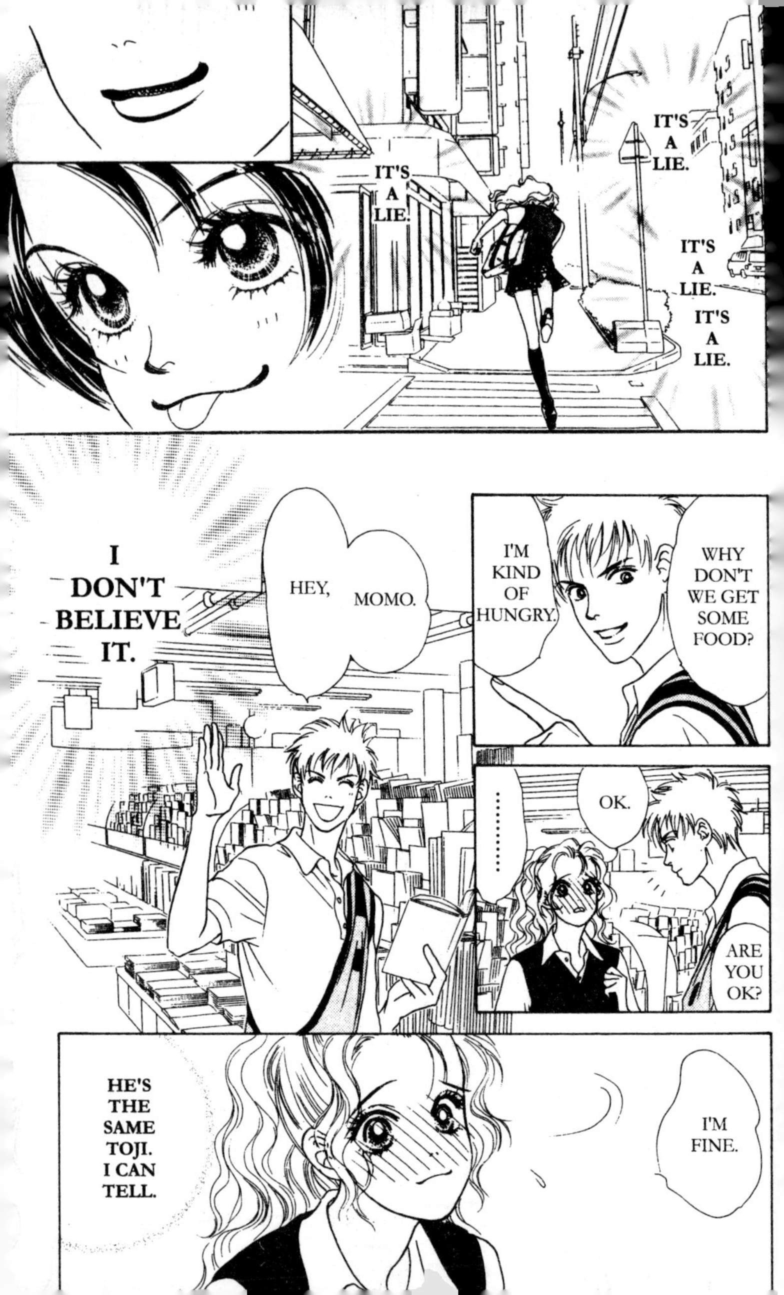

IT'S A LIE.
IT'S A LIE.
IT'S A LIE.
IT'S A LIE.
I DON'T BELIEVE IT.
HEY, MOMO.
I'M KIND OF HUNGRY.
WHY DON'T WE GET SOME FOOD?
......
OK.
ARE YOU OK?
HE'S THE SAME TOJI. I CAN TELL.
I'M FINE.

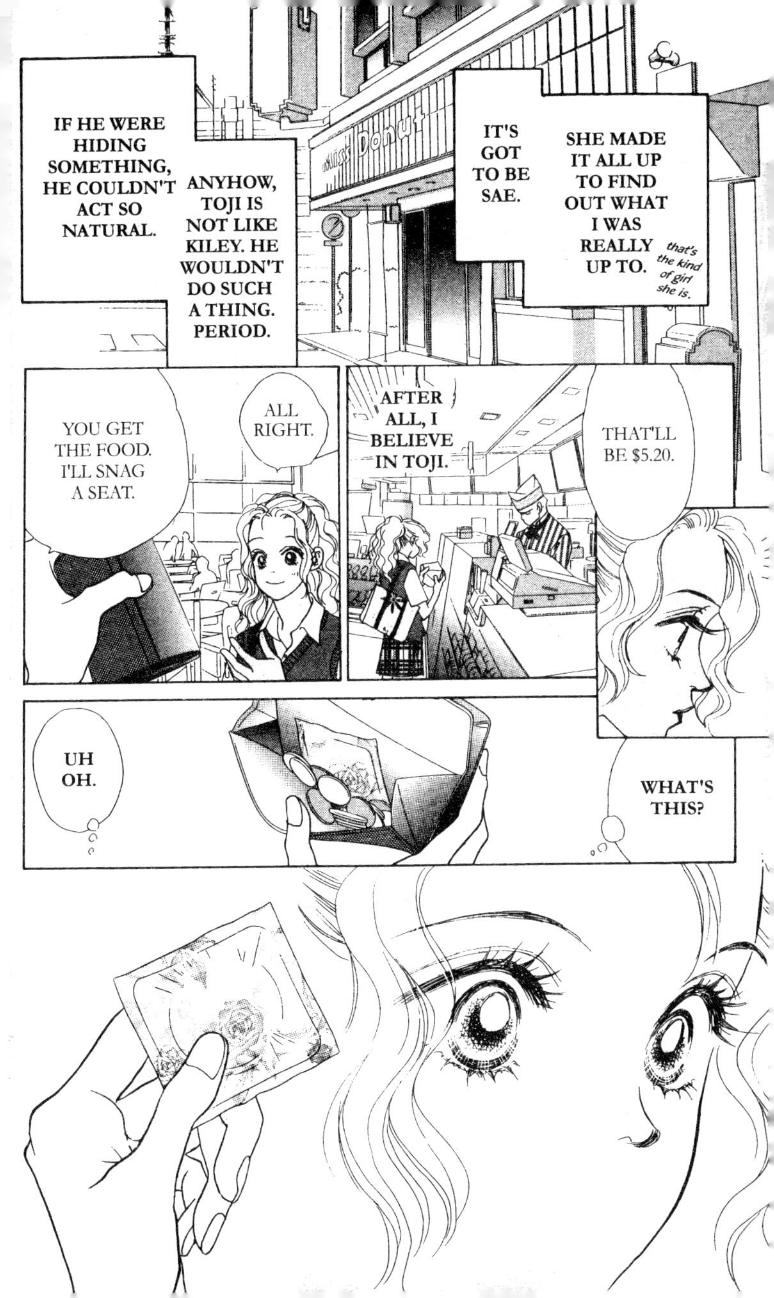
IF HE WERE HIDING SOMETHING, HE COULDN'T ACT SO NATURAL.
ANYHOW, TOJI IS NOT LIKE KILEY. HE WOULDN'T DO SUCH A THING. PERIOD.
Miss Donut
IT'S GOT TO BE SAE.
SHE MADE IT ALL UP TO FIND OUT WHAT I WAS REALLY UP TO.
that's the kind of girl she is.
YOU GET THE FOOD. I'LL SNAG A SEAT.
ALL RIGHT.
AFTER ALL, I BELIEVE IN TOJI.
THAT'LL BE $5.20.
UH OH.
WHAT'S THIS?

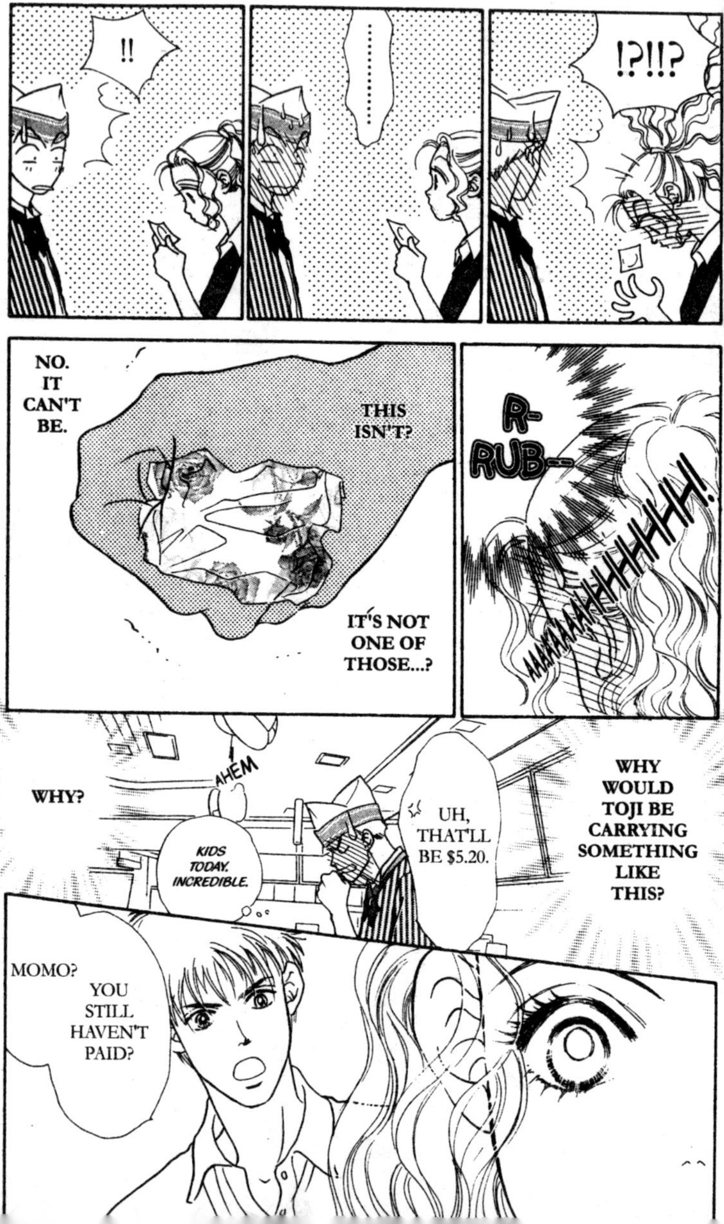
!!
....
!?!!?
NO. IT CAN'T BE.
THIS ISN'T?
IT'S NOT ONE OF THOSE...?
R-RUB--
AAAAAAAAHHHHHHH!
WHY?
AHEM
KIDS TODAY. INCREDIBLE.
UH, THAT'LL BE $5.20.
WHY WOULD TOJI BE CARRYING SOMETHING LIKE THIS?
MOMO? YOU STILL HAVEN'T PAID?

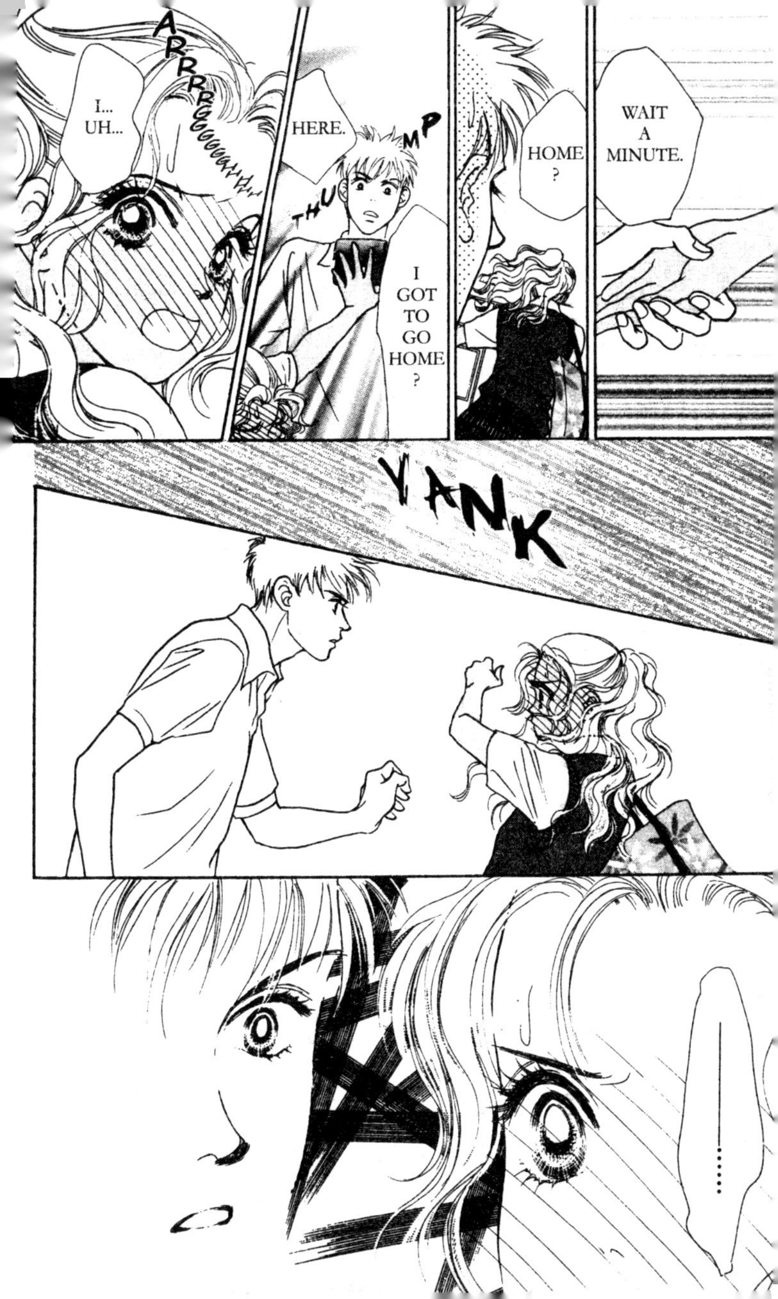
ARRRRGGGGGGGH
I... UH...
HERE.
THUMP
I GOT TO GO HOME?
HOME?
WAIT A MINUTE.
YANK
......

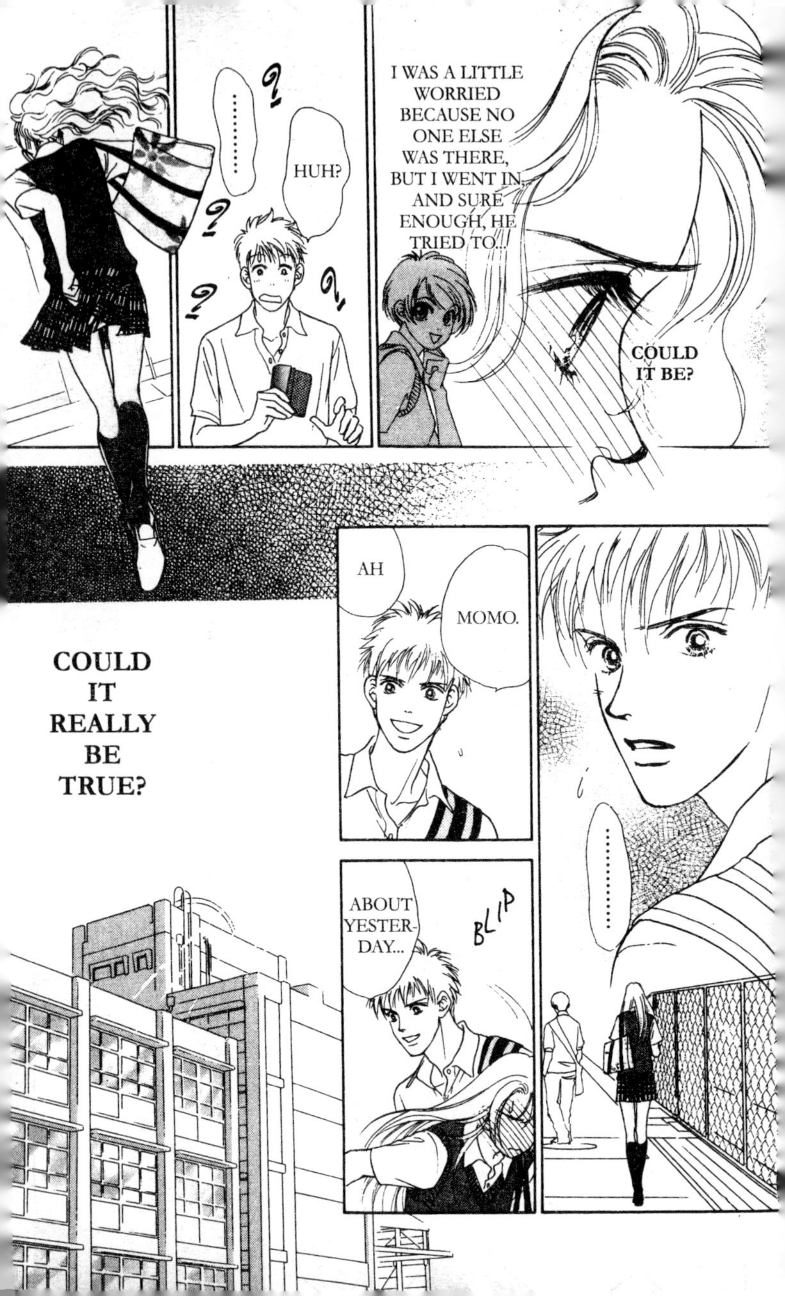

……
HUH?
I WAS A LITTLE WORRIED BECAUSE NO ONE ELSE WAS THERE, BUT I WENT IN, AND SURE ENOUGH, HE TRIED TO...
COULD IT BE?
COULD IT REALLY BE TRUE?
AH
MOMO.
ABOUT YESTERDAY...
BLIP
……

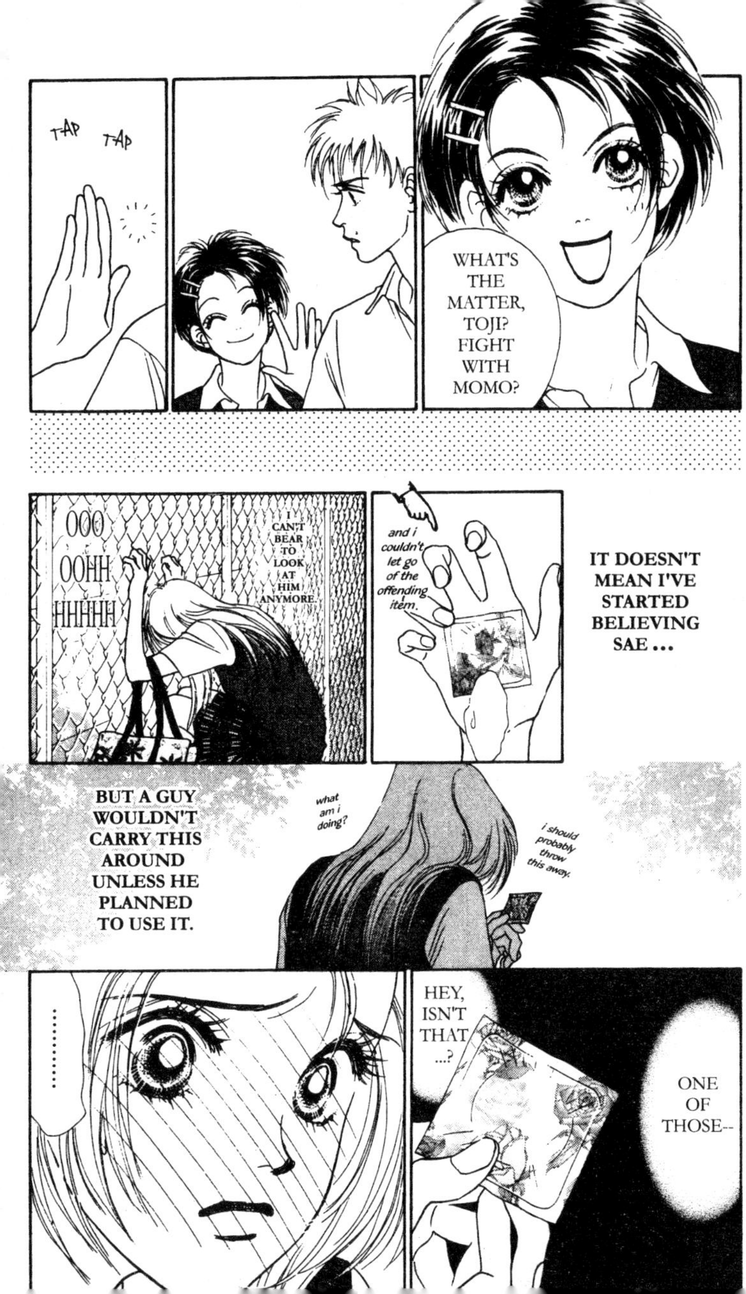
TAP TAP
WHAT'S THE MATTER, TOJI? FIGHT WITH MOMO?
OOOOOHHHHHHH
I CAN'T BEAR TO LOOK AT HIM ANYMORE.
and i couldn't let go of the offending item.
IT DOESN'T MEAN I'VE STARTED BELIEVING SAE ...
BUT A GUY WOULDN'T CARRY THIS AROUND UNLESS HE PLANNED TO USE IT.
what am i doing?
i should probably throw this away.
....
HEY, ISN'T THAT ...?
ONE OF THOSE--

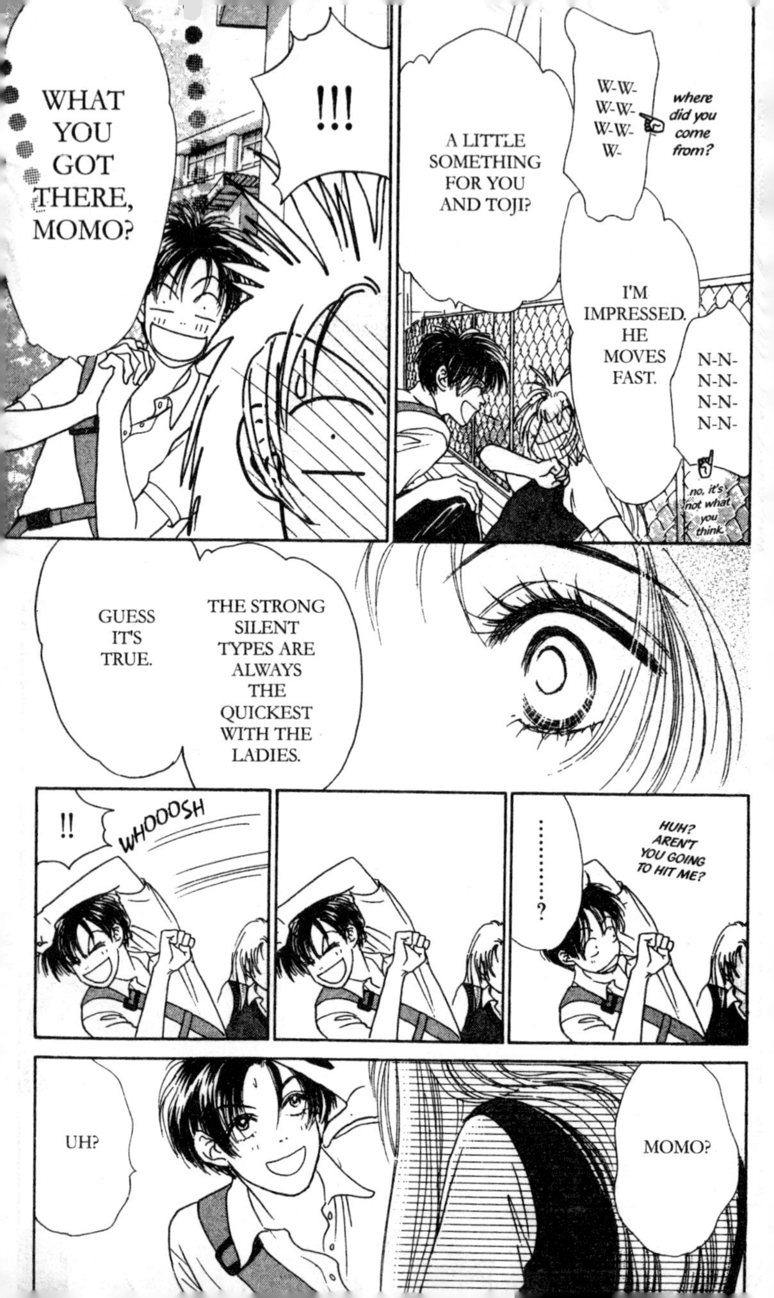

WHAT YOU GOT THERE, MOMO?
!!!
A LITTLE SOMETHING FOR YOU AND TOJI?
W-W-W-W-W-W-W-
where did you come from?
I'M IMPRESSED. HE MOVES FAST.
N-N-N-N-N-N-N-N-
no, it's not what you think.
GUESS IT'S TRUE.
THE STRONG SILENT TYPES ARE ALWAYS THE QUICKEST WITH THE LADIES.
!!
WHOOOSH
.........?
HUH? AREN'T YOU GOING TO HIT ME?
UH?
MOMO?

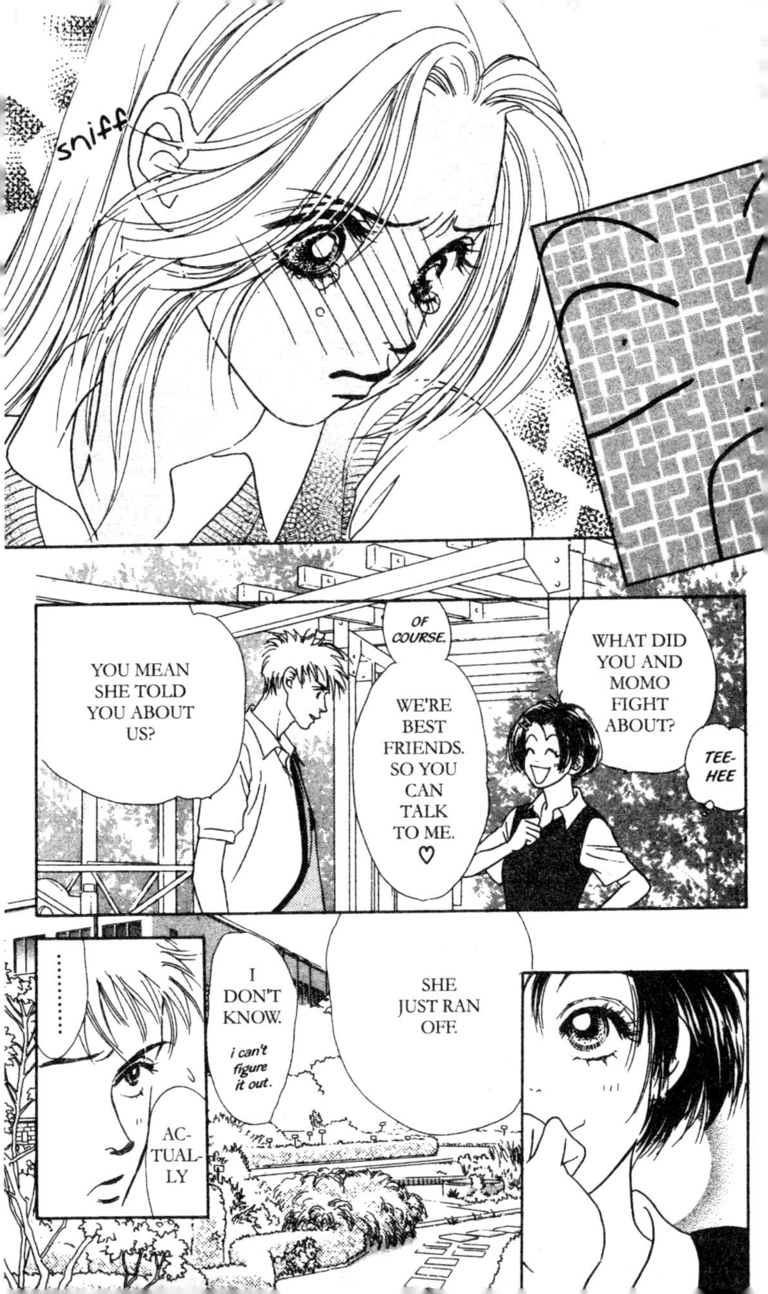
sniff
YOU MEAN SHE TOLD YOU ABOUT US?
OF COURSE.
WE'RE BEST FRIENDS. SO YOU CAN TALK TO ME. ♡
WHAT DID YOU AND MOMO FIGHT ABOUT?
TEE-HEE
....
ACTUALLY
I DON'T KNOW.
i can't figure it out.
SHE JUST RAN OFF.

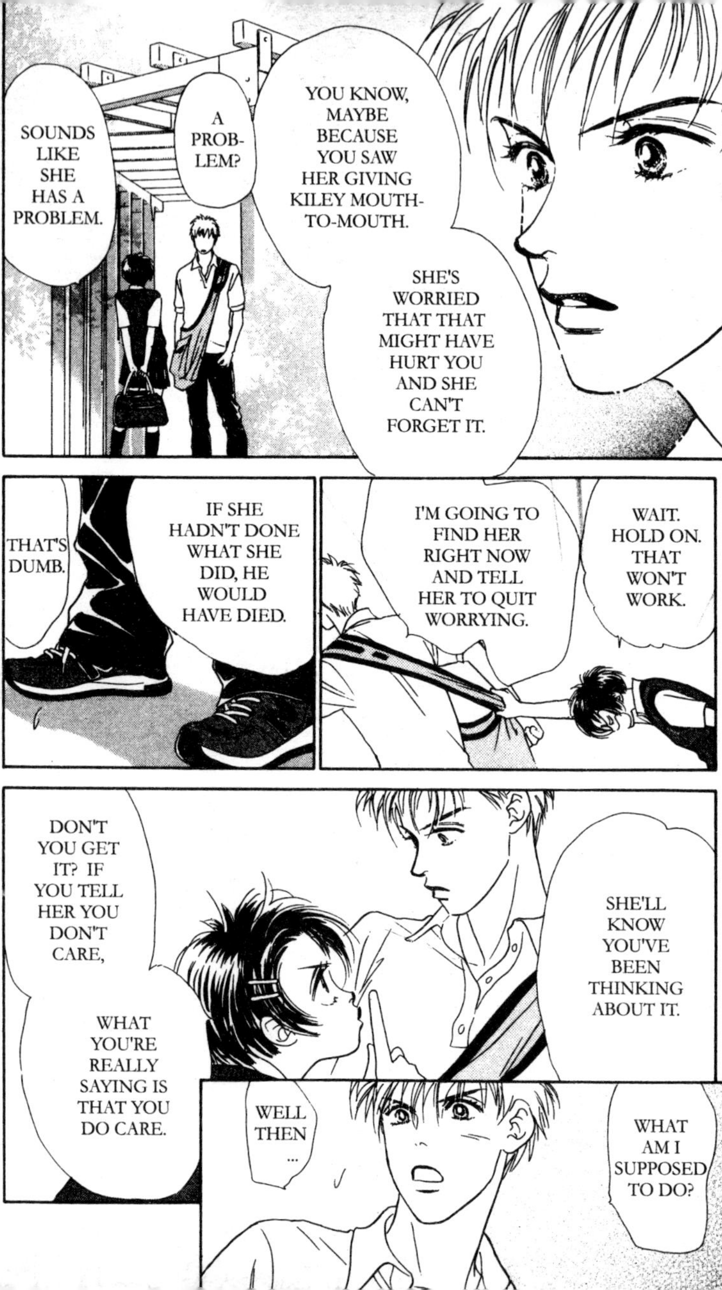
SOUNDS LIKE SHE HAS A PROBLEM.
A PROB-LEM?
YOU KNOW, MAYBE BECAUSE YOU SAW HER GIVING KILEY MOUTH-TO-MOUTH.
SHE'S WORRIED THAT THAT MIGHT HAVE HURT YOU AND SHE CAN'T FORGET IT.
THAT'S DUMB.
IF SHE HADN'T DONE WHAT SHE DID, HE WOULD HAVE DIED.
I'M GOING TO FIND HER RIGHT NOW AND TELL HER TO QUIT WORRYING.
WAIT. HOLD ON. THAT WON'T WORK.
DON'T YOU GET IT? IF YOU TELL HER YOU DON'T CARE,
WHAT YOU'RE REALLY SAYING IS THAT YOU DO CARE.
SHE'LL KNOW YOU'VE BEEN THINKING ABOUT IT.
WELL THEN ...
WHAT AM I SUPPOSED TO DO?

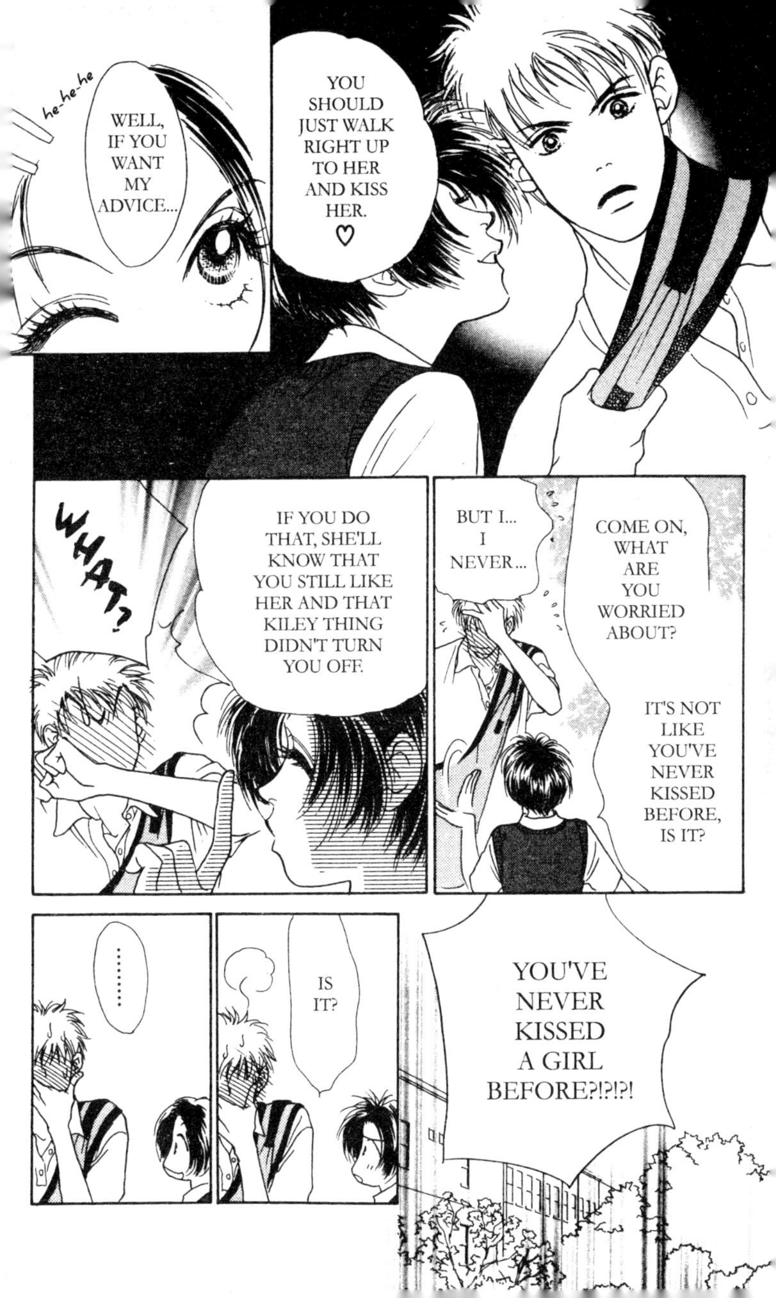
he-he-he
WELL, IF YOU WANT MY ADVICE...
YOU SHOULD JUST WALK RIGHT UP TO HER AND KISS HER. ♡
WHAT?
IF YOU DO THAT, SHE'LL KNOW THAT YOU STILL LIKE HER AND THAT KILEY THING DIDN'T TURN YOU OFF.
BUT I... I NEVER...
COME ON, WHAT ARE YOU WORRIED ABOUT?
IT'S NOT LIKE YOU'VE NEVER KISSED BEFORE, IS IT?
....
IS IT?
YOU'VE NEVER KISSED A GIRL BEFORE?!?!?!

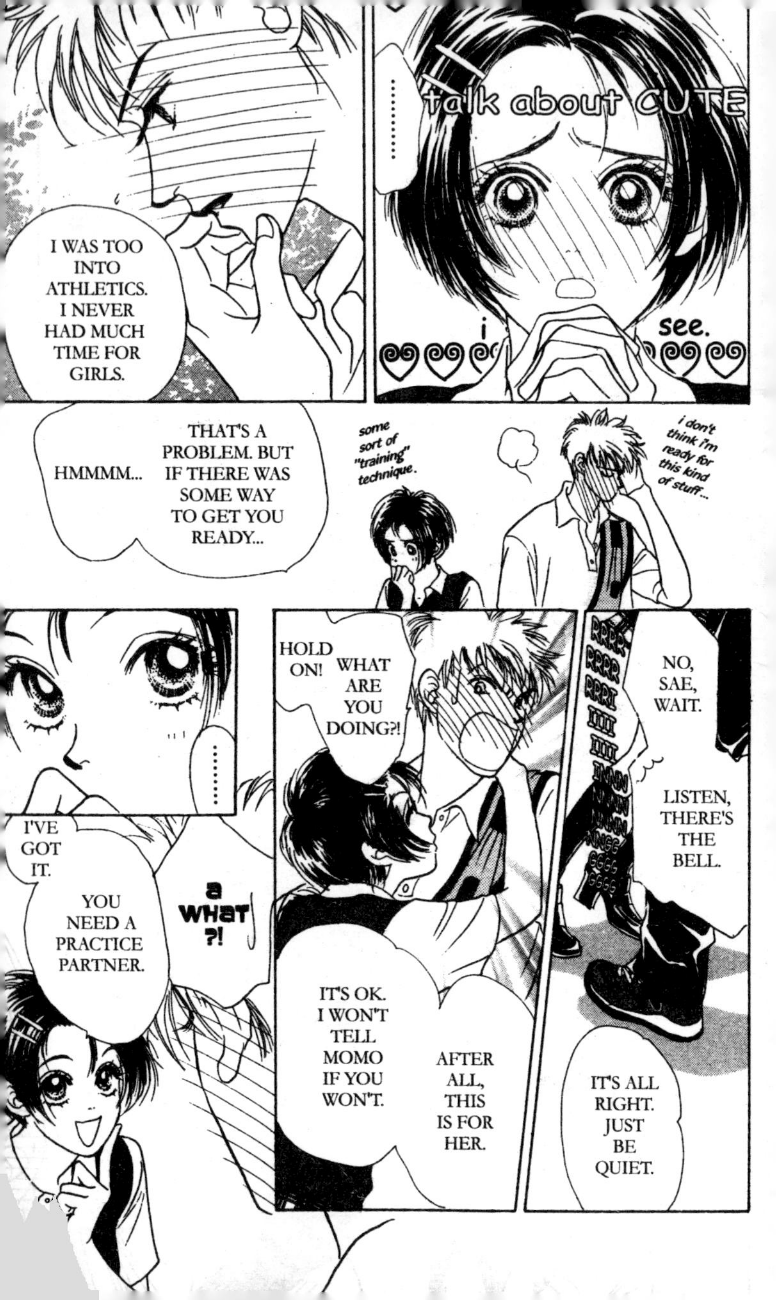
I WAS TOO INTO ATHLETICS. I NEVER HAD MUCH TIME FOR GIRLS.
......
talk about CUTE
i see.
HMMMM...
THAT'S A PROBLEM. BUT IF THERE WAS SOME WAY TO GET YOU READY...
some sort of "training" technique.
i don't think i'm ready for this kind of stuff...
......
I'VE GOT IT.
YOU NEED A PRACTICE PARTNER.
a WHAT ?!
HOLD ON!
WHAT ARE YOU DOING?!
IT'S OK. I WON'T TELL MOMO IF YOU WON'T.
AFTER ALL, THIS IS FOR HER.
RRRR RRRR RRRI IIII IIII INNN NNNN NNNN NNGG GGGG GGGG
NO, SAE, WAIT.
LISTEN, THERE'S THE BELL.
IT'S ALL RIGHT. JUST BE QUIET.

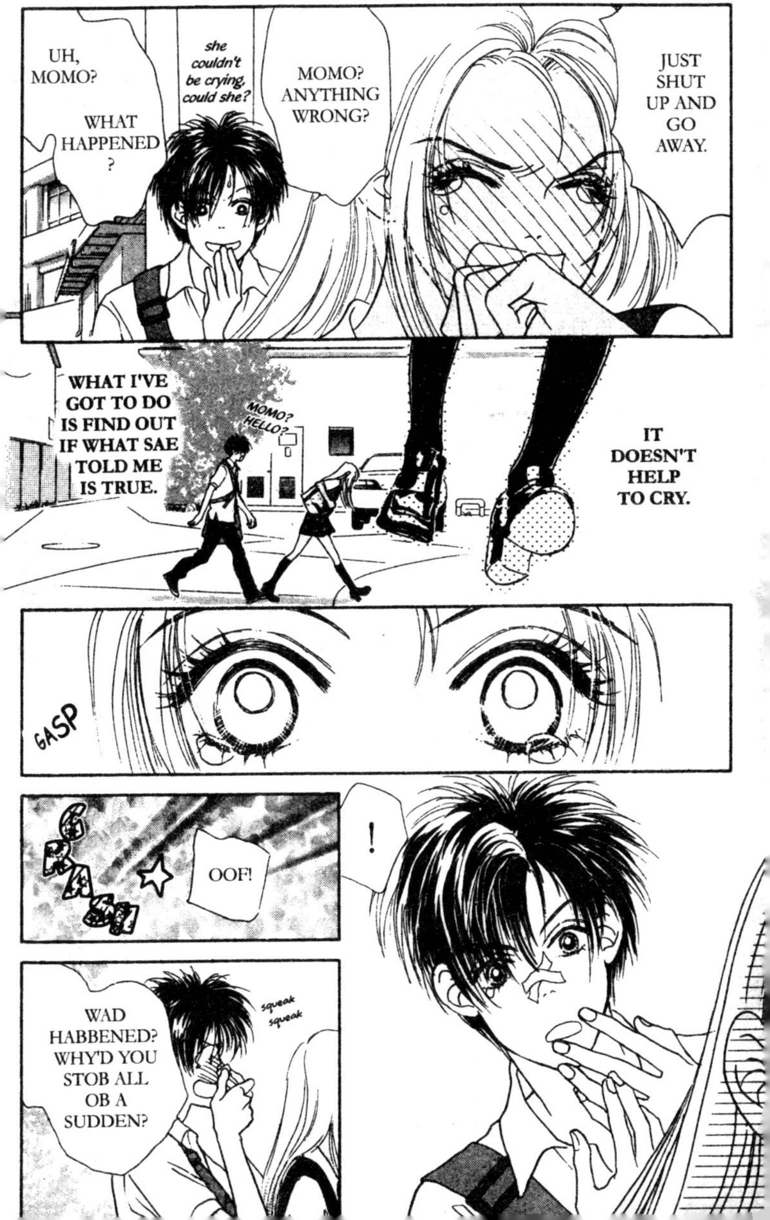
UH, MOMO?
WHAT HAPPENED?
she couldn't be crying, could she?
MOMO? ANYTHING WRONG?
JUST SHUT UP AND GO AWAY.
WHAT I'VE GOT TO DO IS FIND OUT IF WHAT SAE TOLD ME IS TRUE.
MOMO? HELLO?
IT DOESN'T HELP TO CRY.
GASP
OOF!
WAD HABBENED? WHY'D YOU STOB ALL OB A SUDDEN?
squeak squeak
!

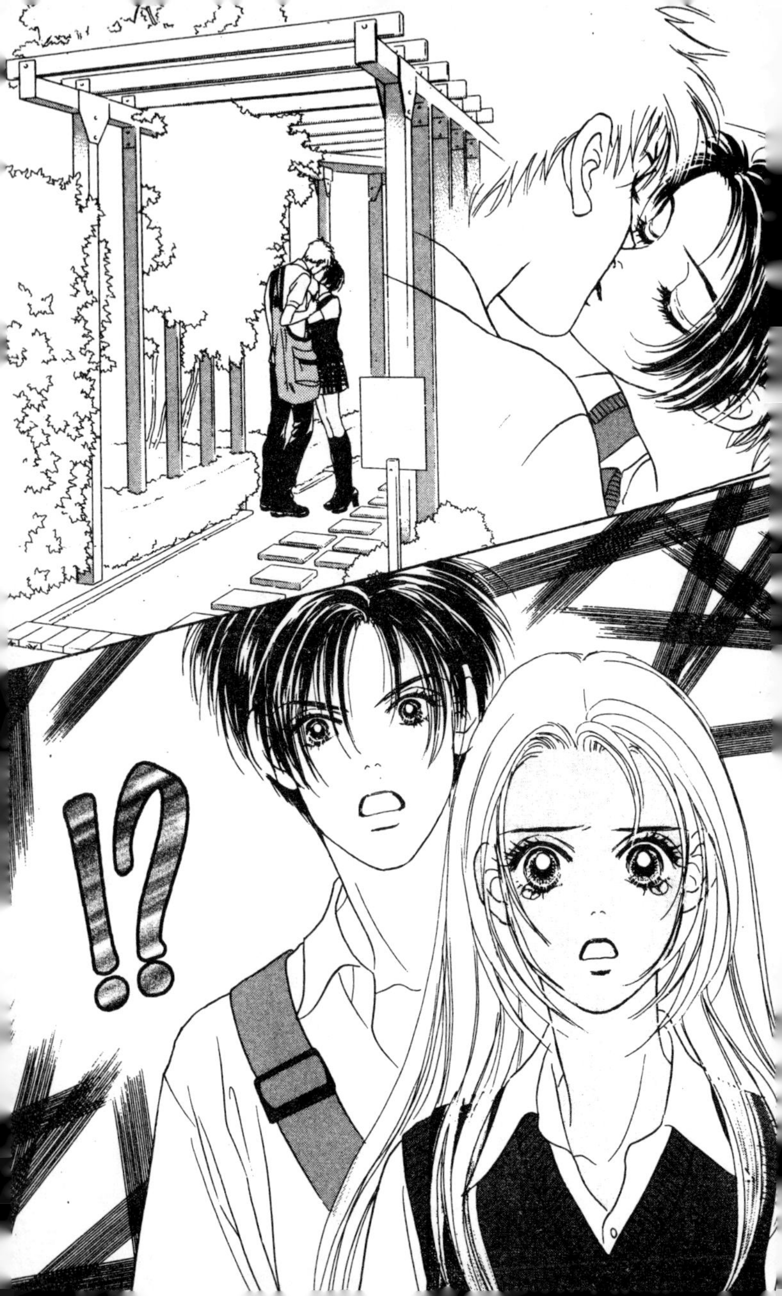
!?

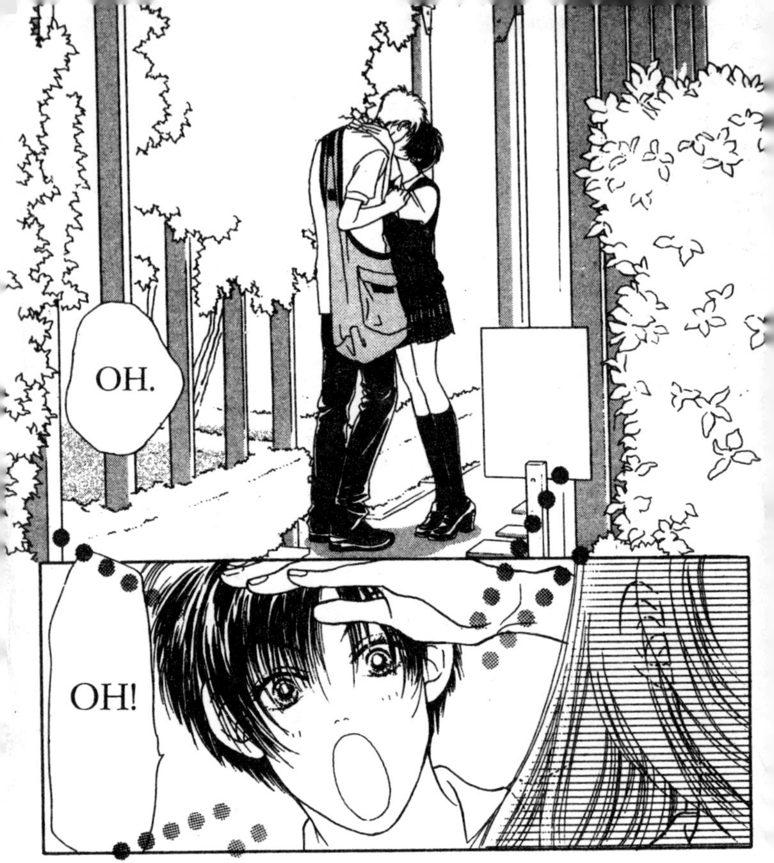
OH.
OH!

PEACH CLUB CORNER

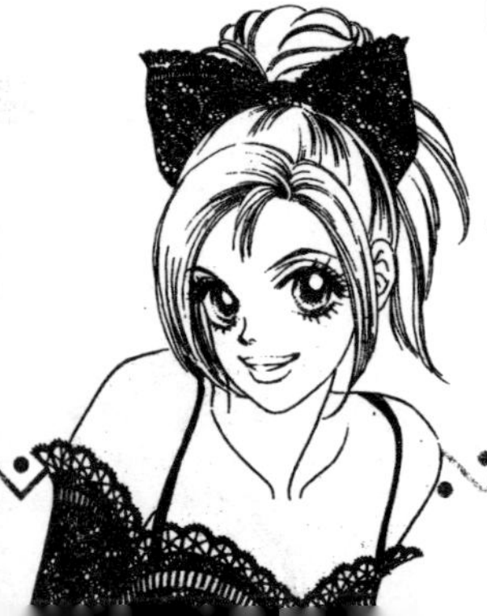

QUESTION: WILL MOMO EVER FULFILL HER DREAM OF LIGHTENING HER SKIN COLOR?

ANSWER: NO, SHE WON'T. IF HER SKIN COLOR WERE TO CHANGE, HER PERSONALITY WOULD CHANGE. YES, MAYBE SOMEDAY, AFTER SHE'S GRADUATED FROM HIGH SCHOOL, SHE'LL SETTLE DOWN SOMEWHERE AND SHE'LL HAVE LIGHTER SKIN. BUT THE LESSON MOMO HAS TO LEARN BEFORE THEN IS TO ACCEPT HERSELF FOR WHAT'S INSIDE.

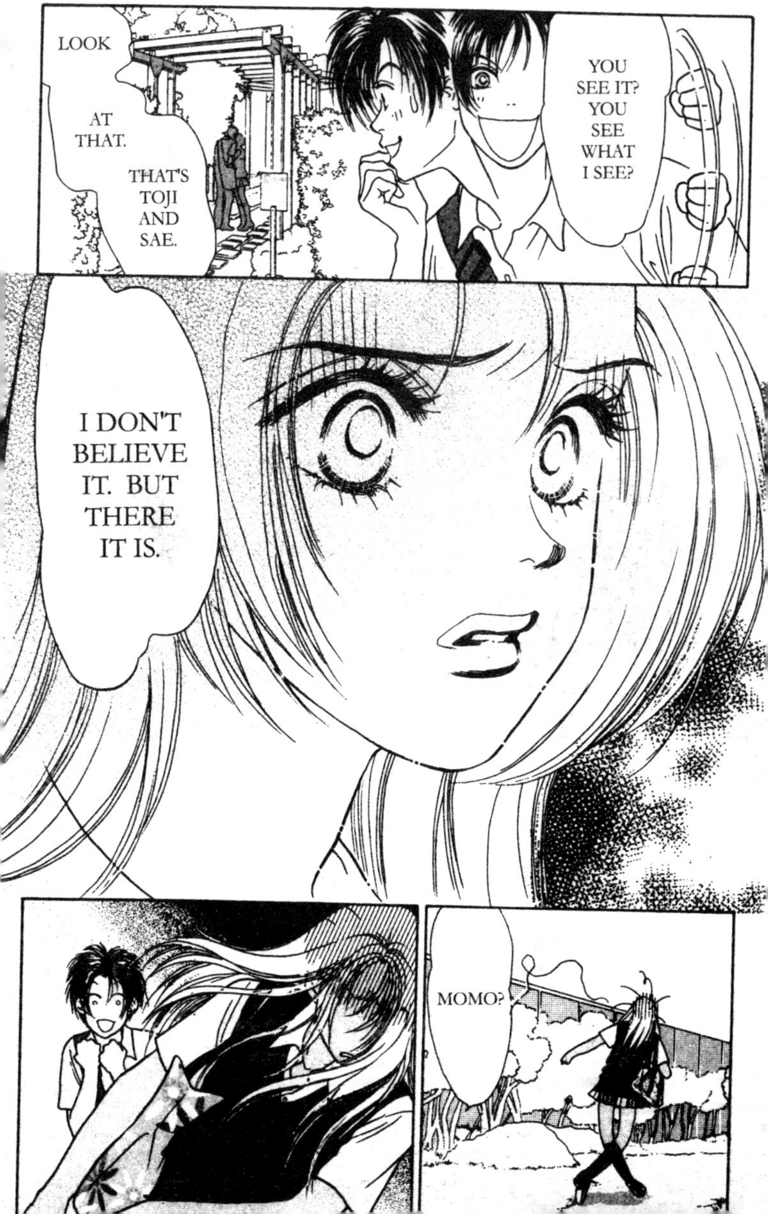
YOU SEE IT? YOU SEE WHAT I SEE?
LOOK AT THAT.
THAT'S TOJI AND SAE.
I DON'T BELIEVE IT. BUT THERE IT IS.
MOMO?

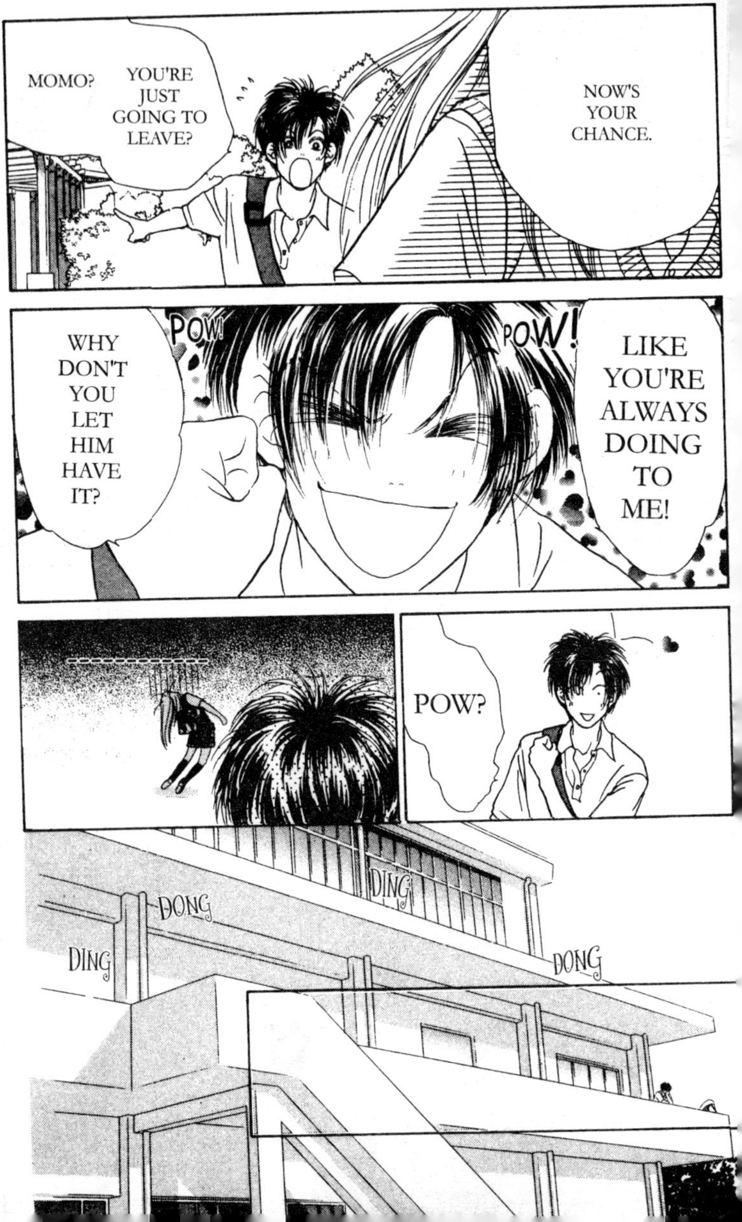
MOMO? YOU'RE JUST GOING TO LEAVE?
NOW'S YOUR CHANCE.
WHY DON'T YOU LET HIM HAVE IT?
POW!
POW!
LIKE YOU'RE ALWAYS DOING TO ME!
POW?
DING
DONG
DING
DONG

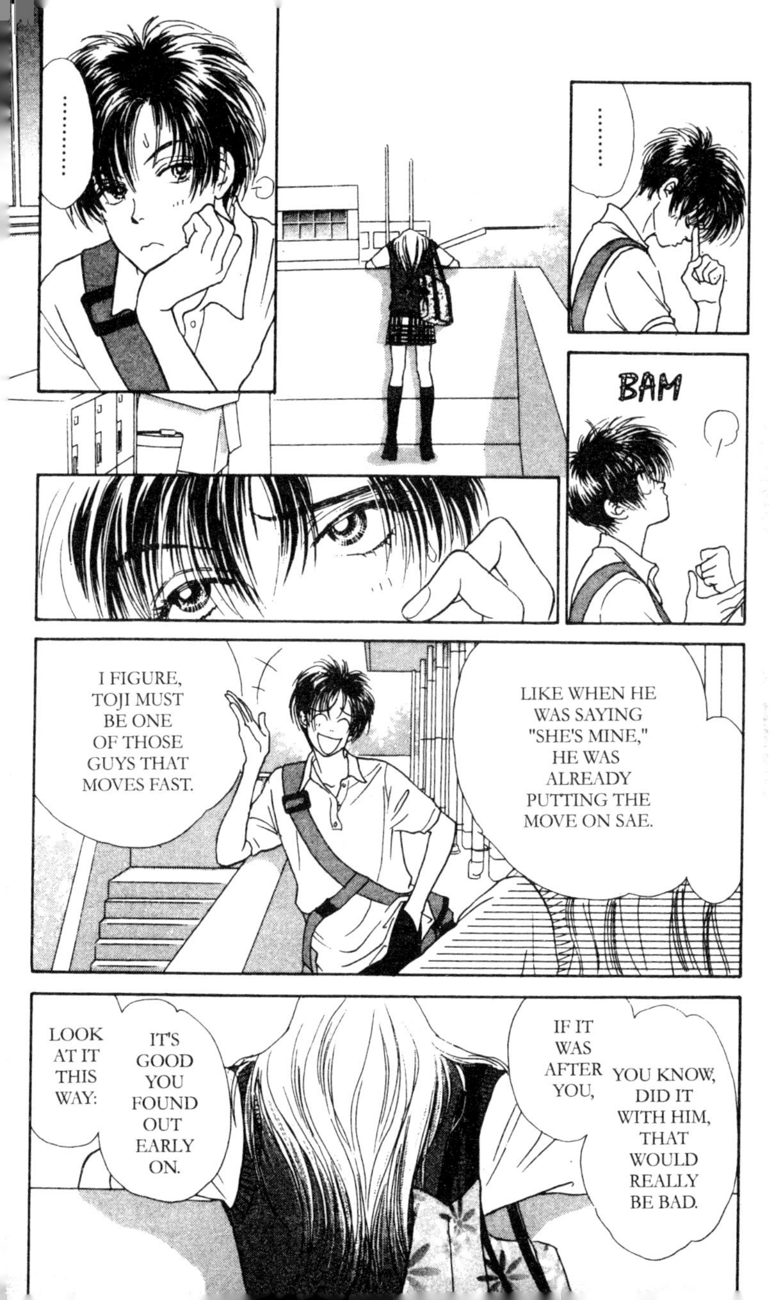
......
......
BAM
I FIGURE, TOJI MUST BE ONE OF THOSE GUYS THAT MOVES FAST.
LIKE WHEN HE WAS SAYING "SHE'S MINE," HE WAS ALREADY PUTTING THE MOVE ON SAE.
LOOK AT IT THIS WAY:
IT'S GOOD YOU FOUND OUT EARLY ON.
IF IT WAS AFTER YOU,
YOU KNOW, DID IT WITH HIM, THAT WOULD REALLY BE BAD.

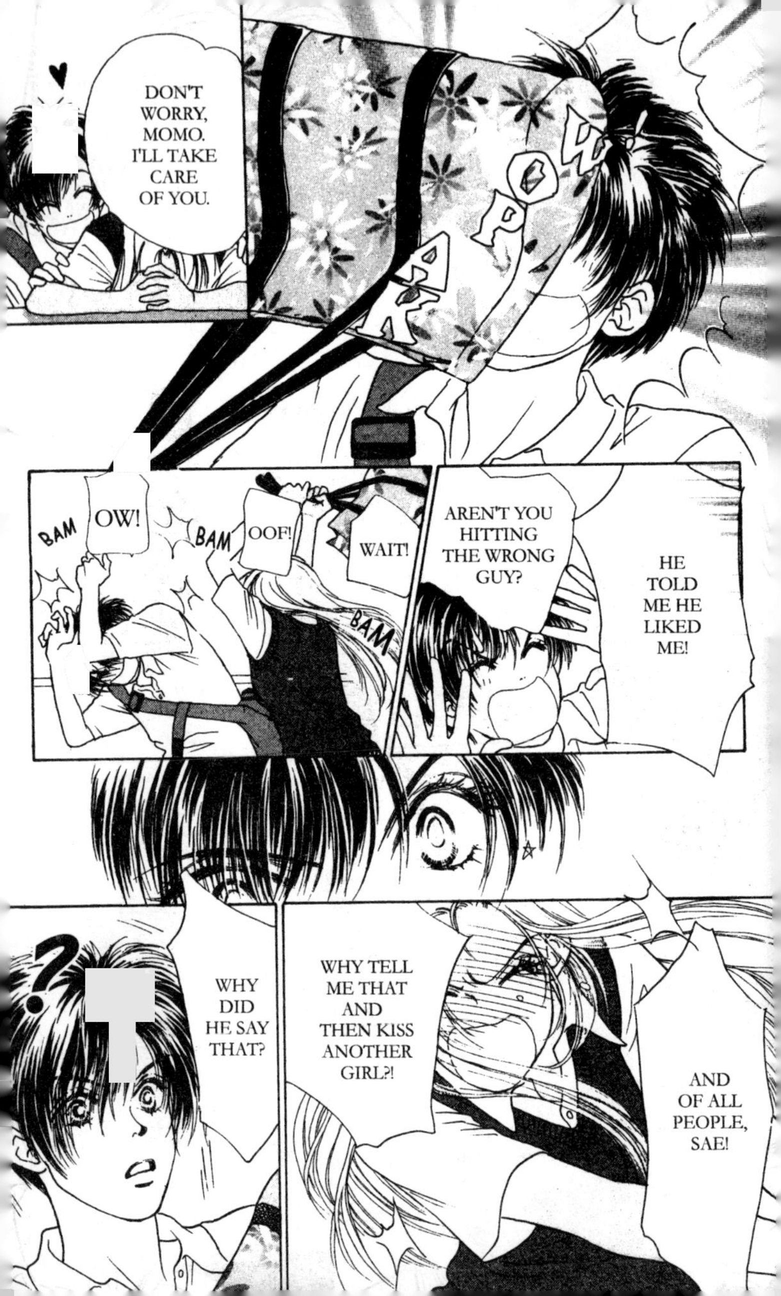
DON'T WORRY, MOMO. I'LL TAKE CARE OF YOU.
KAPOW
BAM
OW!
BAM
OOF!
BAM
WAIT!
AREN'T YOU HITTING THE WRONG GUY?
HE TOLD ME HE LIKED ME!
WHY DID HE SAY THAT?
WHY TELL ME THAT AND THEN KISS ANOTHER GIRL?!
AND OF ALL PEOPLE, SAE!

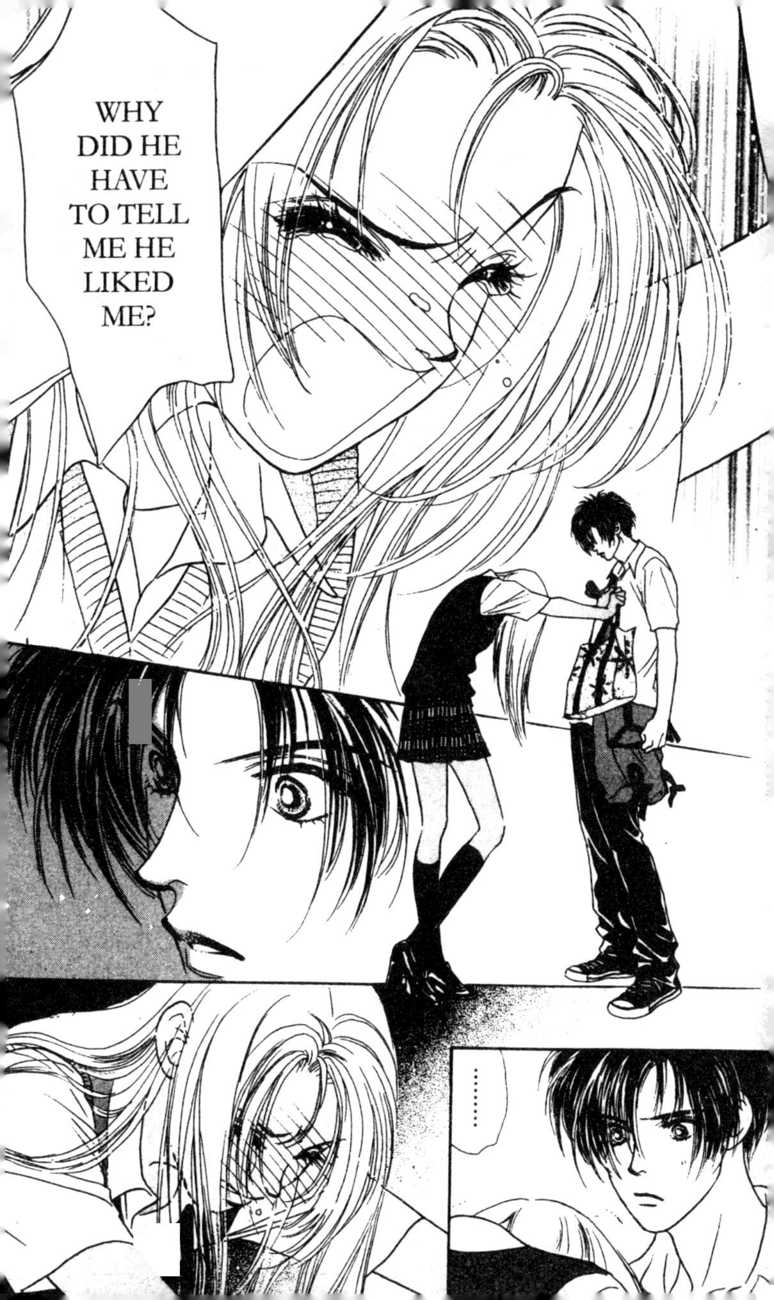
WHY DID HE HAVE TO TELL ME HE LIKED ME?
....

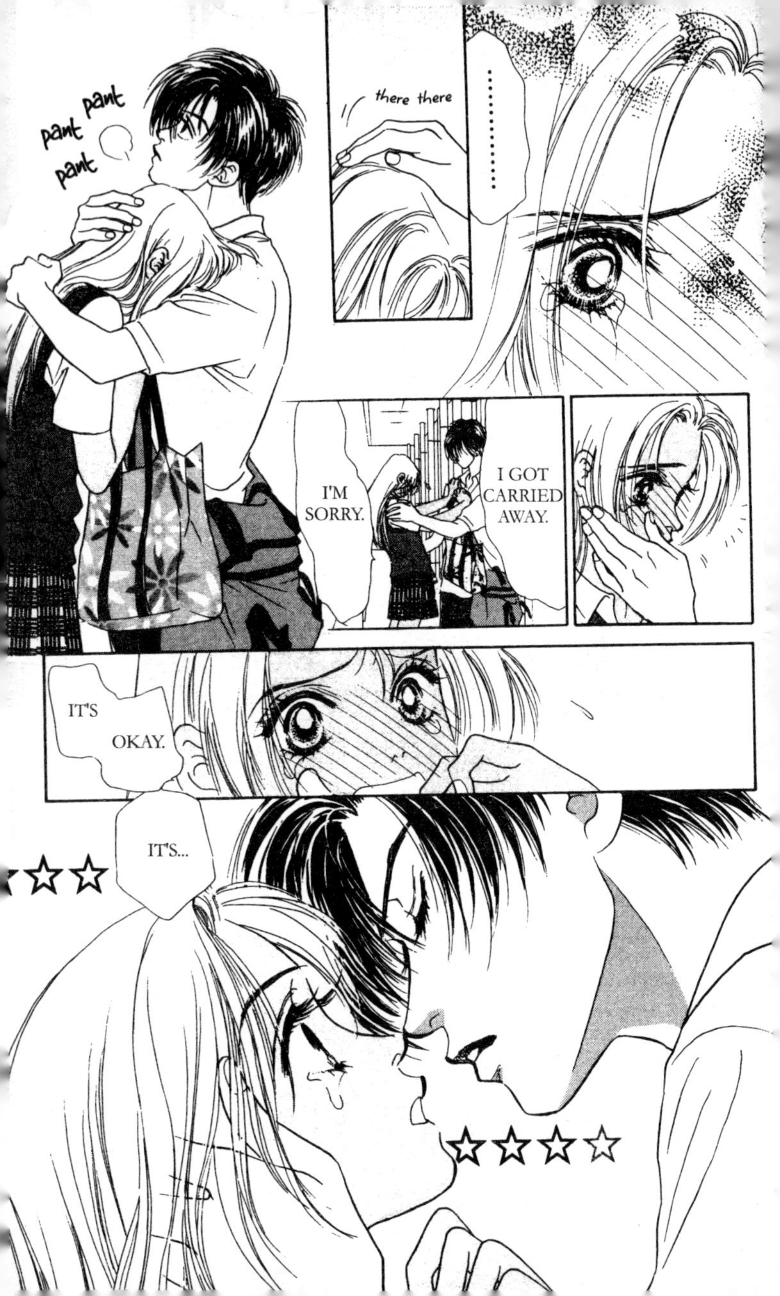
pant pant
pant
there there
....
I'M SORRY.
I GOT CARRIED AWAY.
IT'S OKAY.
IT'S...

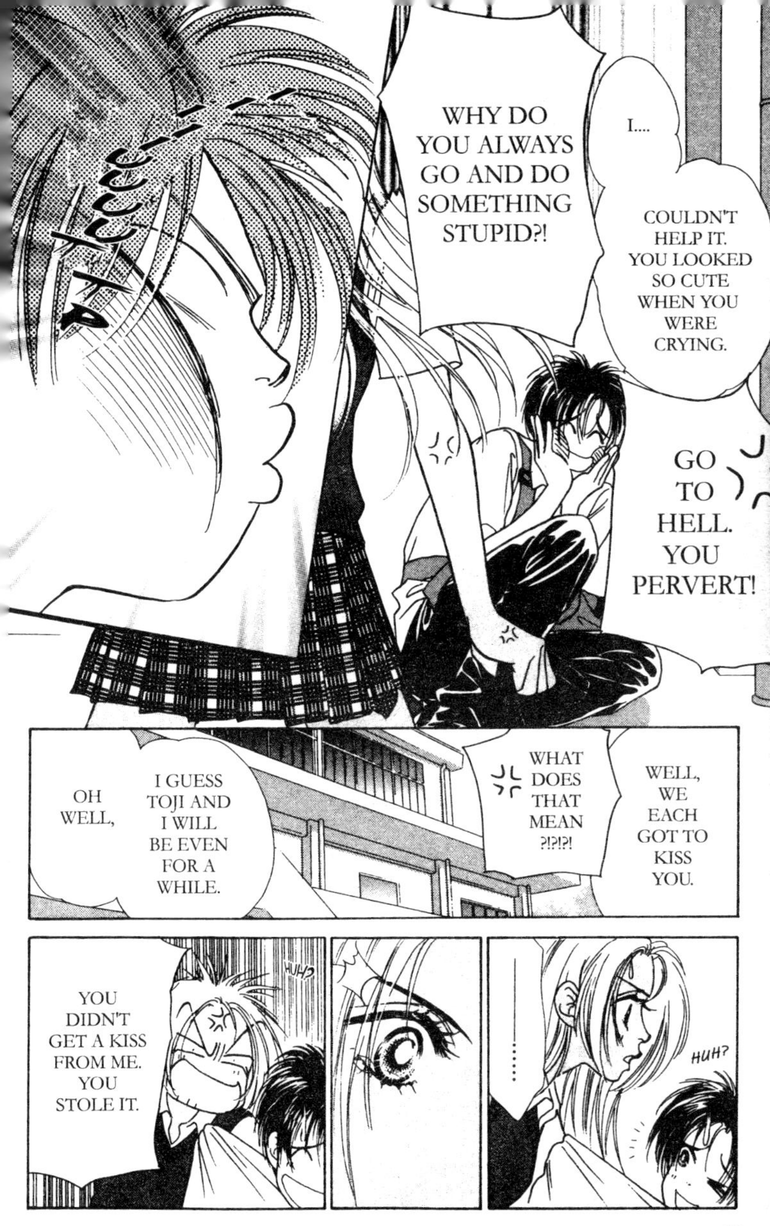
WHY DO YOU ALWAYS GO AND DO SOMETHING STUPID?!
I....
COULDN'T HELP IT. YOU LOOKED SO CUTE WHEN YOU WERE CRYING.
GO TO HELL. YOU PERVERT!
OH WELL,
I GUESS TOJI AND I WILL BE EVEN FOR A WHILE.
WHAT DOES THAT MEAN ?!?!?!
WELL, WE EACH GOT TO KISS YOU.
YOU DIDN'T GET A KISS FROM ME. YOU STOLE IT.
HUH?
......
HUH?

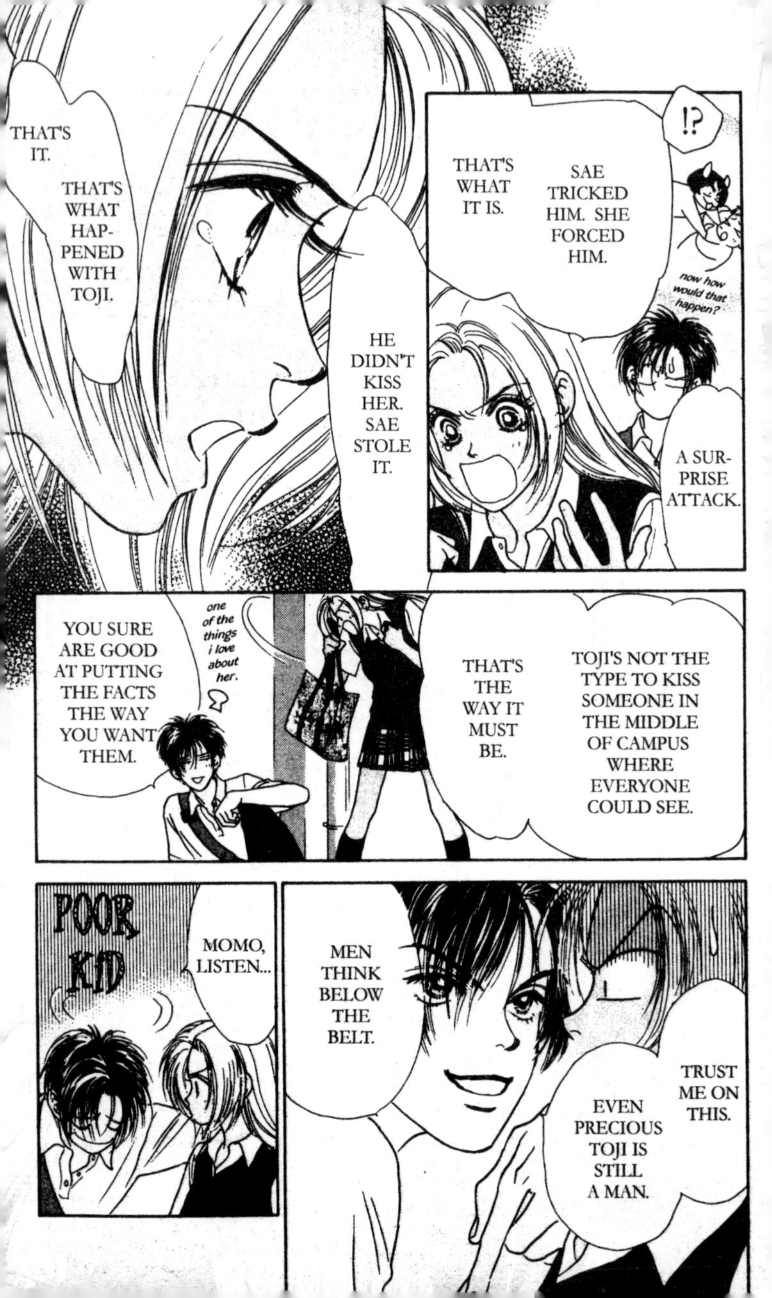
THAT'S IT.
THAT'S WHAT HAP-PENED WITH TOJI.
HE DIDN'T KISS HER. SAE STOLE IT.
THAT'S WHAT IT IS.
SAE TRICKED HIM. SHE FORCED HIM.
!?
now how would that happen?
A SUR-PRISE ATTACK.
YOU SURE ARE GOOD AT PUTTING THE FACTS THE WAY YOU WANT THEM.
one of the things i love about her.
THAT'S THE WAY IT MUST BE.
TOJI'S NOT THE TYPE TO KISS SOMEONE IN THE MIDDLE OF CAMPUS WHERE EVERYONE COULD SEE.
POOR KID
MOMO, LISTEN...
MEN THINK BELOW THE BELT.
TRUST ME ON THIS.
EVEN PRECIOUS TOJI IS STILL A MAN.

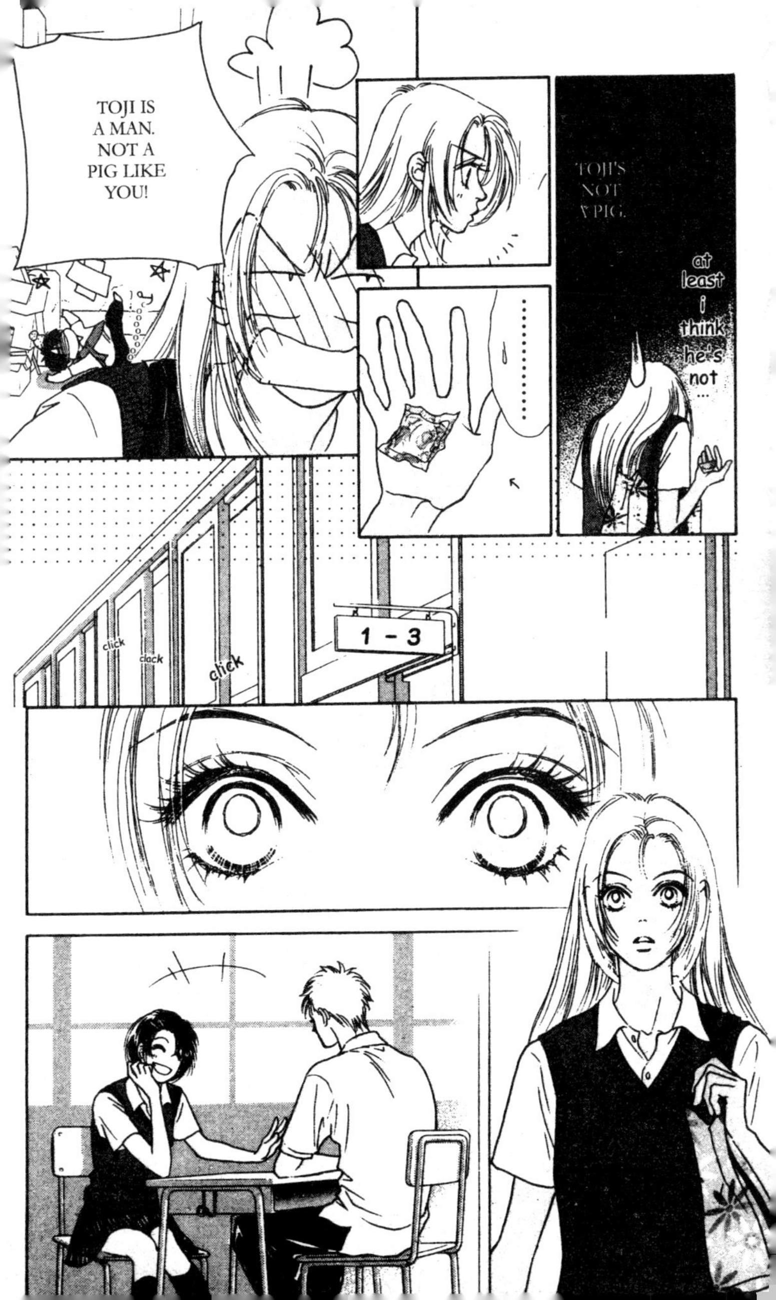
TOJI IS A MAN. NOT A PIG LIKE YOU!
TOJI'S NOT A PIG.
at least i think he's not ...
click
clack
click
1 - 3

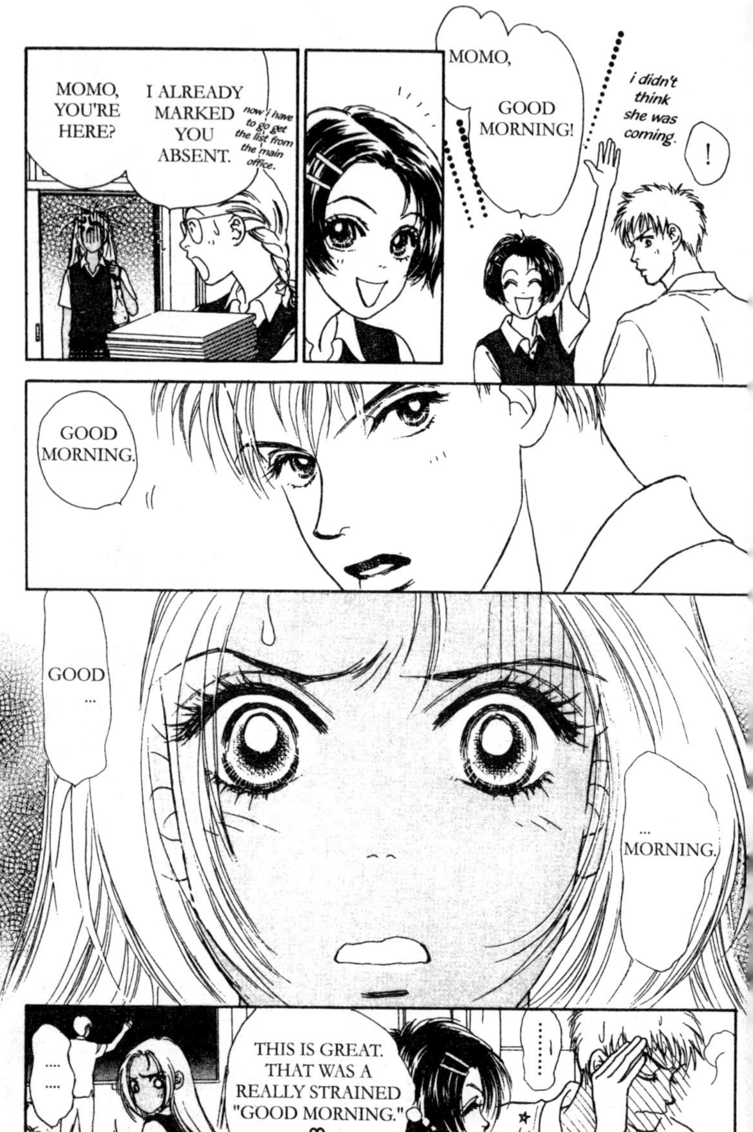
MOMO, YOU'RE HERE?
I ALREADY MARKED YOU ABSENT.
now i have to go get the list from the main office.
MOMO, GOOD MORNING!
i didn't think she was coming.
!
GOOD MORNING.
GOOD ...
... MORNING.
....
THIS IS GREAT. THAT WAS A REALLY STRAINED "GOOD MORNING." ♡
......
hooray hooray

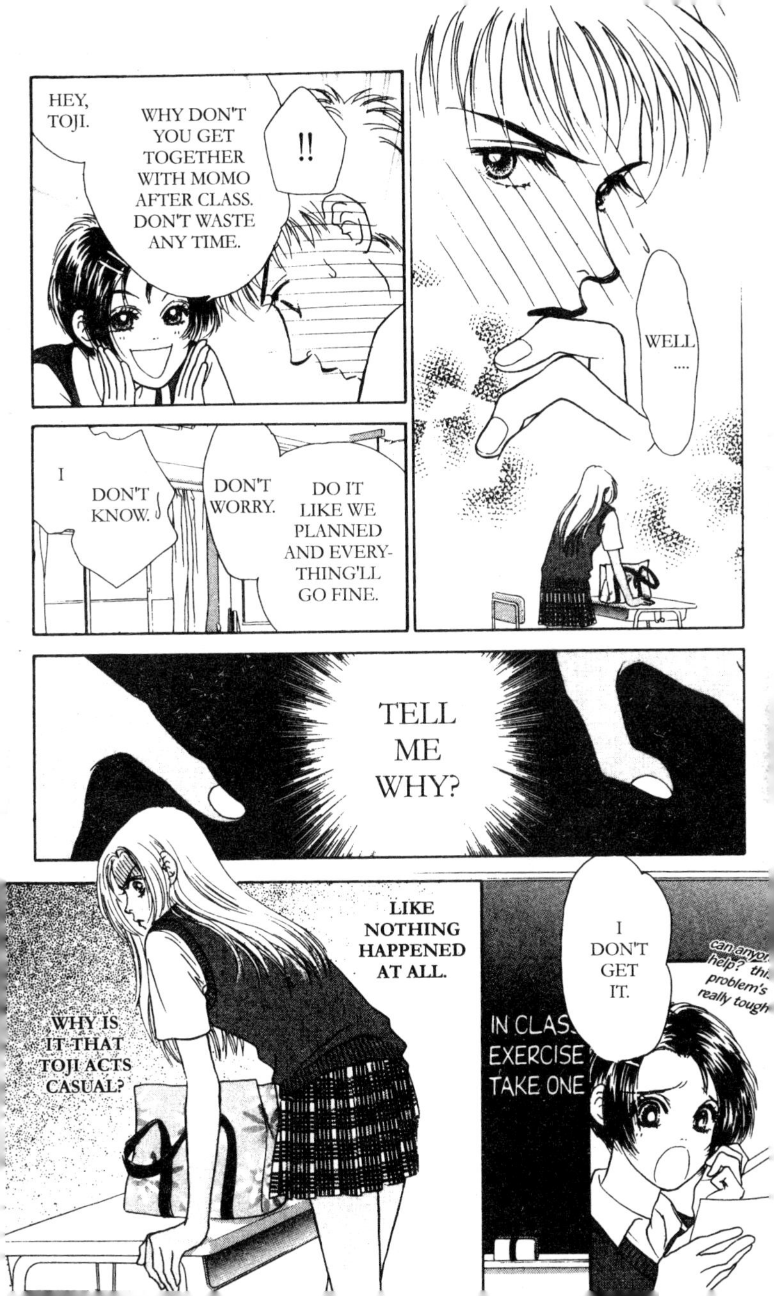
HEY, TOJI.
WHY DON'T YOU GET TOGETHER WITH MOMO AFTER CLASS. DON'T WASTE ANY TIME.
!!
I
DON'T KNOW.
DON'T WORRY.
DO IT LIKE WE PLANNED AND EVERY-THING'LL GO FINE.
WELL ....
TELL ME WHY?
LIKE NOTHING HAPPENED AT ALL.
WHY IS IT THAT TOJI ACTS CASUAL?
I DON'T GET IT.
IN CLAS
EXERCISE
TAKE ONE
can anyo
help? thi
problem's
really tough

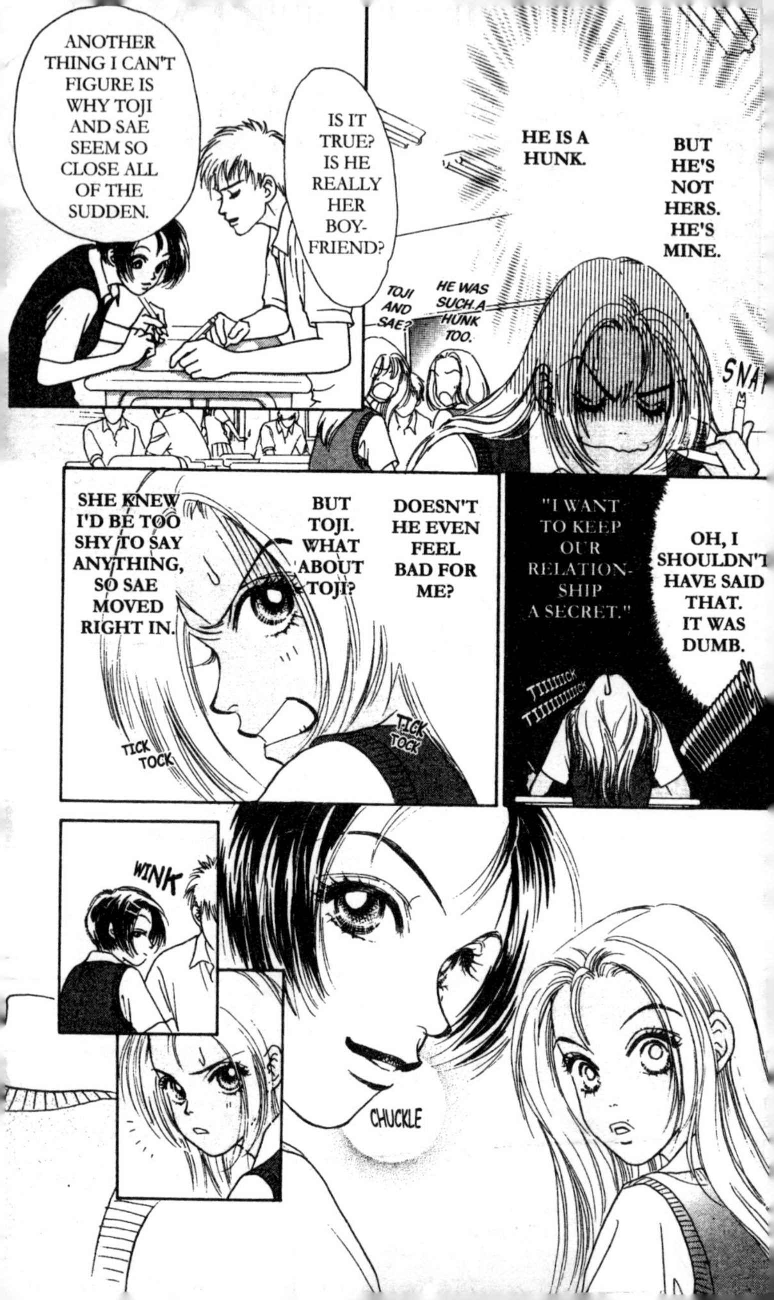
ANOTHER THING I CAN'T FIGURE IS WHY TOJI AND SAE SEEM SO CLOSE ALL OF THE SUDDEN.
IS IT TRUE? IS HE REALLY HER BOY-FRIEND?
HE IS A HUNK.
BUT HE'S NOT HERS. HE'S MINE.
TOJI AND SAE?
HE WAS SUCH A HUNK TOO.
SNAP
SHE KNEW I'D BE TOO SHY TO SAY ANYTHING, SO SAE MOVED RIGHT IN.
BUT TOJI. WHAT ABOUT TOJI?
DOESN'T HE EVEN FEEL BAD FOR ME?
TICK TOCK
TICK TOCK
"I WANT TO KEEP OUR RELATION-SHIP A SECRET."
OH, I SHOULDN'T HAVE SAID THAT. IT WAS DUMB.
TIIIIIICK TIIIIIIIICK
WINK
CHUCKLE

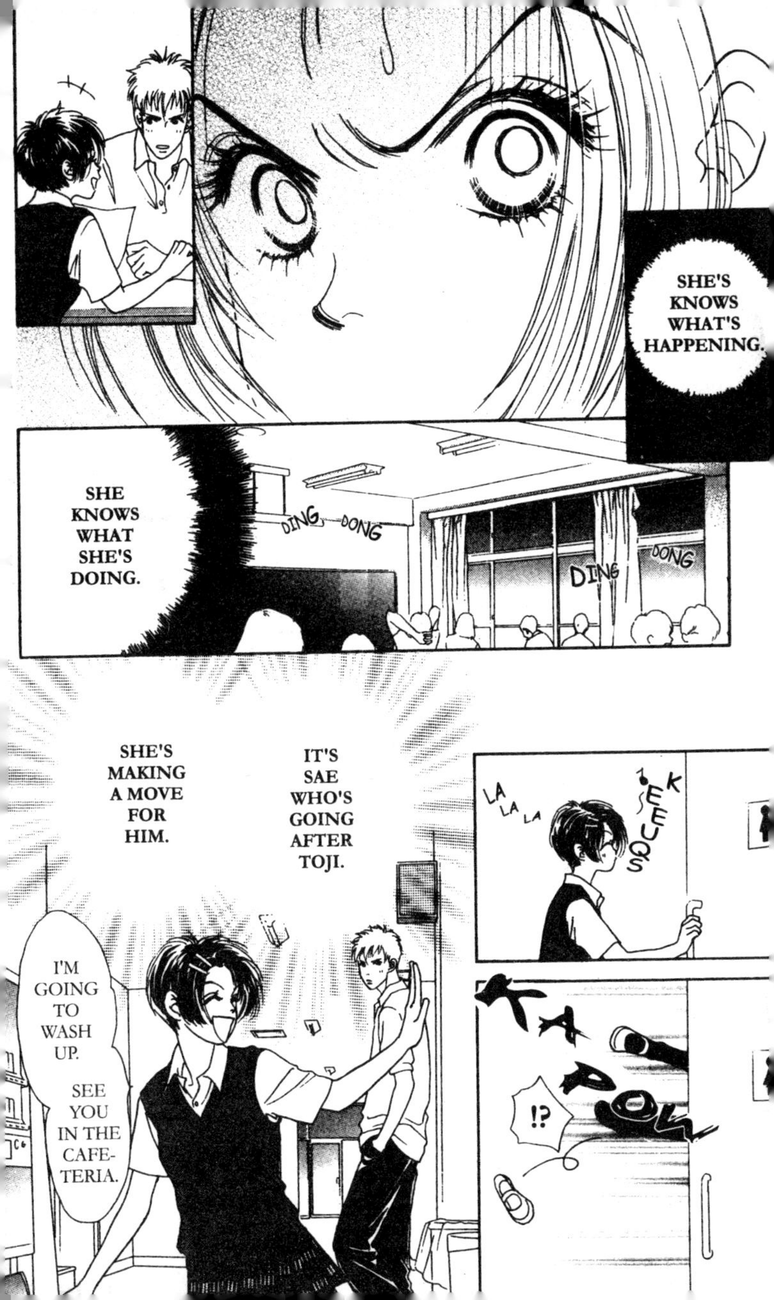
SHE'S KNOWS WHAT'S HAPPENING.
SHE KNOWS WHAT SHE'S DOING.
DING DONG
DING DONG
SHE'S MAKING A MOVE FOR HIM.
IT'S SAE WHO'S GOING AFTER TOJI.
I'M GOING TO WASH UP.
SEE YOU IN THE CAFE-TERIA.
LA LA LA
SQUEEK
KAPOW
!?

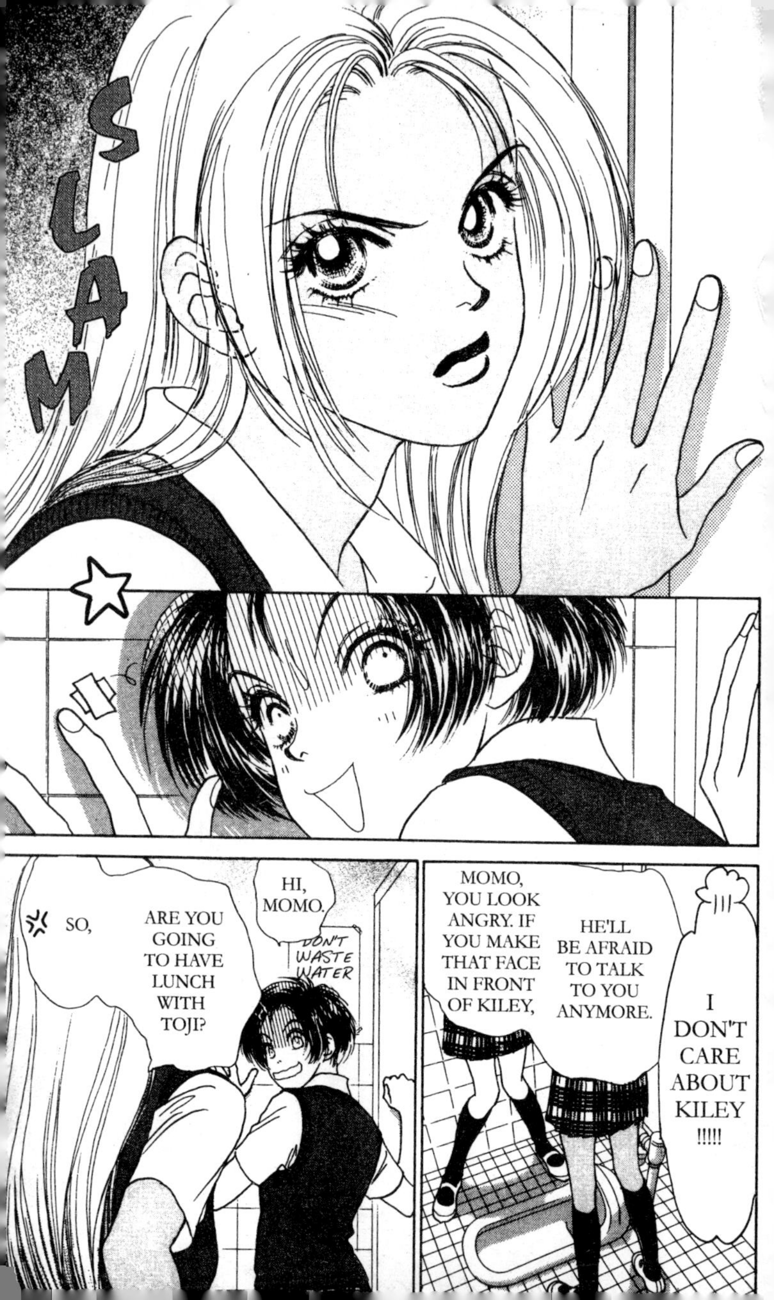
SLAM
SO,
ARE YOU GOING TO HAVE LUNCH WITH TOJI?
HI, MOMO.
DON'T WASTE WATER
MOMO, YOU LOOK ANGRY. IF YOU MAKE THAT FACE IN FRONT OF KILEY,
HE'LL BE AFRAID TO TALK TO YOU ANYMORE.
I DON'T CARE ABOUT KILEY !!!!!

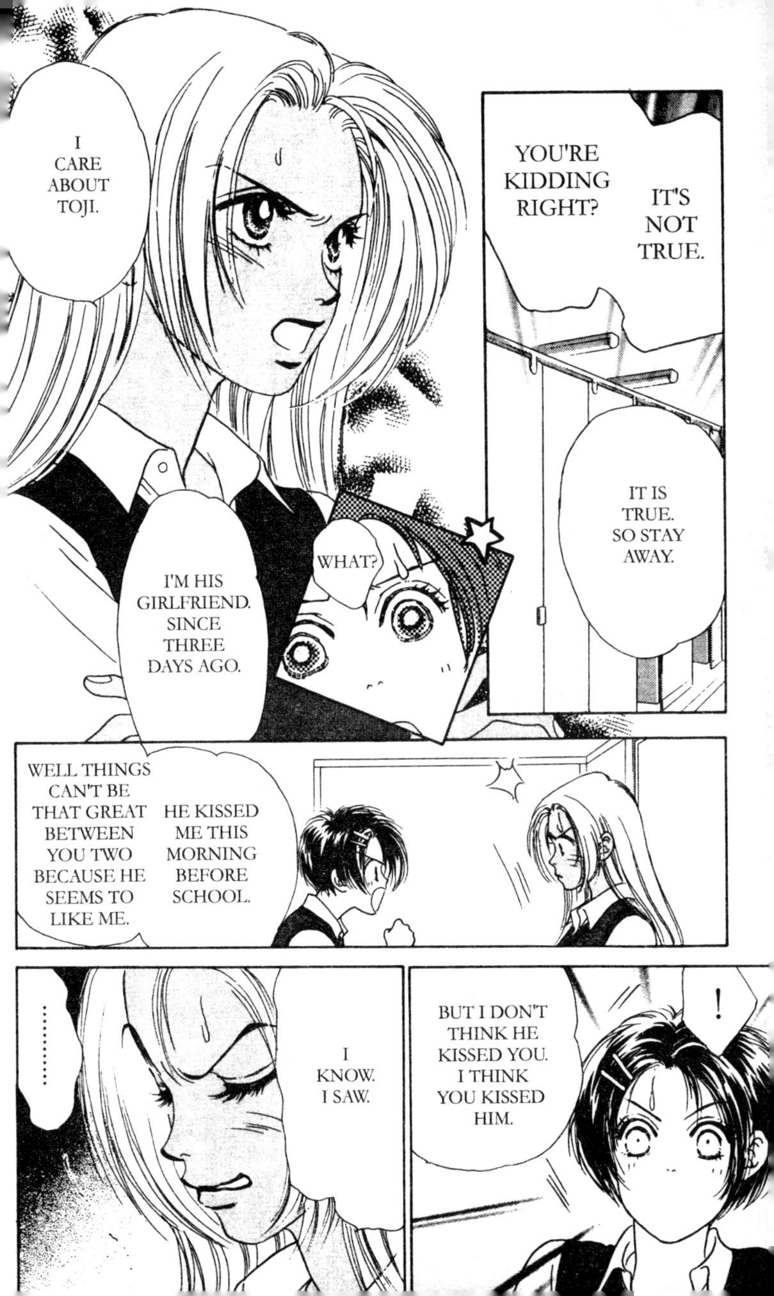
I CARE ABOUT TOJI.
I'M HIS GIRLFRIEND. SINCE THREE DAYS AGO.
WHAT?
YOU'RE KIDDING RIGHT?
IT'S NOT TRUE.
IT IS TRUE. SO STAY AWAY.
WELL THINGS CAN'T BE THAT GREAT BETWEEN YOU TWO BECAUSE HE SEEMS TO LIKE ME.
HE KISSED ME THIS MORNING BEFORE SCHOOL.
....
I KNOW. I SAW.
BUT I DON'T THINK HE KISSED YOU. I THINK YOU KISSED HIM.
!

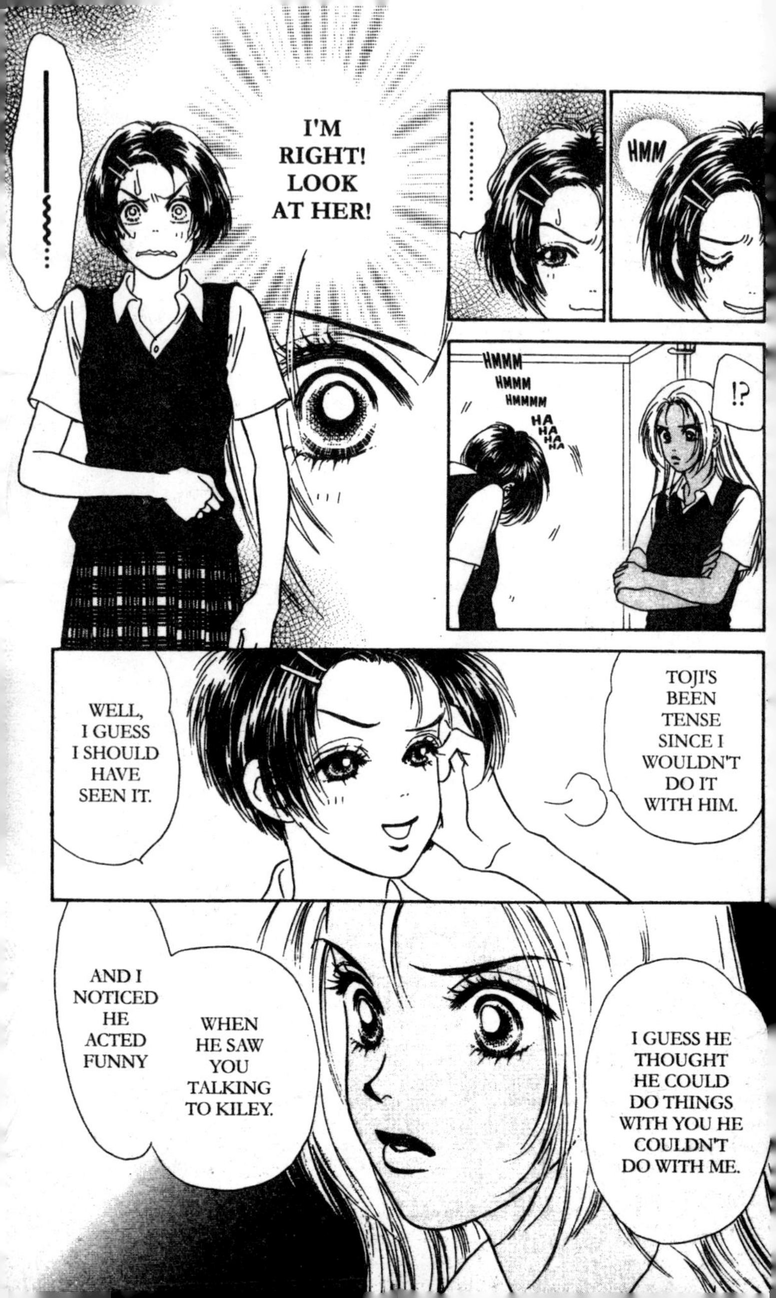

―――…
I'M RIGHT! LOOK AT HER!
……
HMM
HMMM HMMM HMMMM
HA HA HA HA
!?
WELL, I GUESS I SHOULD HAVE SEEN IT.
TOJI'S BEEN TENSE SINCE I WOULDN'T DO IT WITH HIM.
AND I NOTICED HE ACTED FUNNY
WHEN HE SAW YOU TALKING TO KILEY.
I GUESS HE THOUGHT HE COULD DO THINGS WITH YOU HE COULDN'T DO WITH ME.

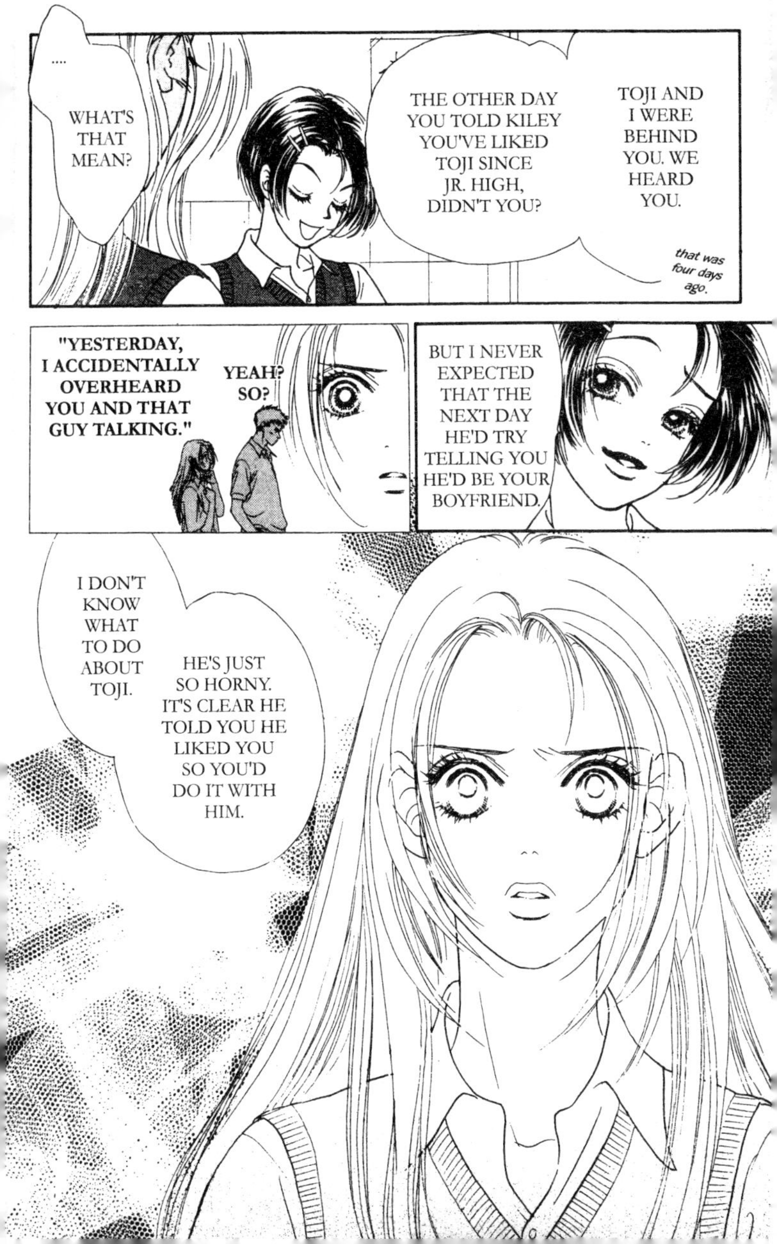
....
WHAT'S THAT MEAN?
THE OTHER DAY YOU TOLD KILEY YOU'VE LIKED TOJI SINCE JR. HIGH, DIDN'T YOU?
TOJI AND I WERE BEHIND YOU. WE HEARD YOU.
that was four days ago.
"YESTERDAY, I ACCIDENTALLY OVERHEARD YOU AND THAT GUY TALKING."
YEAH? SO?
BUT I NEVER EXPECTED THAT THE NEXT DAY HE'D TRY TELLING YOU HE'D BE YOUR BOYFRIEND.
I DON'T KNOW WHAT TO DO ABOUT TOJI.
HE'S JUST SO HORNY. IT'S CLEAR HE TOLD YOU HE LIKED YOU SO YOU'D DO IT WITH HIM.

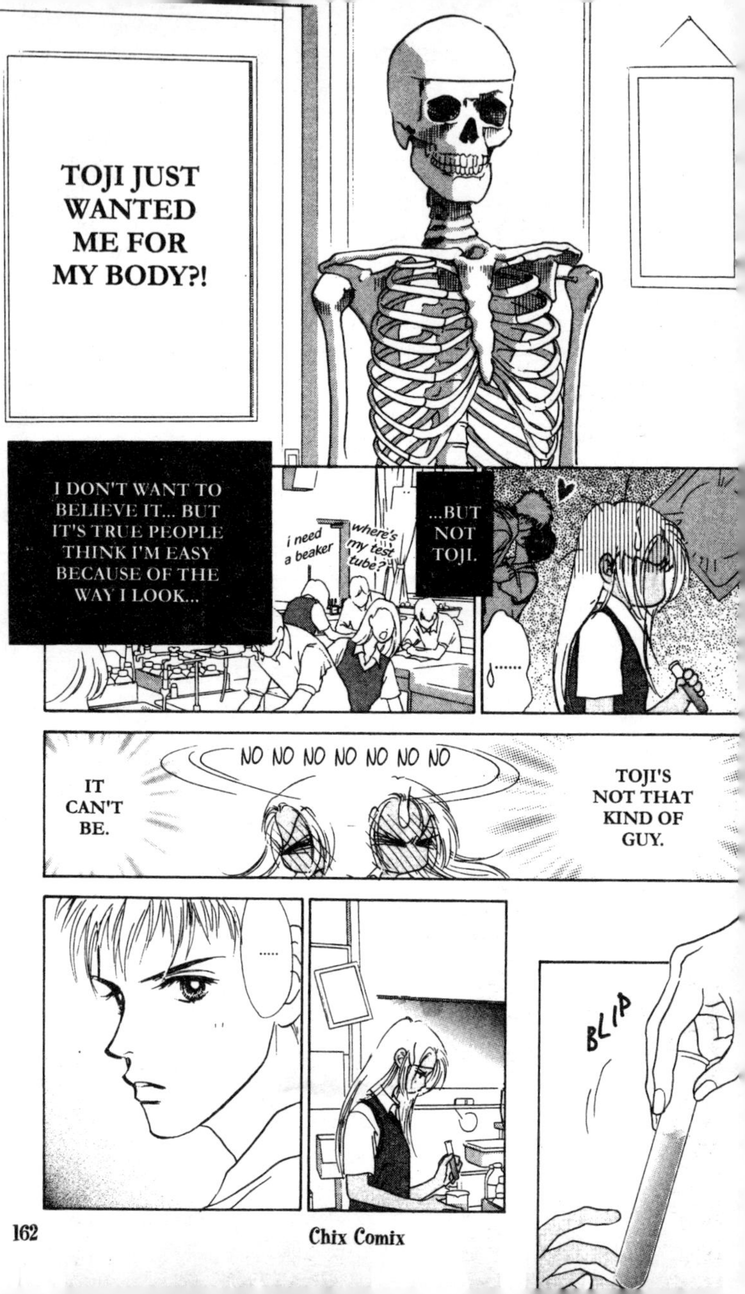

TOJI JUST WANTED ME FOR MY BODY?!
I DON'T WANT TO BELIEVE IT... BUT IT'S TRUE PEOPLE THINK I'M EASY BECAUSE OF THE WAY I LOOK...
i need a beaker
where's my test tube?
...BUT NOT TOJI.
......
IT CAN'T BE.
NO NO NO NO NO NO NO
TOJI'S NOT THAT KIND OF GUY.
.....
BLIP

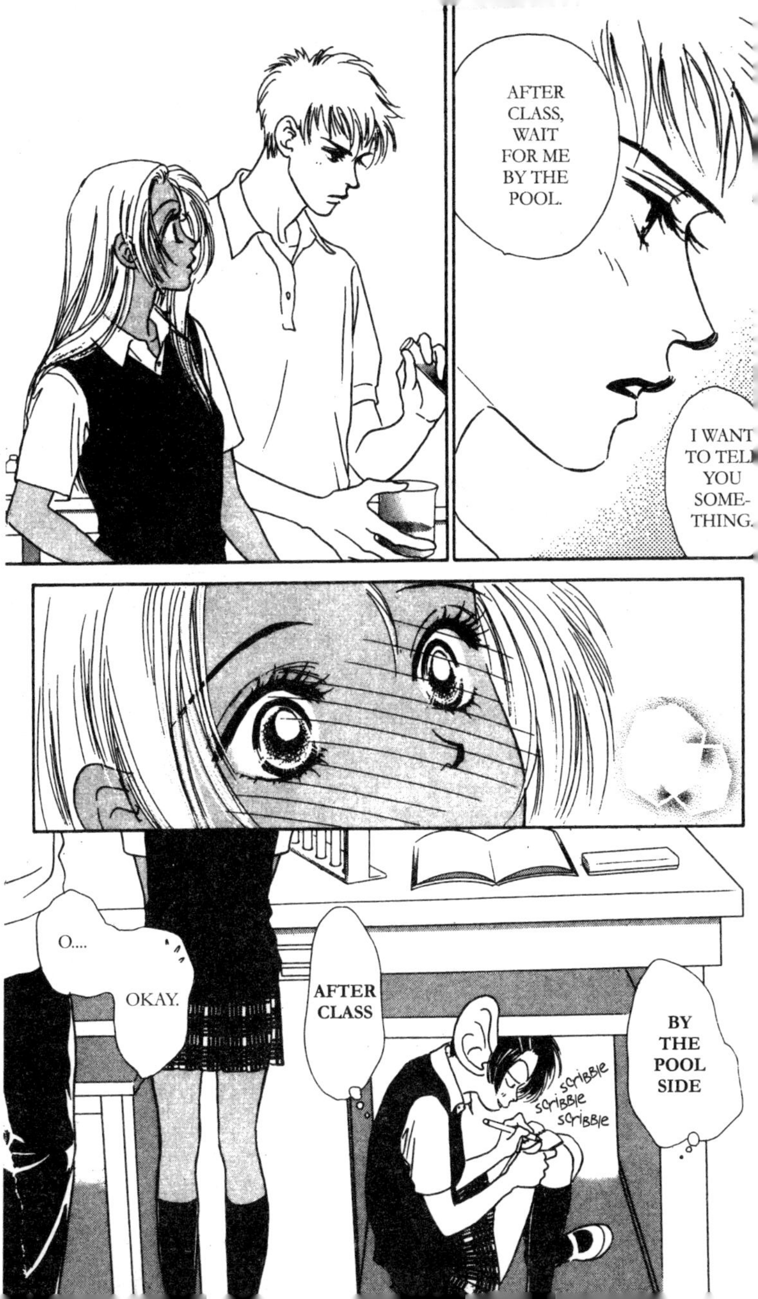
AFTER CLASS, WAIT FOR ME BY THE POOL.
I WANT TO TELL YOU SOME-THING.
O....
OKAY.
AFTER CLASS
BY THE POOL SIDE
SCRIBBLE SCRIBBLE SCRIBBLE

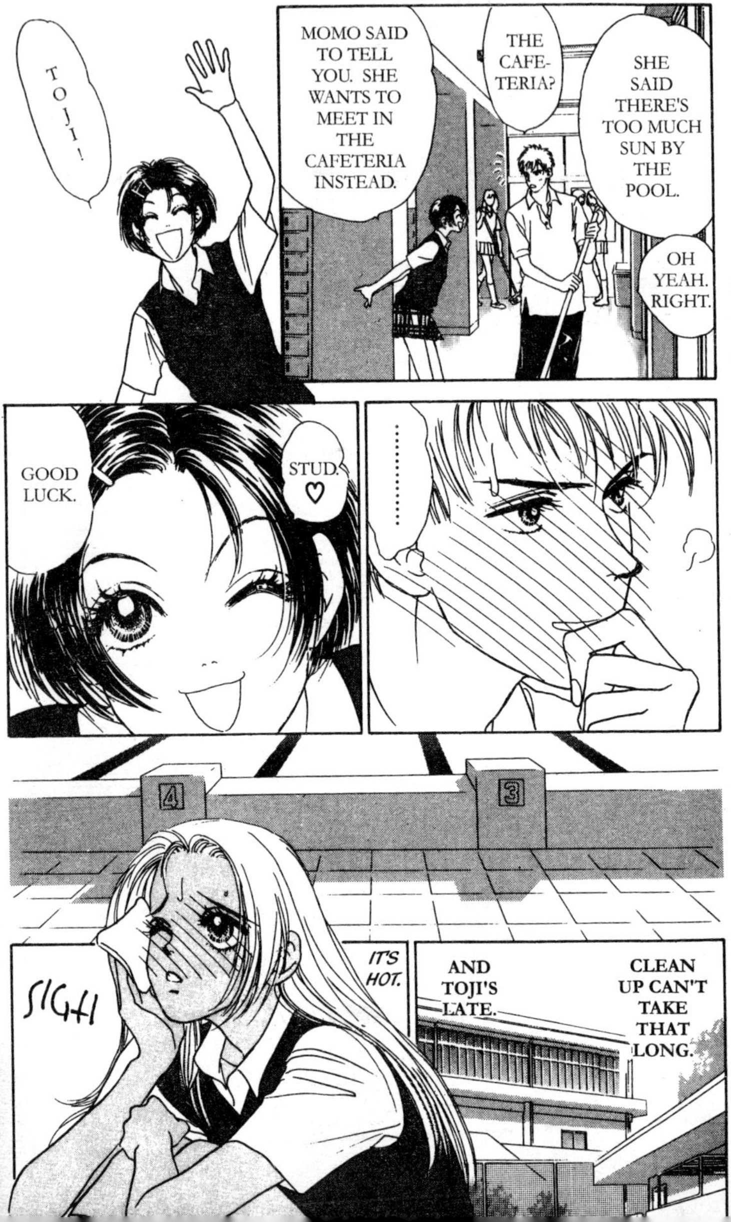
TOJI!
MOMO SAID TO TELL YOU. SHE WANTS TO MEET IN THE CAFETERIA INSTEAD.
THE CAFE-TERIA?
SHE SAID THERE'S TOO MUCH SUN BY THE POOL.
OH YEAH. RIGHT.
GOOD LUCK.
STUD. ♡
......
SIGH
IT'S HOT.
AND TOJI'S LATE.
CLEAN UP CAN'T TAKE THAT LONG.

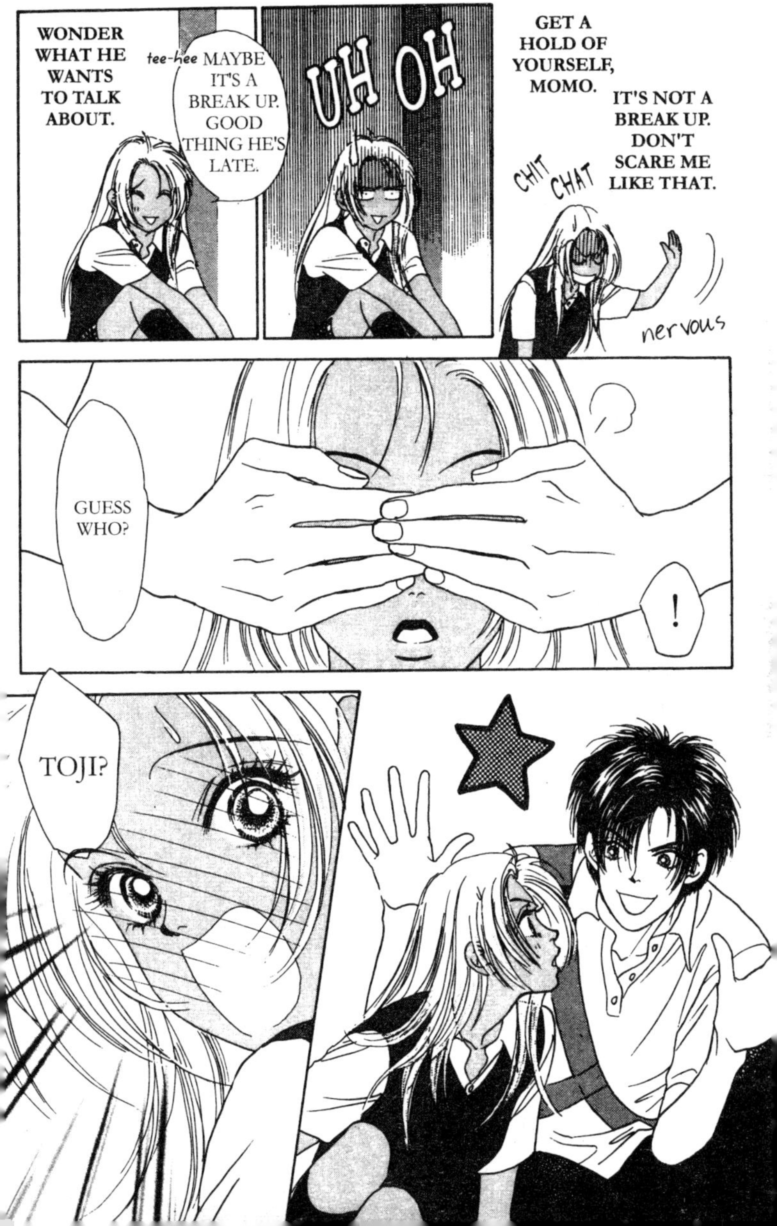
WONDER WHAT HE WANTS TO TALK ABOUT.
tee-hee
MAYBE IT'S A BREAK UP. GOOD THING HE'S LATE.
UH OH
GET A HOLD OF YOURSELF, MOMO.
IT'S NOT A BREAK UP. DON'T SCARE ME LIKE THAT.
CHIT CHAT
nervous
GUESS WHO?
!
TOJI?

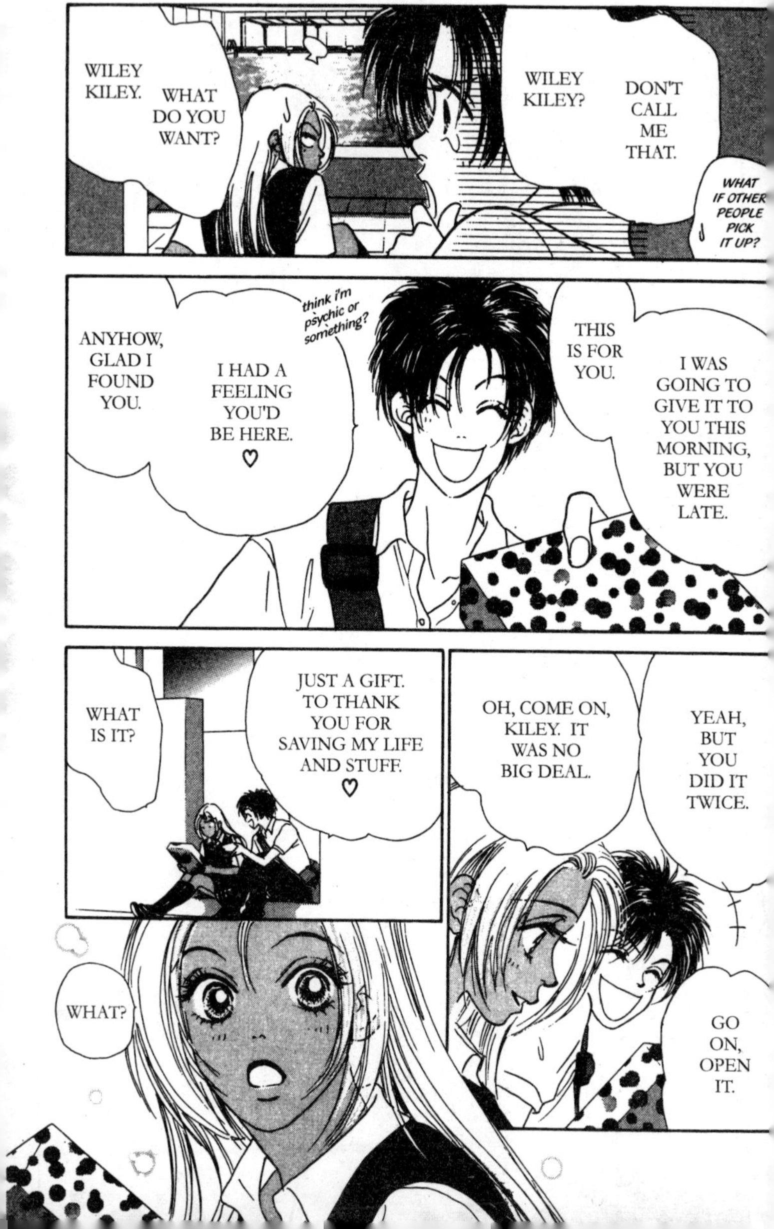
WILEY KILEY.
WHAT DO YOU WANT?
WILEY KILEY?
DON'T CALL ME THAT.
WHAT IF OTHER PEOPLE PICK IT UP?
ANYHOW, GLAD I FOUND YOU.
I HAD A FEELING YOU'D BE HERE. ♡
think i'm psychic or something?
THIS IS FOR YOU.
I WAS GOING TO GIVE IT TO YOU THIS MORNING, BUT YOU WERE LATE.
WHAT IS IT?
JUST A GIFT. TO THANK YOU FOR SAVING MY LIFE AND STUFF. ♡
WHAT?
OH, COME ON, KILEY. IT WAS NO BIG DEAL.
YEAH, BUT YOU DID IT TWICE.
GO ON, OPEN IT.

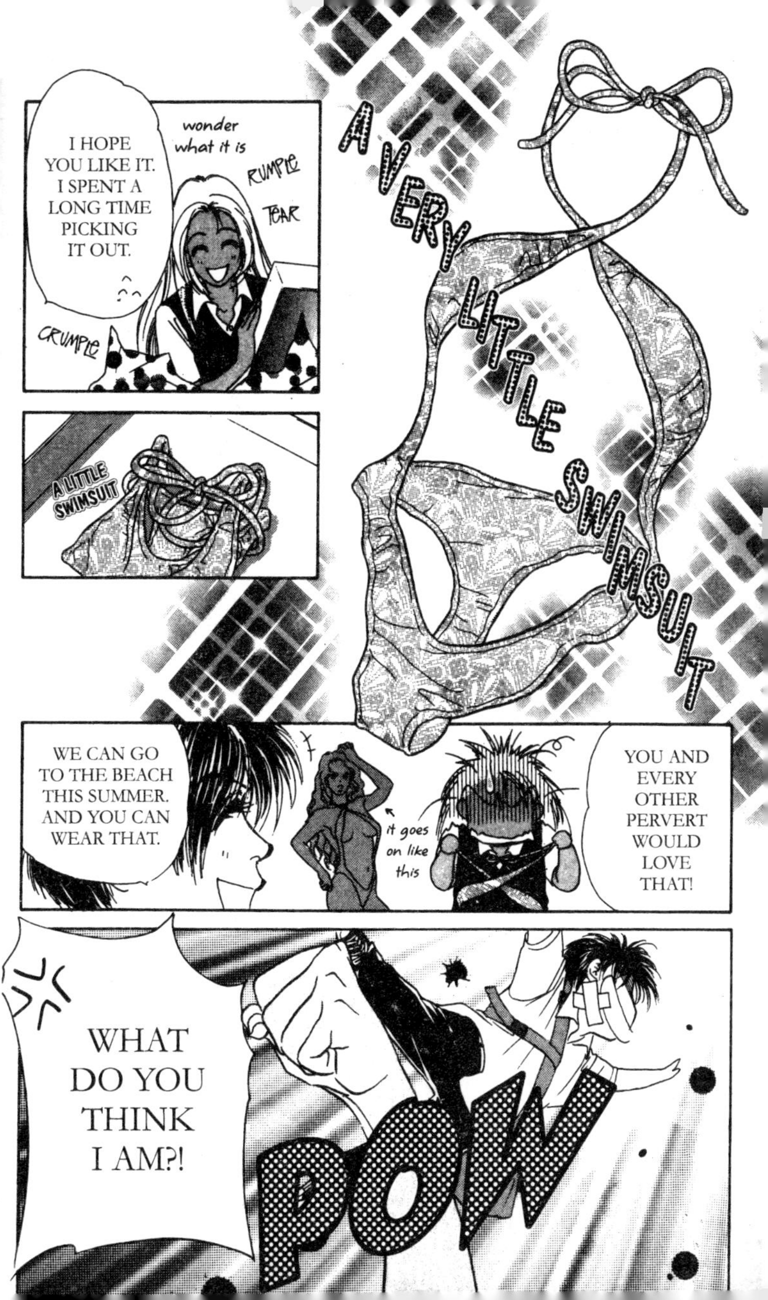
I HOPE YOU LIKE IT. I SPENT A LONG TIME PICKING IT OUT.
wonder what it is
RUMPLE
TEAR
CRUMPLE
A VERY LITTLE SWIMSUIT
A LITTLE SWIMSUIT
WE CAN GO TO THE BEACH THIS SUMMER. AND YOU CAN WEAR THAT.
it goes on like this
YOU AND EVERY OTHER PERVERT WOULD LOVE THAT!
WHAT DO YOU THINK I AM?!
POW

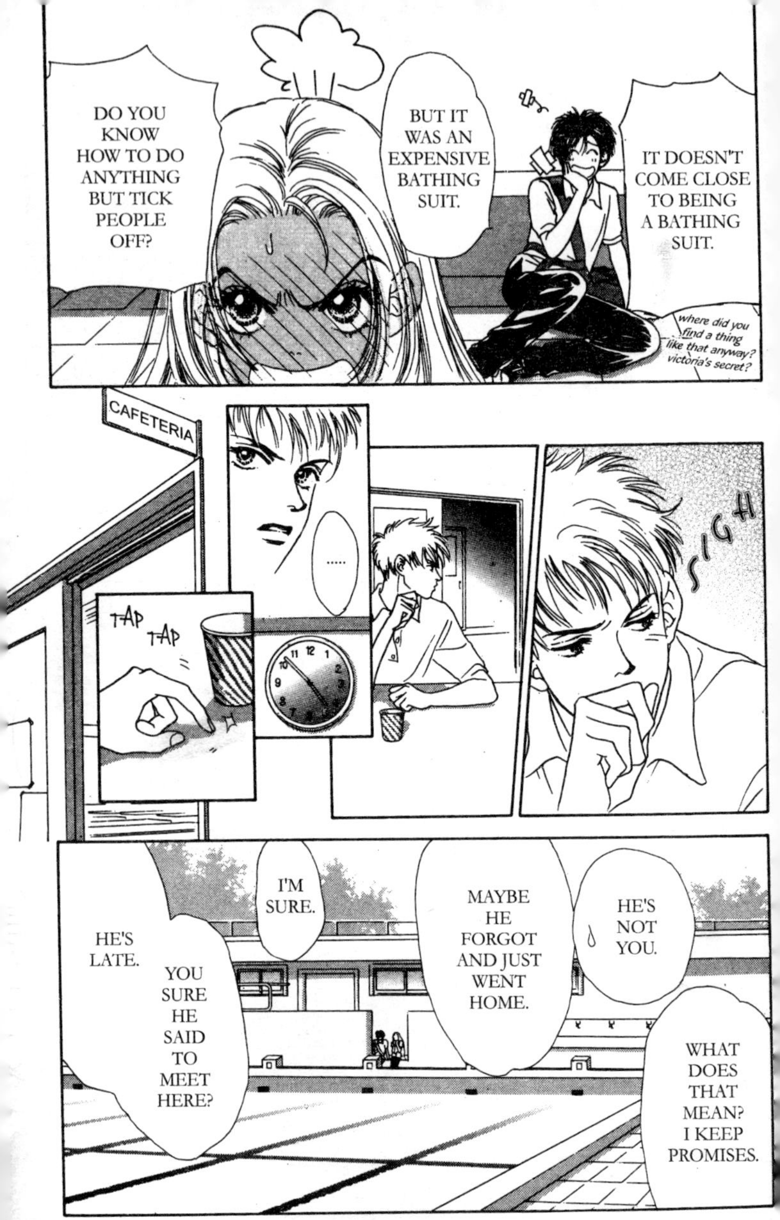
DO YOU KNOW HOW TO DO ANYTHING BUT TICK PEOPLE OFF?
BUT IT WAS AN EXPENSIVE BATHING SUIT.
IT DOESN'T COME CLOSE TO BEING A BATHING SUIT.
where did you find a thing like that anyway? victoria's secret?
CAFETERIA
TAP TAP
.....
SIGH
HE'S LATE.
YOU SURE HE SAID TO MEET HERE?
I'M SURE.
MAYBE HE FORGOT AND JUST WENT HOME.
HE'S NOT YOU.
WHAT DOES THAT MEAN? I KEEP PROMISES.

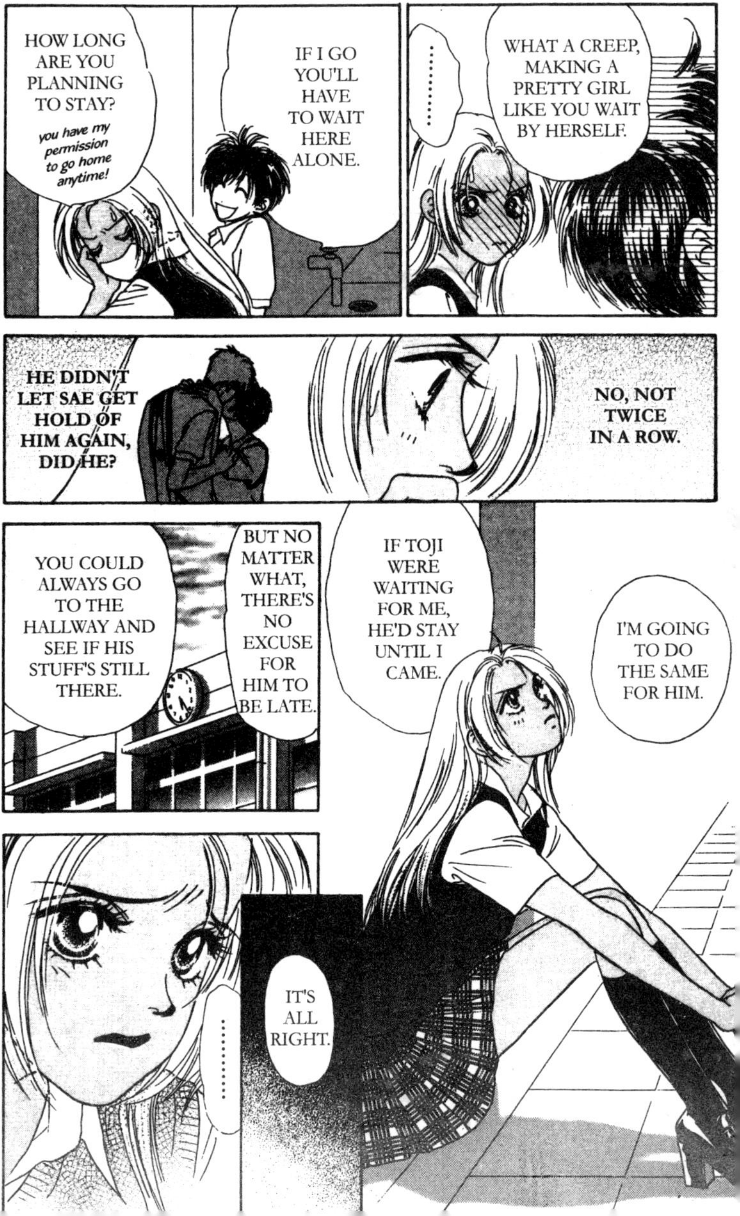
HOW LONG ARE YOU PLANNING TO STAY?
you have my permission to go home anytime!
IF I GO YOU'LL HAVE TO WAIT HERE ALONE.
......
WHAT A CREEP, MAKING A PRETTY GIRL LIKE YOU WAIT BY HERSELF.
HE DIDN'T LET SAE GET HOLD OF HIM AGAIN, DID HE?
NO, NOT TWICE IN A ROW.
YOU COULD ALWAYS GO TO THE HALLWAY AND SEE IF HIS STUFF'S STILL THERE.
BUT NO MATTER WHAT, THERE'S NO EXCUSE FOR HIM TO BE LATE.
......
IF TOJI WERE WAITING FOR ME, HE'D STAY UNTIL I CAME.
I'M GOING TO DO THE SAME FOR HIM.
IT'S ALL RIGHT.

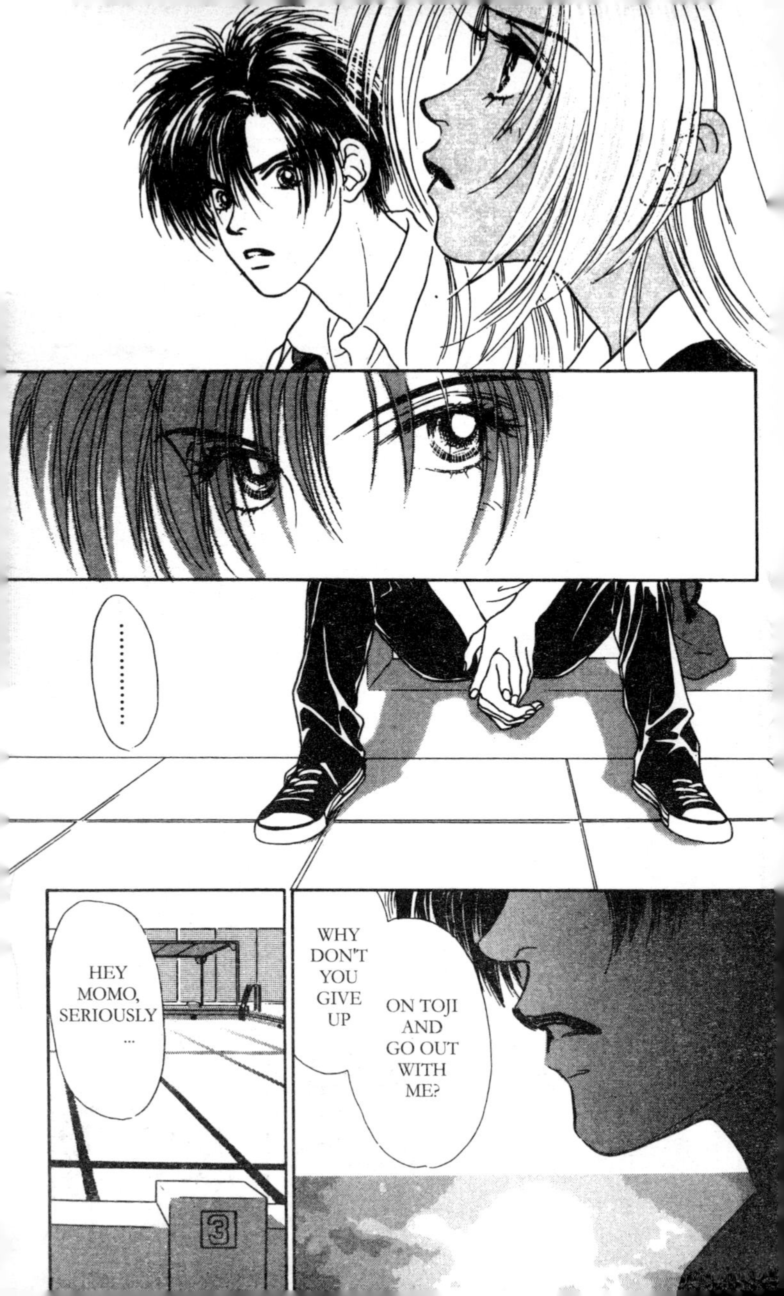
....
HEY MOMO, SERIOUSLY ...
WHY DON'T YOU GIVE UP
ON TOJI AND GO OUT WITH ME?

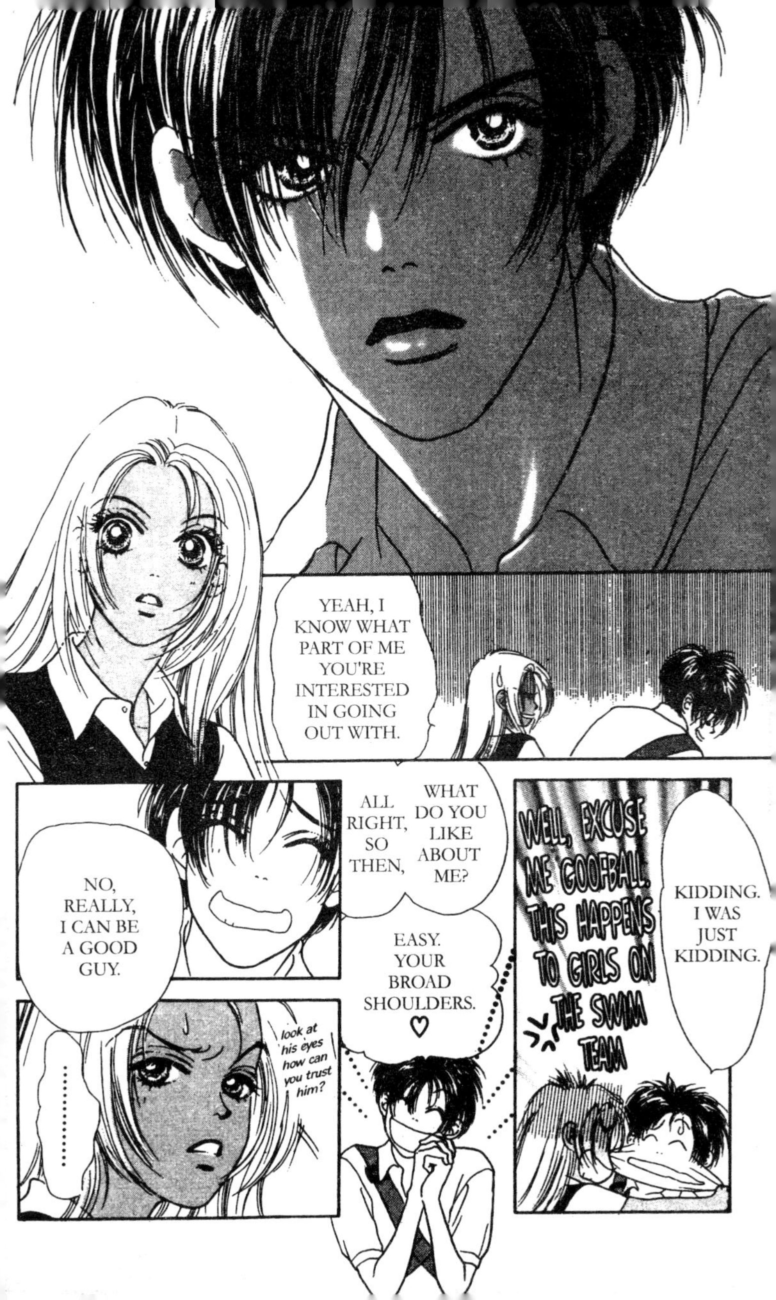
YEAH, I KNOW WHAT PART OF ME YOU'RE INTERESTED IN GOING OUT WITH.
NO, REALLY, I CAN BE A GOOD GUY.
......
look at his eyes how can you trust him?
ALL RIGHT, SO THEN,
WHAT DO YOU LIKE ABOUT ME?
EASY. YOUR BROAD SHOULDERS. ♡
WELL, EXCUSE ME GOOFBALL. THIS HAPPENS TO GIRLS ON THE SWIM TEAM
KIDDING. I WAS JUST KIDDING.

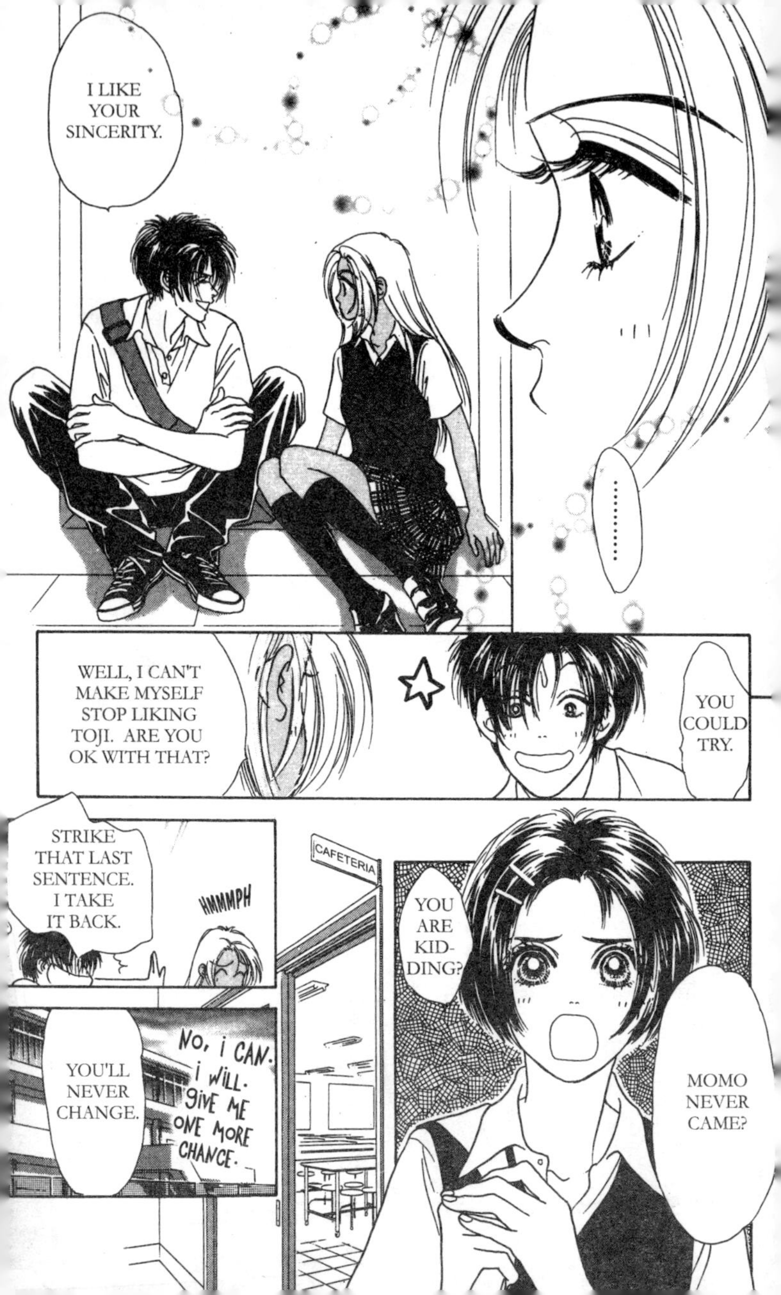
I LIKE YOUR SINCERITY.
......
WELL, I CAN'T MAKE MYSELF STOP LIKING TOJI. ARE YOU OK WITH THAT?
YOU COULD TRY.
STRIKE THAT LAST SENTENCE. I TAKE IT BACK.
HMMMPH
YOU'LL NEVER CHANGE.
No, i CAN. i WILL. give ME ONE MORE CHANCE.
CAFETERIA
YOU ARE KID-DING?
MOMO NEVER CAME?

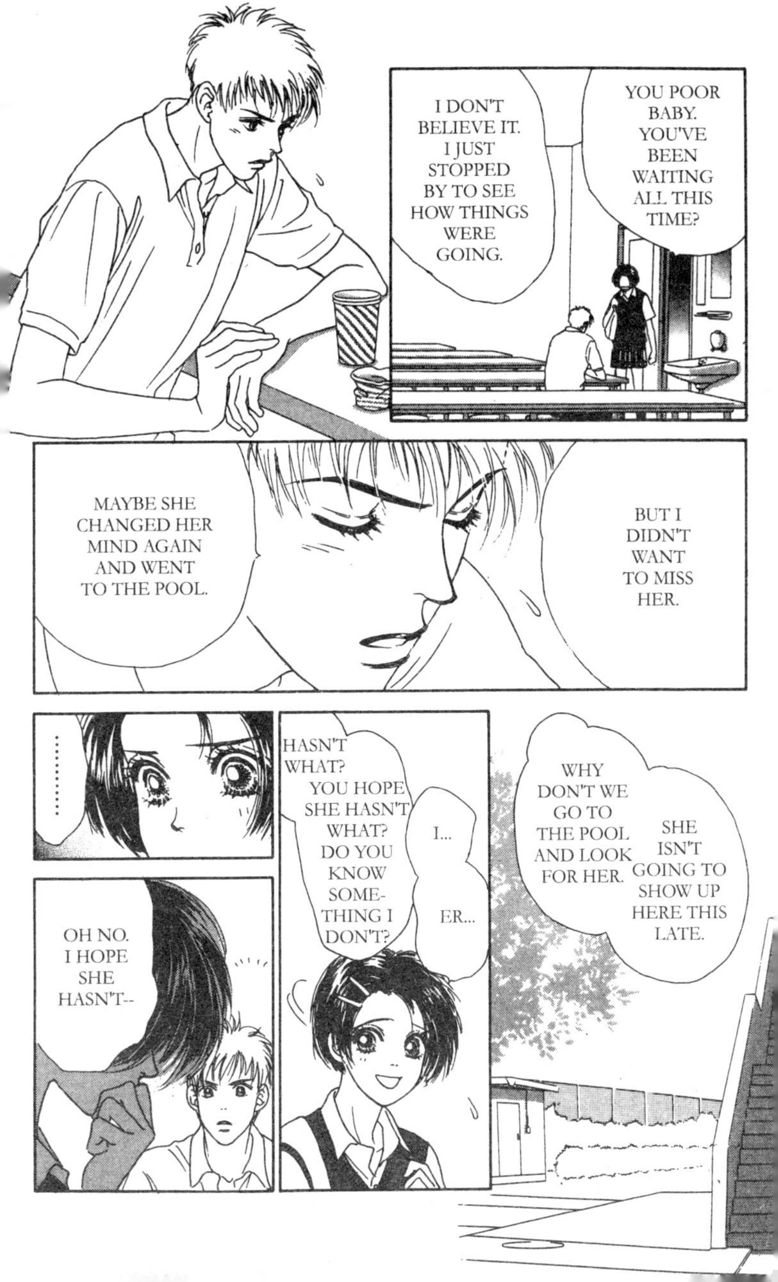

I DON'T BELIEVE IT. I JUST STOPPED BY TO SEE HOW THINGS WERE GOING.
YOU POOR BABY. YOU'VE BEEN WAITING ALL THIS TIME?
MAYBE SHE CHANGED HER MIND AGAIN AND WENT TO THE POOL.
BUT I DIDN'T WANT TO MISS HER.
....
OH NO. I HOPE SHE HASN'T--
HASN'T WHAT?
YOU HOPE SHE HASN'T WHAT? DO YOU KNOW SOME-THING I DON'T?
I...
ER...
WHY DON'T WE GO TO THE POOL AND LOOK FOR HER.
SHE ISN'T GOING TO SHOW UP HERE THIS LATE.

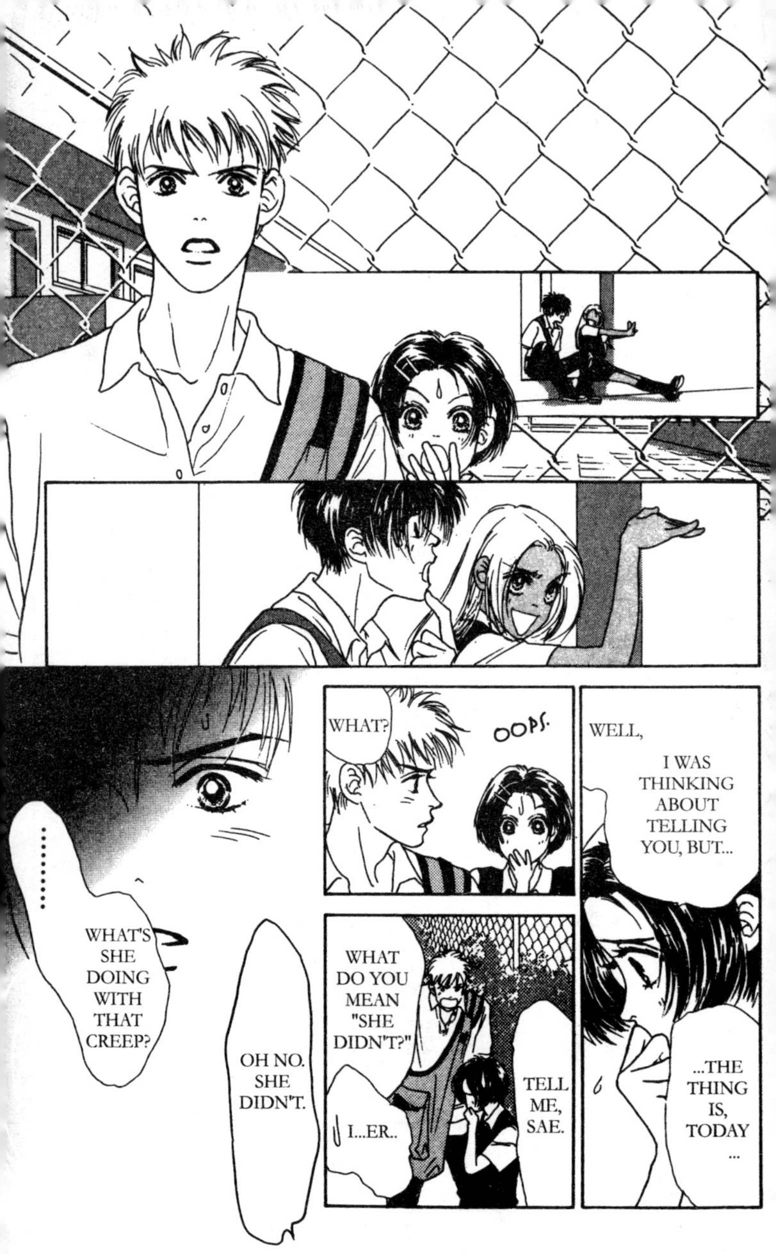

......
WHAT'S SHE DOING WITH THAT CREEP?
OH NO. SHE DIDN'T.
WHAT?
OOPS.
WHAT DO YOU MEAN "SHE DIDN'T?"
TELL ME, SAE.
I...ER..
WELL,
I WAS THINKING ABOUT TELLING YOU, BUT...
...THE THING IS, TODAY ...

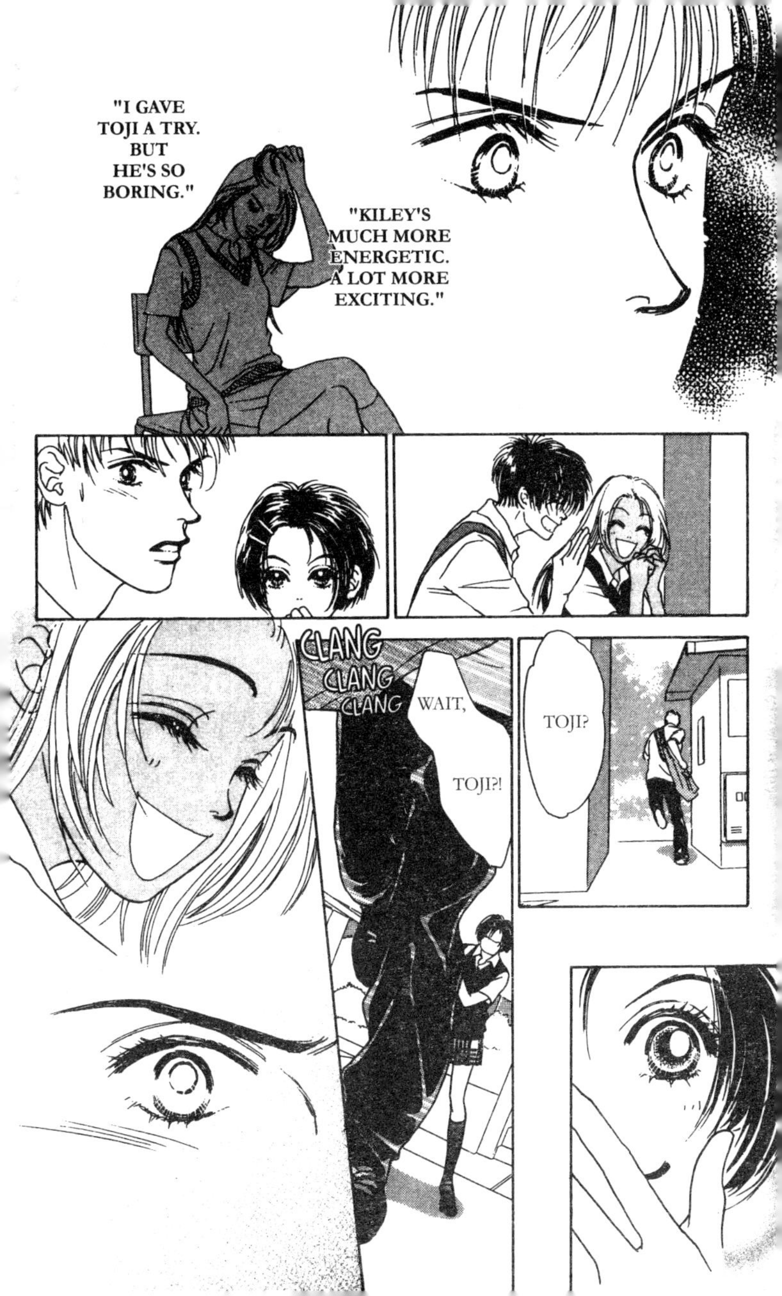
"I GAVE TOJI A TRY. BUT HE'S SO BORING."
"KILEY'S MUCH MORE ENERGETIC. A LOT MORE EXCITING."
CLANG CLANG CLANG
WAIT,
TOJI?!
TOJI?

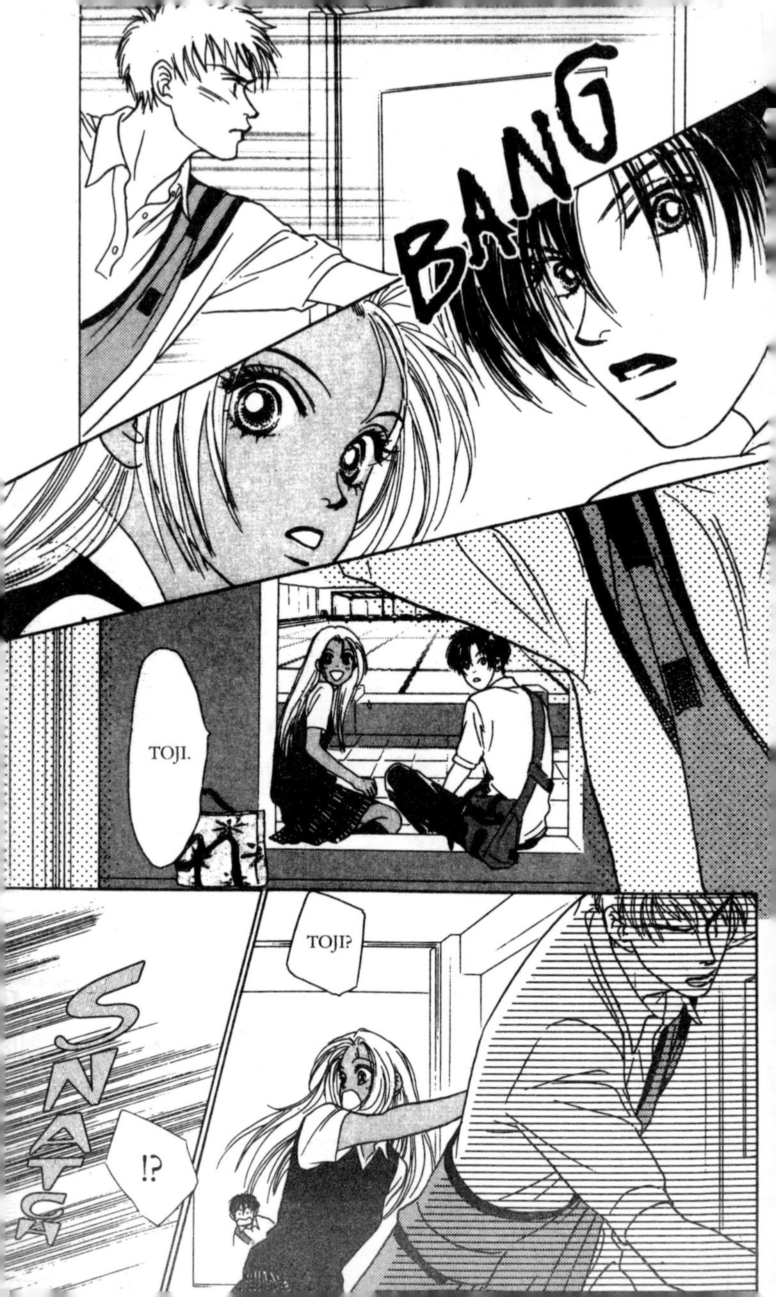
BANG
TOJI.
SNATCH
!?
TOJI?

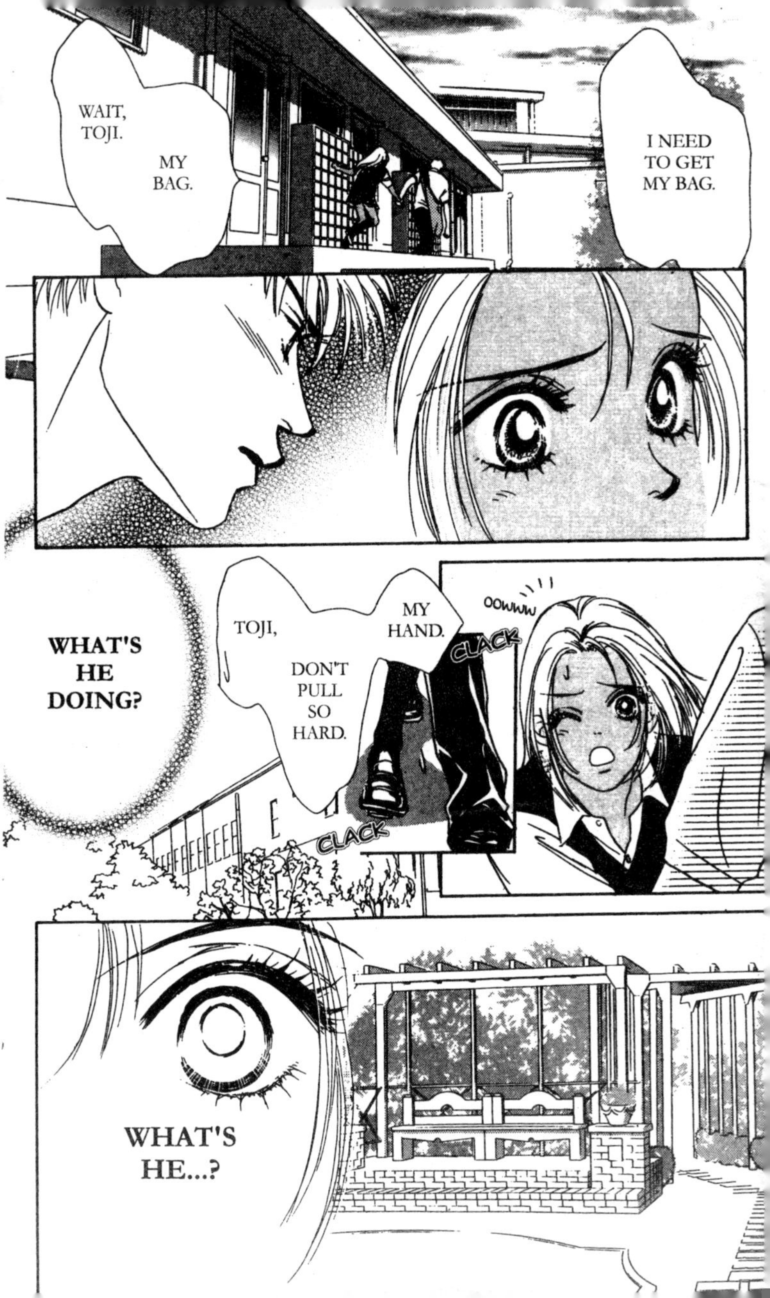
WAIT, TOJI.
MY BAG.
I NEED TO GET MY BAG.
WHAT'S HE DOING?
TOJI,
DON'T PULL SO HARD.
MY HAND.
CLACK
CLACK
OOWWW
WHAT'S HE...?

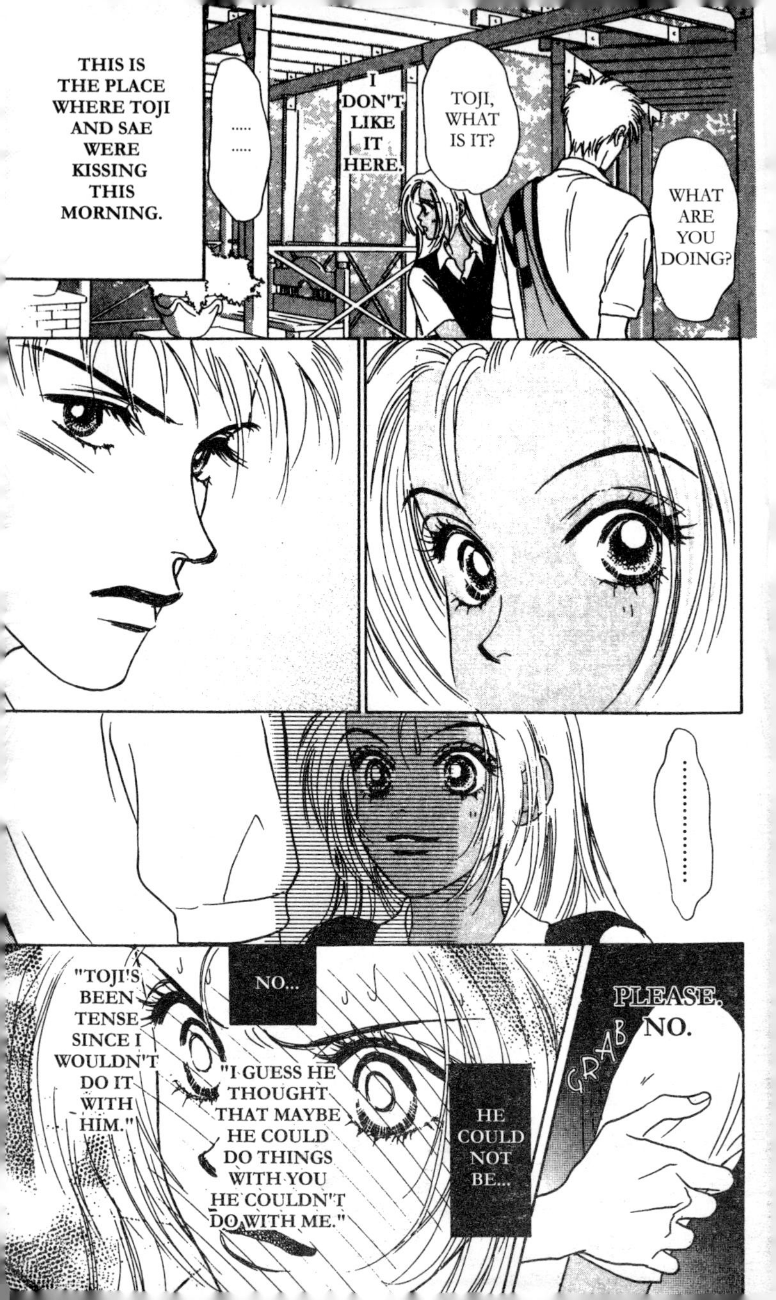
THIS IS THE PLACE WHERE TOJI AND SAE WERE KISSING THIS MORNING.
....
I DON'T LIKE IT HERE.
TOJI, WHAT IS IT?
WHAT ARE YOU DOING?
....
"TOJI'S BEEN TENSE SINCE I WOULDN'T DO IT WITH HIM."
NO...
"I GUESS HE THOUGHT THAT MAYBE HE COULD DO THINGS WITH YOU HE COULDN'T DO WITH ME."
HE COULD NOT BE...
PLEASE.
NO.
GRAB

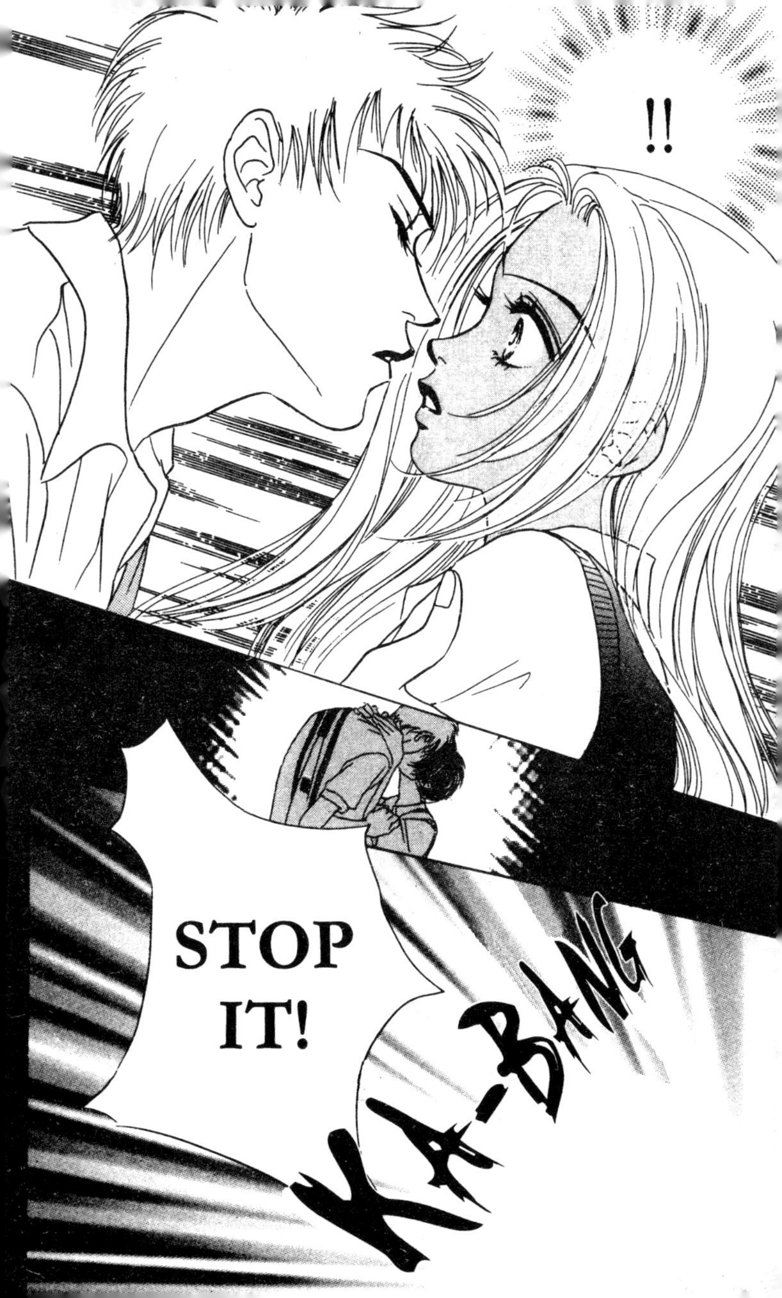
!!
STOP IT!
KA-BANG

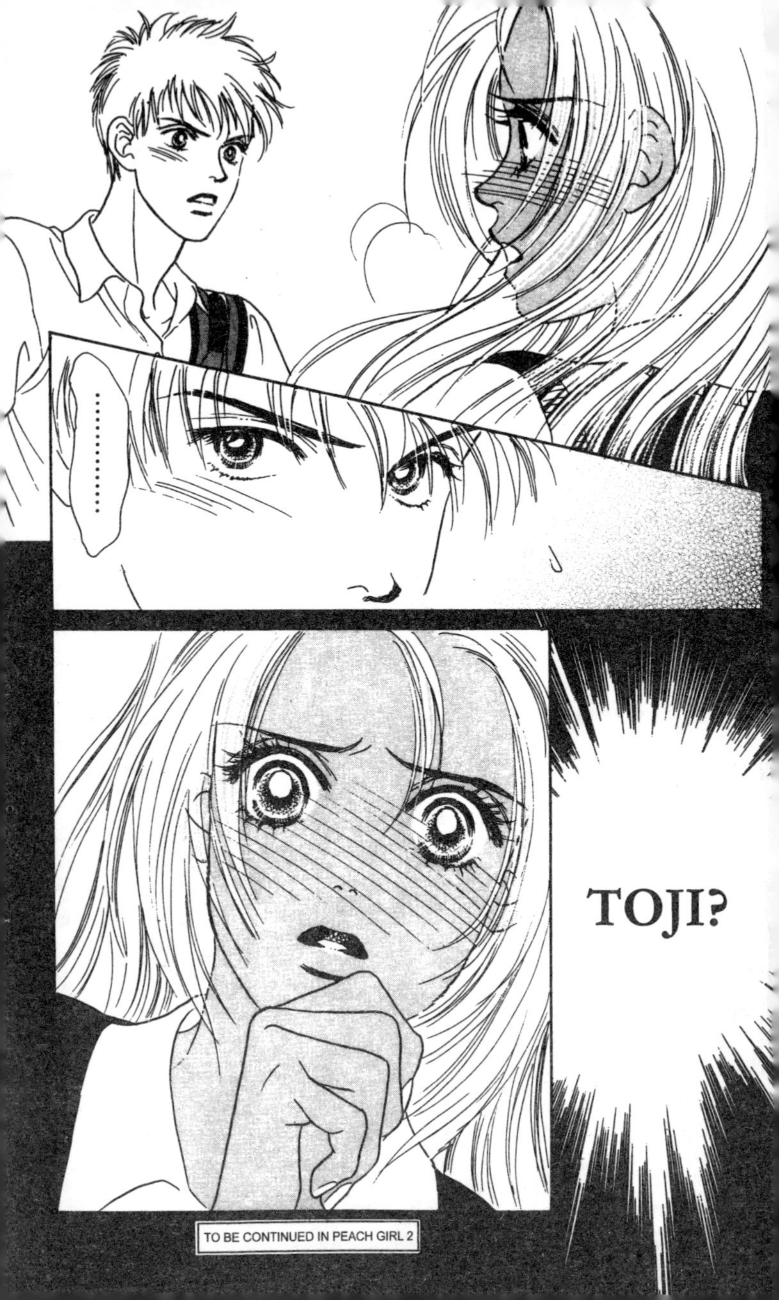
....
TOJI?
TO BE CONTINUED IN PEACH GIRL 2

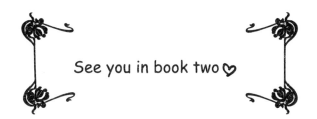

See you in book two ♡

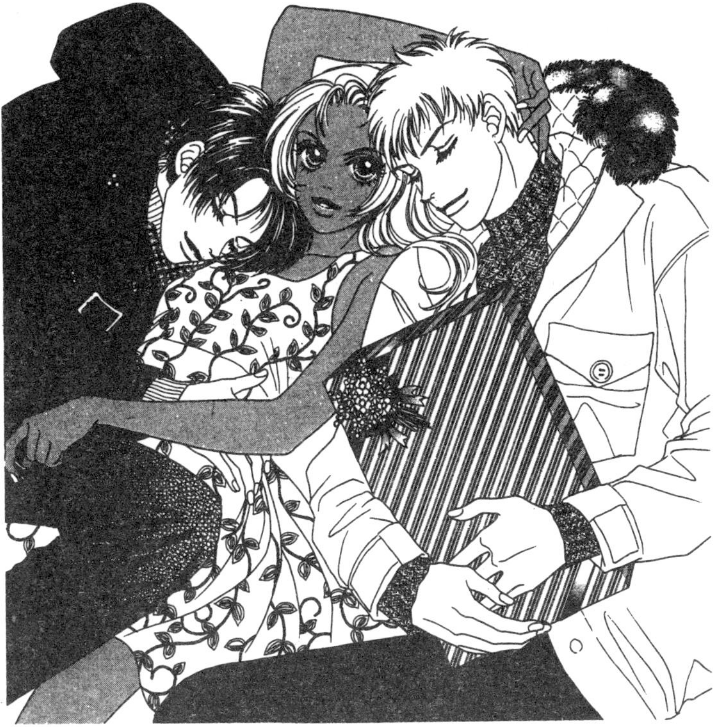

Staff : Aiko Amemori
Tomomi Kasue
Shiho Murahira
Eri Noda
Mami Haruki

Editor T. Tanaka

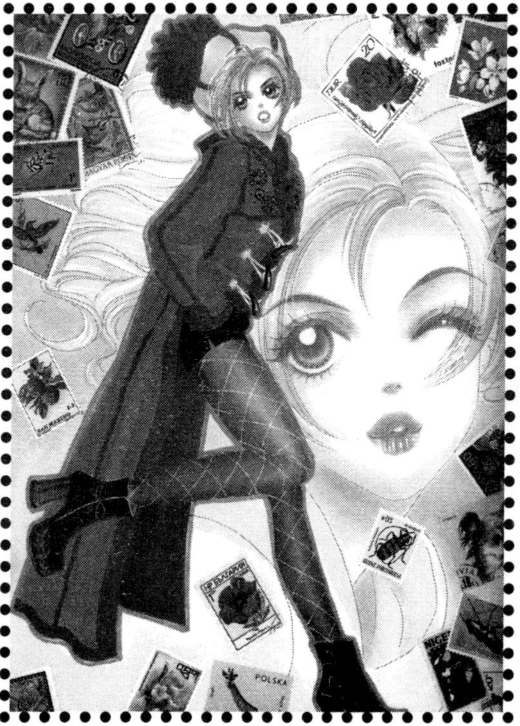
POLSKA

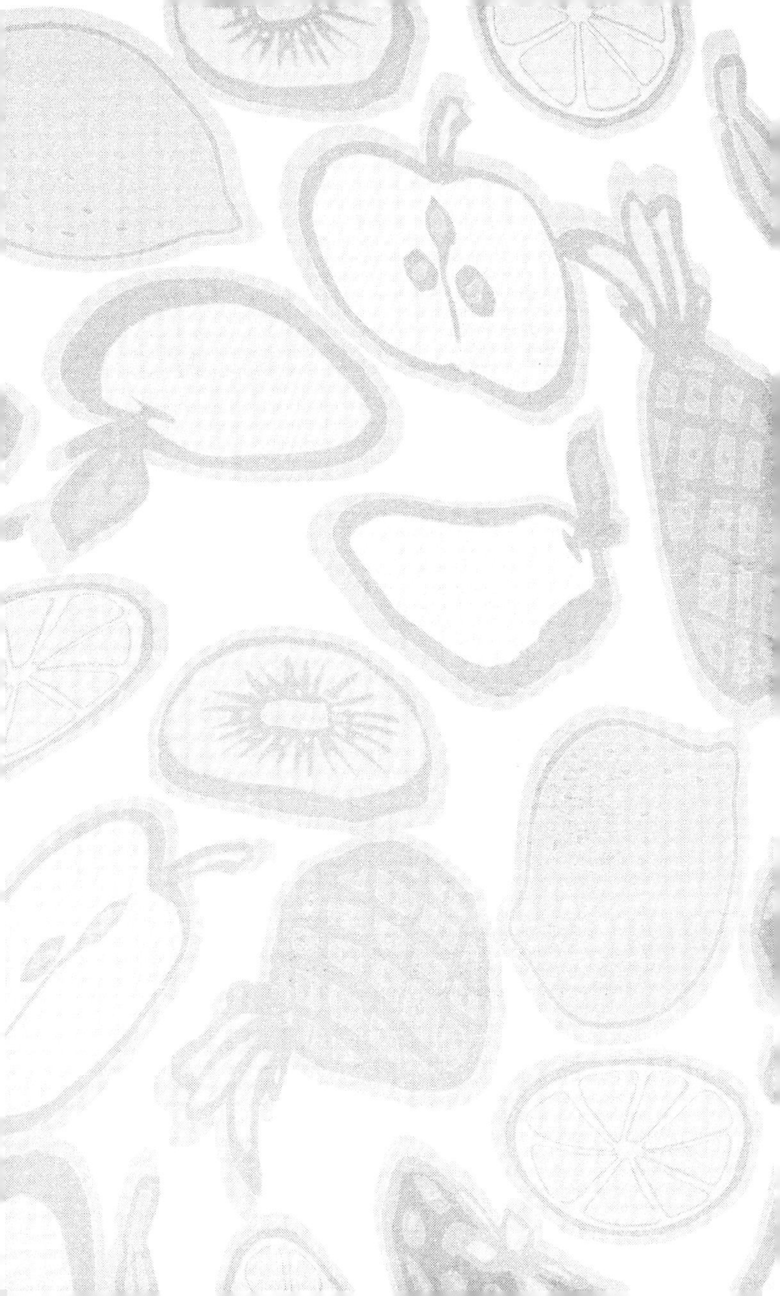

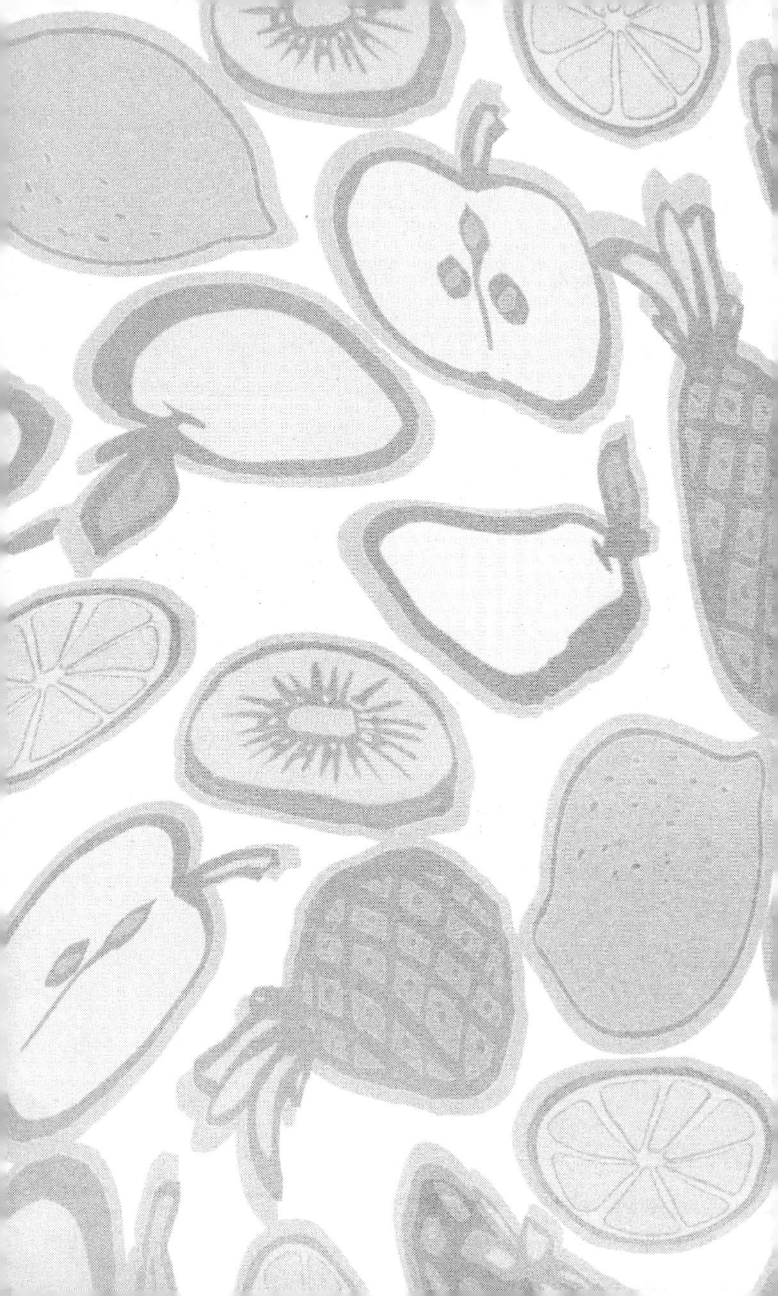